Meaning, Truth, and God

Leroy S. Rouner, editor

Boston University Studies
in Philosophy and Religion

The distinction between meaning and truth has become a critical issue for contemporary philosophy of religion. These essays by eminent scholars express a concern not only with the logic of religious belief and the effect of social context on religious meaning, but with the truth-claim concerning the reality of God.

Traditionally, the challenge of theology, Professor Rouner explains in the Introduction, was to make the affirmations of religious belief meaningful to believers. The truth of these beliefs is presupposed by the theological system. Philosophers of religion, on the other hand, have been mindful not only of the truth-question of religion, but of the increasing importance of that question in a religiously pluralistic world. Rouner asserts that especially when religious cults turn bizarre, or authoritarian fundamentalisms threaten basic human rights, the truth question becomes unavoidable. Therefore, there is a new urgency for integrating meaning and truth in the philosophy of religion.

Meaning, Truth, and God is also a reinterpretation of major nineteenth-century thinkers. This review lends perspective to future work on these problems as well as gives evidence that nineteenth-century philosophy was more mindful of the meaning/truth problem than some have supposed.

Contributors are Charles Hartshorne, David B. Burrell, Robert R. Williams, Paul Ricoeur, John B. Cobb, Jr., Howard Clark Kee, John E. Smith, Marx W. Wartofsky, J. N. Findlay, Ernest L. Fortin, Thomas F. O'Meara, and Leroy S. Rouner.

Leroy S. Rouner is professor of philosophical theology and director of the Institute for Philosophy and Religion at Boston University.

MEANING, TRUTH, AND GOD

BOSTON UNIVERSITY STUDIES IN PHILOSOPHY AND RELIGION

General Editor: Leroy S. Rouner

Volume Three

Volume Two
Transcendence and the Sacred
Alan M. Olson and Leroy S. Rouner, Editors

Volume One
Myth, Symbol, and Reality
Alan M. Olson, Editor

Meaning, Truth, and God

Edited by
Leroy S. Rouner

UNIVERSITY OF NOTRE DAME PRESS
Notre Dame & London

Library of Congress Cataloging in Publication Data

Main entry under title:

Meaning, truth, and God.

(Boston University studies in philosophy and
religion; v. 3)
   1. Religion — Philosophy — Addresses, essays,
lectures. I. Rouner, Leroy S. II. Series.
BL51.M483   200'.1   82-7023
ISBN 0-268-01355-1   AACR2

Contents

Preface

Boston University Studies in Philosophy and Religion is a joint project of the Boston University Institute for Philosophy and Religion and the University of Notre Dame Press. The series includes an annual volume edited from the previous year's program of the Institute, as well as other occasional volumes dealing with critical issues in the philosophy of religion. In preparation are volumes on foundations of ethics, and on religious and cultural pluralism.

The Boston University Institute for Philosophy and Religion is sponsored jointly by the School of Theology, the Department of Philosophy, the Department of Religion, and the Graduate School of Boston University. As an interdisciplinary and ecumenical forum it does not represent any philosophical school or religious tradition. Within the academic community it is committed to dialogue on questions of value, truth, and ultimate meaning, which transcend the narrow specialization of academic life. Outside the university community it seeks to recover the "public tradition" of philosophical discourse which was a lively part of American intellectual life in the early years of this century, before the professionalization of both philosophy and religious studies.

Our themes are purposely broad and inclusive. Our essays focus on analyses of specific issues, and we encourage our authors to make an autobiographical connection with their analysis. We also emphasize the need for comparative studies. Humane scholarship in world religions makes a small but significant contribution to mutual understanding among the world's various believers.

The Institute program receives support from several sources. We are especially grateful to the United Methodist Board of

Higher Education and Ministry. The Board's recent contributions have made it possible for us to expand our program considerably.

It is our hope that these volumes may be a resource for critical reflection on fundamental human issues both within the academic community and beyond.

For

HANS-GEORG GADAMER

His work has taught us how philosophy and religious reflection discover truth. His lectures to the Institute for Philosophy and Religion have given that teaching humane urgency, personal depth, and intellectual immediacy.

Acknowledgments

The editor wishes to express his appreciation to the authors of these essays for their cooperation and to members of the Institute staff for their help, especially to Irena Makarushka, who prepared the manuscript for the publishers, and Janet Byers who helped her. Most of all, however, my thanks go once again to Barbara Darling Smith, my Assistant, who was ultimately responsible for technical editing and whose effectiveness and indefatigable cheer make our work together a continuing delight. Once again our friends and colleagues at the University of Notre Dame Press have given evidence of the privilege it is to work with them. Ann Rice has transformed the manuscript into a book with her special blend of patient professionalism and good-humored warmth. And the series owes a continuing debt to Jim Langford, Director of the Press. It was his encouragement and vision which made this series possible, and he continues to be the publisher *par excellence*.

Contributors

DAVID B. BURRELL, C.S.C., is Professor of Theology at the University of Notre Dame. He received his S.T.L. from the Gregorian University, Rome, in 1960, and his Ph.D. from Yale University in 1965. Professor Burrell has been the recipient of both the Fulbright and the Woodrow Wilson Fellowships (1954). His books include *Analogy and Philosophical Language* (1973) and *Aquinas: God and Action* (1979). He is also the author of numerous essays, articles, and reviews.

JOHN B. COBB, JR., is Ingraham Professor of Theology at the School of Theology at Claremont and Avery Professor of Religion at Claremont Graduate School, as well as Director of Process Studies there. Born in Kobe, Japan, Professor Cobb received M.A. and Ph.D. degrees from the University of Chicago. Among his books are *A Christian Natural Theology* (1965), and *The Structure of Christian Existence* (1967). More recently he coauthored (with David Ray Griffin) *Process Theology: An Introductory Exposition* (1976). His latest book, coauthored with Charles Birch, is *The Liberation of Life* (1982).

J. N. FINDLAY is University Professor and Borden Parker Bowne Professor of Philosophy at Boston University. He has studied at Transvaal University College, South Africa, and at Balliol College, Oxford. His doctorate is from the University of Graz, Austria, in 1933. Professor Findlay has written nu-

merous books, including *Meinong's Theory of Objects* (1933);
Hegel: A Reexamination (1958); *Values and Intentions*
(1961); two series of Gifford Lectures entitled *The Discipline
of the Cave* (1966) and *The Transcendence of the Cave*
(1967); *Ascent to the Absolute* (1970); *Plato: The Written
and Unwritten Doctrines* (1974); and *Kant and the Transcendental Object* (1981). He has held the Chair of Philosophy at King's College, London, and has taught at Yale University and the University of Texas. Professor Findlay is a
Fellow of the British Academy and of the American Academy of Arts and Sciences.

ERNEST L. FORTIN is the author of numerous articles in both
English and French on medieval and renaissance theology
and philosophy. His books include *Political Idealism and
Christianity in the Thought of Saint Augustine* (1972), and
*Dissidence et philosophie au moyen âge: Dante et ses antécé-
dents* (1981). Professor Fortin received his S.T.L. at the Uni-
versity of Saint Thomas, Rome, in 1950, and his Ph.D. at the
University of Paris in 1955. He has been the recipient of sev-
eral grants, including a French Government Travel Grant,
North Africa (1954), a Fulbright Travel and Study Grant,
India (1966), and a Publication Grant from the Canadian
Arts Council (1980). He is Professor of Theology at Boston
College.

CHARLES HARTSHORNE is a Fellow of the American Academy of Arts and Sciences. Educated at Harvard, he received
his Ph.D. there in 1923. He did postgraduate study at the
University of Freiburg and the University of Marburg, and
has taught most recently at the University of Texas. Honorary degrees have been conferred on him by Haverford College (1967), Emory University (1969), Episcopal Seminary of
the Southwest (1977), and the University of Louvain, Bel-
gium (1978). Professor Hartshorne is the author of over four
hundred articles and his books include *The Philosophy and*

Psychology of Sensation (1934); *The Divine Relativity* (1948); *Reality as Social Process* (1953); *The Logic of Perfection* (1962), for which he won the Lecomte du Noüy Award; and *Aquinas to Whitehead: Seven Centuries of Metaphysics of Religion* (1976). He is also the editor (with Paul Weiss) of *The Collected Papers of Charles S. Peirce.*

HOWARD CLARK KEE received his Ph.D. from Yale University in 1951. He was named Aurelio Professor of Biblical Studies at Boston University in 1982. Among his most recent books are *Jesus in History* (1970), *The Origins of Christianity: Sources and Documents* (1973), *Community of the New Age: Studies in Mark's Gospel* (1977), and *Christian Origins in Sociological Perspective* (1980). He is also the author of numerous articles and reviews. Professor Kee has been guest lecturer at the University of Marburg, the University of Tübingen, Brown University, and Tel Aviv University. He taught at Drew University and Bryn Mawr College before coming to Boston University in 1977.

THOMAS F. O'MEARA, O.P., is Professor of Theology and Director of the Master of Divinity program at the University of Notre Dame. He has taught at Weston School of Theology, Wartburg Lutheran Seminary, and the Aquinas Institute of Theology. He received his doctorate from the University of Munich. His books include *Holiness and Radicalism in Religious Life* (1970), *Paul Tillich's Theology of God* (1971), and, most recently, *Romantic Idealism and Roman Catholicism: Schelling and the Theologians* (1982). He has also written many articles for scholarly publications. Professor O'Meara is past President of the Catholic Theological Society of America.

PAUL RICOEUR is Professor of Philosophy at the Sorbonne and John Nuveen Professor of Philosophy and Theology at the

University of Chicago. He studied at the University of Rennes and the University of Paris, where he is agrégé in philosophy and holds a doctorate in letters (1950). Professor Ricoeur has taught at the University of Strasbourg and at the University of Paris-Nanterre. His books include *Freedom and Nature: The Voluntary and the Involuntary* (1966), *Husserl: An Analysis of His Phenomenology* (1967), *The Symbolism of Evil* (1969), *Freud and Philosophy: An Essay on Interpretation* (1970), *Biblical Hermeneutics* (1975), *Interpretation Theory* (1976), and *Rule of Metaphor* (1977).

LEROY S. ROUNER is Professor of Philosophical Theology at Boston University, Director of the Boston University Institute for Philosophy and Religion, and General Editor of Boston University Studies in Philosophy and Religion. He graduated from Harvard College (A.B.) in 1953; Union Theological Seminary (B.D., *summa cum laude*) in 1958; and Columbia University (Ph.D.) in 1961. Professor Rouner taught for five years in Bangalore, India. He edited the Hocking Festschrift, *Philosophy, Religion, and the Coming World Civilization* (1966), and is author of *Within Human Experience: The Philosophy of William Ernest Hocking* (1969); *The Discovery of Humankind* (1976); and *Return Home in Peace* (forthcoming). In 1972 he was elected an honorary member of the Harvard College chapter of Phi Beta Kappa.

JOHN E. SMITH has taught at Yale University since 1952 and was named Clark Professor of Philosophy in 1972. He has written extensively on American philosophy and philosophy of religion. His books include *The Spirit of American Philosophy* (1963), *Experience and God* (1968), and *The Analogy of Experience* (1973). He has been Dudleian Lecturer at Harvard (1960), Suarez Lecturer at Fordham (1963), Aquinas Lecturer at Marquette (1967), and Warfield Lecturer at Princeton Theological Seminary (1970). Professor Smith received his B.A. from Columbia University in 1942, his B.D.

as an Auburn Fellow from Union Theological Seminary in 1945, and his Ph.D. from Columbia University in 1948. He also received an honorary LL.D. from the University of Notre Dame in 1964.

MARX W. WARTOFSKY is Professor of Philosophy at Boston University, editor of *The Philosophical Forum*, coeditor (with Robert S. Cohen) of *Boston Studies in the Philosophy of Science* and (with Carol Gould) of *Women and Philosophy: Toward a Theory of Liberation* (1976). He has written numerous articles on aesthetics and on the philosophy of science. His books include *Conceptual Foundations of Scientific Thought* (1968), which has been translated into a number of languages; *Feuerbach* (1977); and *Models: Representation and the Scientific Understanding* (1979). Professor Wartofsky received his B.A. in 1948, M.A. in 1949, and Ph.D. in 1952, from Columbia University.

ROBERT R. WILLIAMS is Associate Professor of Philosophy at Hiram College, Ohio. He received his Ph.D. from Columbia University in 1970 and has done postdoctoral research at the University of Chicago (1975) and at Purdue University (1978) as a recipient of two National Endowment for the Humanities grants. Professor Williams has written a book on *Schleiermacher, the Theologian: The Construction of the Doctrine of God* (1978). He is also the author of several articles that have appeared in scholarly journals. Since 1977 he has chaired the Department of Philosophy at Hiram College.

Introduction

LEROY S. ROUNER

THE DISTINCTION BETWEEN meaning and truth has become a critical issue for contemporary philosophy of religion. What Hans Reichenbach has called *The Rise of Scientific Philosophy* challenged religious thinkers with fundamental questions: How can one verify the religious truth-claim? What evidence would count against such a claim? If no empirical data could conceivably falsify the religious truth-claim, how can such a claim be meaningful? Scientific philosophers understood philosophy primarily as a method for analyzing the uses of language. Religious thinkers, on the other hand, usually understood philosophy more traditionally as a systematic statement of knowable truth. As a result, conversations between scientific philosophers and religious thinkers have been confused, and often antagonistic. The confusion arose partly from the distinction within the company of religious thinkers themselves between the theologians and the philosophers of religion. Theology claims revelation as a source of knowledge. Therefore theology never asks, "Is there a God?" It begins with the affirmation, "Thus saith the Lord." Because philosophy of religion, like all other specializations within philosophy, is rational reflection on experience, the truth-question about the existence and reality of God is crucial, even though the philosopher may personally believe in a religious tradition.

As a result, theology proper has been less concerned with the challenge to its truth-claim than it has been with the challenge to make its statements meaningful. Especially after it became apparent that even scientific philosophy required certain axiomatic assumptions in order to get its inquiry underway, theology tended to absorb the truth-question into its understanding of revelation.

1

In the highly influential Protestant Christian theology of Karl Barth, for example, the theological task was to make the affirmations of religious belief meaningful to believers. The truth of these beliefs is presupposed by the theological system.

Philosophers of religion, on the other hand, were mindful not only of the traditional truth-question which is any philosopher's commitment, but of the increasing importance of that question in a religiously pluralistic world. Especially when religious cults turned bizarre, or authoritarian fundamentalisms threatened basic human rights, the truth question became unavoidable. The Boston University Institute for Philosophy and Religion chose this theme with the conviction that there is a new urgency for integrating meaning and truth in the philosophy of religion. The essays which follow express a concern not only with the logic of religious belief, and the effect of social context on religious meanings, but with the truth-claim concerning the reality of God.

The book is also a reinterpretation of major nineteenth-century thinkers. A careful examination of the recent past helps in charting new directions for the future. We are usually influenced by our predecessors rather more than we realize, and this review not only lends perspective to future work on these problems, but gives evidence that nineteenth-century philosophy was more mindful of the meaning/truth problem than some have supposed.

Since the major challenge in recent years has been less concerned with the substance of religious belief than it has been with the logic of religious affirmations, we begin with Charles Hartshorne's essay on "Grounds for Believing in God's Existence." Perhaps more than any living philosopher, Hartshorne has concerned himself with an analysis and defense of logical argument for the existence of God. His paper is a concise conspectus of his views on such fundamental issues as the nature of valid proof for the existence of God, the problems of suffering and evil, and an understanding of value and human freedom. Hartshorne has probably given more sustained attention to the ontological argument than any philosopher in history. When he makes the claim, therefore, that neither Anselm's defenders nor his critics have ever made the important distinction between the abstract existence of a defined essence, and the concrete how of this existence, we find ourselves enlightened by a new perspective on a fundamental issue, instructed by the most qualified of all possible mentors.

The second part of Hartshorne's paper is a running dialogue with the views of Willard V. Quine. When Hartshorne first presented his paper to the Institute's audience, Quine was the critic and responded with a carefully reasoned statement of his own on points of fundamental disagreement. For some time after the meeting was adjourned, their congenial debate continued, and Professor Hartshorne subsequently rewrote his paper in the light of that conversation with Quine. While Hartshorne's argument is logically sophisticated, he points out that it is a matter of informal rather than formal logic, since theistic argument can never be so cogent that any rational person must accept it. Its purpose is to show that the theistic view of life and reality makes better sense than the nontheistic view.

David Burrell is concerned with the same issue which motivates Hartshorne, and which has been central to the challenge of scientific philosophy: How can one verify the religious truth-claim? Hartshorne's response is that it can be verified logically. While that logic is informal, in the technical sense, and does not lay claim to all possible rational ground, it is nonetheless strict. Burrell suggests, on the other hand, that the verification of religious belief is more experiential than strictly logical. His introductory paragraph is particularly noteworthy in clarifying the distinction between meaning and truth. Announcing that his essay is a constructive thesis on how to verify such religious statements as "God created the heavens and the earth," he admits that he has heretofore been concerned to avoid the issue by trying to find "acceptable ways to parse the statement itself." Analyses and explanations of such statements, in terms of the logical coherence internal to the sentence itself, make the statement, *qua* statement, meaningful. Whether the statement refers to anything actual in the real world or not — that is, whether or not it is true — is another question. Somewhat ruefully, Burrell confesses that pressure from his philosophical colleagues and from his own philosophical concerns have joined forces "to bring me around to meet the issue of truth after all."

He is persuaded, however, that the truth-question has never been as simple or monolithic as some earlier discussions assumed, and that verification of any statement depends on an understanding of "what those who use them intend them to mean." Although this focus on use and purpose is precisely the concern which motivated Peirce and James in the development of American pragmatism, and the criteria of his constructive thesis have parallels in James's essay on "The Will to Believe," Burrell's grounding is in the traditions of Roman Catholic philosophy, and he gains critical perspective on those traditions primarily from Wittgenstein and his later followers. He argues that creedal statements or revelations are true when they "confirm in a discriminating manner those aspirations which set one seeking," and continue to be realized in "a supereminent way." Community confirmation is a primary dimension of this supereminence, since religious belief always has a communal dimension.

Our concern for the logic of theological inquiry then moves back to the heart of nineteenth-century thought and the conflict between Schleiermacher and Hegel. Schleiermacher's theology of feeling prompted sarcastic invective from Hegel — if religion is a feeling of absolute dependence then "a dog would be the best Christian" — and Robert Williams's essay sorts out some of the confusion and identifies the critical issues in a controversy which has been subject to persistent misinterpretation. A theology based on feeling almost invites the kind of caricature with which Hegel responds, but Williams argues that Hegel knew better. He is further persuaded that contemporary Hegel scholars have been too uncritical in their acceptance of Hegel's views on Schleiermacher's theological program. The heart of Hegel's criticism was that Schleiermacher had lost his theological nerve in trying to accommodate modernity's critique of religious truth-claims. By turning to noncognitive and emotivist criteria for theology, Hegel argued that Schleiermacher had made Christian faith meaningful to modernity by giving up any coherent claim to truth.

Williams's essay is partly a defense of Schleiermacher on this issue, but it is not anti-Hegelian, since his primary interest is in the issue of theological truth itself. He rejects Hegel's portrayal of Schleiermacher's views on the feeling of utter dependence as irresponsible caricature and a bogus issue. He then goes on to show that there are legitimate differences between Hegel and Schleiermacher on describing and interpreting the process of theological reflection. Hegel tended to identify the essence of Christianity with its historic doctrines, while Schleiermacher finds the essence of Christianity in the self-consciousness of a particular historical-cultural form of life. Williams is persuaded that this conflict is far from resolved, and that a clearer understanding of the differences between Hegel and Schleiermacher can enlighten our encounter with these same issues in contemporary philosophy of religion.

This first section then concludes with a landmark essay by Paul Ricoeur on the role of "figurative thinking" in Hegel's philosophy. Hartshorne's defense of informal logic, Burrell's appeal to use and intention as criteria for verification, and Williams's defense of feeling as a way of knowing the truth — all are responses to the challenge to rethink the issue of meaning and truth and show how one verifies the truth of one's views. Ricoeur joins that conversation with a classic example of how careful analysis of our predecessors' views can aid critical construction in contemporary philosophy. As to historical interpretation, Ricoeur's thesis is simply that this notion of *Vorstellung*, or pictorial thinking, is central to Hegel's philosophy of religion. He notes that religion and philosophy have the same speculative content, as Hegel understands it, but that religion grasps it figuratively, while philosophy grasps it conceptually. However, the figurative and the speculative are dynamically interrelated. Speculation generates the movement of representation toward the concept. The continuing issue for Ricoeur is whether the concept must abolish the figure, or whether the philosophical concept may still require the support of the religiously oriented figure or picture or myth in order to assert itself and remain meaningful as a concept.

Ricoeur's solution, following Hegel, is to divide religious reflection into three stages: immediacy, figurative mediation, and conceptualization. Immediacy is revelation, that moment of religious experience which generates the need to understand and hence interpret. In Christianity, the moment of immediacy becomes specific in the appearance of Jesus as a historical figure. Figurative mediation is required by the passing of immediacy.

When the historical Jesus is no longer present, the community knows what the revelation means through the figurative thinking of narrative and symbolic representations. Conceptualization is "the endless death of the representation" in that the idea draws out the meaning and truth of the representation and therefore transcends it. At the same time, however, the concept keeps returning to the immediacy of religion for the generation of new stories, interpretations, and symbols which, again, keep aiming at concepts without losing their rooting in the initial immediacy of religion or in the mediating shapes of figurative thought.

Quoting Gadamer, Ricoeur notes that this theory of interpretation follows Hegel rather than Schleiermacher, since it holds together the three moments of immediate manifestation, figurative interpretation, and conceptualization, without losing the force of any of these necessary components. If Williams's essay has been persuasive, some readers may want to argue with Gadamer/Ricoeur on that point. For his part, however, it is clear that Ricoeur seeks a theory of critical interpretation which will hold these three elements together.

David Burrell and Robert Williams have already noted the communal dimensions of verification, and both Charles Hartshorne and Paul Ricoeur, in their different ways, have noted the dynamism of verification as a historical process. Our second group of essays, therefore, naturally moves into consideration of the community as it is affected by social process. There are two presuppositions which inform this group of essays: one is the conviction that religious meaning is established in a community of belief; the other is that truth is a dynamic and even historical concept. One would expect something of the sort from Weber, Feuerbach, and the process theologians; but John Smith argues persuasively that, the Absolute notwithstanding, the social and historical dimension is also present in the philosophy of Josiah Royce.

John Cobb's essay is primarily a historical account of process theology in America. Those readers who think of Whitehead's thought as determinative for process thinking in this country will be particularly interested in Cobb's argument that the independent development of the Chicago school is equally important to the spirit and agenda of process theology. He begins with comments about Whitehead's influence, then turns in rather more detail to the development of the Chicago school, and concludes with an evaluation of the conjoining of these two influences. By the Chicago school he means the group of scholars who constituted the faculty of the Divinity School at the University of Chicago in the 1890s. Cobb notes that this group showed little concern for the great figures of nineteenth-century European thought. Ritschl and Troeltsch were known and read, but the influence of Kant and Hegel, for example, was minimal. The two major concerns were for the social gospel on the one hand, and critical biblical study on the other, woven together dialectically into a sociohistorical method. Biblical study would give an understanding of how our ancestors in the faith responded to the critical issues of their day. We were to find the secret of their creativity, but not repeat their responses. Christians understand themselves as part of a movement which has its origins in the biblical community. Christianity is a sociohistorical movement which has no fixed doctrinal or conceptual essence. Here Cobb pauses to defend this point, arguing that the longer a movement's history, the more difficult it is for that movement to claim a continuous doctrinal or conceptual identity. Cobb is quite blunt: there is no essence of Christianity.

He concludes that the influence of Whitehead on the successors of the Chicago school has been salutary in several areas: truth is independent of immediate social relevance; it must be concerned with nature as well as society; and it must be concerned with metaphysics, as the grounding of sociohistorical accounts. Cobb concludes that the sociohistorical approach to theology had an important contribution to make; that Whitehead encompassed disparate elements in a unique way; and that contemporary process theologians have not yet learned to follow him in this respect.

Howard Kee picks up on the biblical-historical interest of the Chicago school in a contemporary vein: what of the influence of Max Weber on the sociology of knowledge and current attempts to reconstruct the life of the early Christian community? Once again we have the persuasion which David Burrell first voiced for us, that the verification of belief is a community event and not simply an individual occasion. The strongest emphasis here, however, is the conviction that knowledge is a sociological phenomenon—the interaction of a given community with those historical processes which shape it. After a careful analysis of Weber's place in the scholarly tradition, Kee notes Weber's wide-ranging influence on Husserl's phenomenology, and the phenomenological sociology of Alfred Schutz. His focus, however, is on four areas of thematic interest for any concerned with the historical reconstruction of Christianity. They are (1) Method; (2) Concept; (3) Theory of Knowledge (Epistemology); and (4) Interpretation (Hermeneutics).

As to method, Weber provides a cautioning word against the *post hoc, ergo propter hoc* fallacy. The fact that Y follows X does not mean that Y is caused by X. Kee emphasizes Weber's warning that ideal types are not historical realities, and that an earlier historical phenomenon which is in analogy to a later historical phenomenon does not necessarily "explain" it. In discussing concept, Kee notes the wide influence of Weber's ideas of charismatic leadership and institutionalization, lamenting the numerous distortions to which these ideal types have been submitted because Weber's interpreters lacked Weber's sense of the dynamic interaction between these two seemingly contradictory norms of religious authority. In discussing a theory of religious knowledge, Kee notes Weber's influence on what we now call the sociology of knowledge. Religious phenomena must be analyzed with attention to the symbolic and cognitive order in which people live, as well as the social setting in which they function. Further, there are not only multiple world-views which evolve within a religious community like early Christianity; there are also various processes of transformation at work which must be taken into account. Finally, as to a theory of interpretation or hermeneutics, Weber was concerned to offer various ideal types of orientation which show possible ways of interpreting certain phenomena in a given historical instance. Weber's contribution, therefore, is to the rich possibilities of historical interpretation. Should this conclusion sound like historical relativism, Kee notes his preference for "relative precision" as opposed to some "absolute fuzziness."

This brings us to John Smith's essay on Royce, where the balance shifts toward a more favorable view of the Absolute. Smith's book on *Royce's Social Infinite* was published more than thirty years ago, and eventually initiated a re-evaluation of Royce and his work. His interest here is the relation between the notion of community and the notion of the Absolute. Royce made much of the Absolute in his early books, but the writings subsequent to *The World and the Individual* make little mention of the Absolute, and concentrate instead on doctrines of loyalty, interpretation, and the community. At the end of his life Royce argued that the idea of the community had been there from the beginning. Smith, once skeptical, now finds himself convinced that this was indeed the case. His question is, rather, what is the relation between this continuous notion of community in Royce's thought, and the eventual disappearance, as it were, of the famous doctrine of the Absolute?

Smith argues that the problems posed by time, development, novelty, and individuality gradually worked on Royce's notion of the Absolute so that he shifted his emphasis away from an idea of the Absolute as *totum simul* consciousness toward a notion of community as one which solved the problem of the One and the many without undercutting the experienced realities of the historical process. Royce's fundamental conviction concerned the time-spanning consciousness of a reality to whom all truth and error is known. The meaning, truth, and purpose of any fragmentary experience is to be known finally only by appeal to a whole which is out of sight for any finite knower. Smith's conclusion is that Royce finally was concerned with two historical forms of human relationship, both of which he found to be distorted. They were collectivism and individualism. Collectivism he judged to be a One without a real many. Individualism seemed to him to provide a many without the coherent unity of a real One. Community points to a form of life which transcends these two distortions because it provides a unity of the One and the many without sacrificing the dynamic reality of either.

Marx Wartofsky's essay on Feuerbach will strike many readers as unusual, coming as it does from a Marxist in search of a viable materialist conception of religious transcendence. He begins by sketching Feuerbach's formulation of the problem, first nega-

tively and then positively. He then discusses what is meant by
Feuerbach's notion of "religious materialism." He goes on to
sketch philosophical and theological alternatives to traditional
conceptions of transcendence. In conclusion, he argues that the
Hegelian notion of dialectic in its transformation by Feuerbach
and Marx provides a clue to a materialistic conception of transcendence. He does this first in terms of a dialectic of consciousness and then as a dialectic of praxis.

Those readers informed by the Judeo-Christian tradition of
theological reflection will, I suspect, be intrigued by Wartofsky's
use of the term *materialism*. Because of the Marxist critique of religion, the initial response of these readers is, I suspect, likely to
be characterized by a hermeneutics of suspicion. As the essay pro-
gresses, however, what Wartofsky means by "material" may seem
increasingly congenial to what the Judeo-Christian tradition has
regularly meant by "historical." Wartofsky outlines the spirit of
revolutionary praxis as one which "has as its animating spirit a vision of human possibilities which sees the divine as within the
grasp of our own creative activity, and as the object of our hope.
Such a theory of belief, as a materialist theory, exceeds the bounds
of contemporary materialism, which has as yet no consistent theory of hope, or of this sort of recognition of the transcendent. But
the transcendent, thus conceived, is within the realm of human
possibility. And a theory of hope as active, practical, efficacious
belief in such human possibilities, is needed." Here a materialist
understanding of religion finds common ground with other traditions of world religion, as well as fundamental elements of human experience.

Having been confronted initially with the logic of theological inquiry, an exploration that was then expanded to include the
dynamics of community life and social history as they bear on the
meaning and truth of religious affirmations, we finally come directly to the reality of God. John Findlay initiates this conversation. His subject is Hegel, but his concern is with the Absolute.
Royce may have become historicist in his later years, but John
Findlay's eye is firmly fixed on the Transcendent. Not one to
equivocate, he announces in his second sentence that he aims to
study the Hegelian Absolute "as a concept — or rather an object —

satisfactory to the unconditional dedication and devotion of religion, something that can be unconditionally worshipped if anything at all can." Ricoeur may regard the Hegelian *Vorstellung* as a regularly recurring element in a dialectic of immediacy, figurative mediation, and conceptualization, but Findlay leaves *Vorstellung* behind and focuses on the Hegelian notion of the Absolute as *Begriff*, the supreme concept, and prime ontological category. The body of his essay is an exploration in definition, beginning with the assertion that "a *Begriff* is a subsistent, Platonic entity which exists freely in its own pure medium, though having necessary relation to the acts and attitudes of the human spirit, and to concrete natural realities set out in space and time." While *Begriffe* are the meaning of all historic pluralisms, behind them all is *der Begriff* in the singular, present in them all and transcendently responsible for all their necessary and contingent relations.

And what is the religious value of this idea of God? Findlay argues that the great religions in their more reflective forms move beyond anthropomorphism to a God which is Truth itself, Beauty itself, and Goodness itself. As to the paradoxes of historic incarnation, Findlay argues with characteristic good humor that "the logical gambits of Hegelianism suit the mysteries of religion better than anything else: the presence within us, and also beyond us, of a universal Spirit which both is and isn't ourselves, and which only is the one because it is also the other." He is critical, however, of the wholly this-worldly dimension of Hegelianism, and ends his essay with a vivid picture of final liberation in which the human spirit will be freed to another world beyond the bonds of matter, sense, space, and time.

But what of philosophic challenge to the reality of God? Findlay's celebration of God as Hegel's Absolute is followed by Ernest Fortin's analysis of Nietzsche's counterview that, far from being the ultimate *Begriff*, God is dead because nihilism has negated the possibility of truth itself. Fortin's focus is on the crisis of nihilism as the root cause of the death of God. He notes that nihilism is often explained by the experience of history and its vicissitudes, but he examines the first chapter of *Beyond Good and Evil* and concludes that Nietzsche's nihilism is predicated not on the experience of history as such, but on a particular interpretation of

that experience which grows out of a prior philosophical conviction concerning the impossibility of theoretical knowledge of any
kind.

At the heart of Nietzsche's philosophy are three interrelated
doctrines: the will to power; the superman; and the eternal return. Fortin notes that there are no supporters of these Nietzschean doctrines in the philosophical community today. At the
same time, the fascination with Nietzsche continues, as Fortin's
essay indicates. Many of Nietzsche's central affirmations seem obviously flawed. His insistence that there are no timeless truths
surely runs aground on a simple logical fallacy. Fortin points out
patiently that one cannot assert absolutely the truth of relativism.
Nevertheless, Nietzsche is much concerned with the responsibility
of thought for the direction of human affairs, and Fortin points
out that Nietzsche's ethics of creativity has a popular contemporary analogue in Heidegger's appeal to an existential "authenticity." And in spite of the fact that Nietzsche was the first philosopher to have taken issue with Socrates, Fortin argues that
Nietzsche's philosophic agenda is closer to that of Socrates than
Nietzsche might have us think. This, as much as anything else,
may be the source of contemporary fascination with Nietzsche's
thought.

Having moved from the reality of God as pure transcendent
concept to God as meaningless notion, we conclude with Thomas
O'Meara's essay on Schelling's Christian philosophy. Much of his
essay is devoted to a succinct summary of Schelling's difficult and
relatively unfamiliar system of religious philosophy. Schelling argued that myth is religion, and that Christianity must be understood as part of a history of culture and consciousness. Here
O'Meara's essay touches a theme which Robert Williams explored
in discussing Schleiermacher's understanding of the religious
community. There is also common ground in an attempt to speak
to the cultured despisers of religion. In Schelling's case, this took
the form of what O'Meara calls an overstated identity of idealism
and revelation. O'Meara notes that Schelling interpretation has
been diverse. There are ties to idealism and medieval mysticism,
but Heidegger and Tillich have drawn on Schelling as sources for
their existentialist philosophies. While there is a distinction be-

tween Christianity and other religions in Schelling's philosophy, there are also elements of continuity between primal religion and revelation, nature and grace. O'Meara even suggests that there are affinities between Schelling and Teilhard de Chardin or Whitehead.

Schelling stood in the tradition of Origen, Augustine, Abelard, Hegel, and Tillich in his concern for a philosophy of religion which would break down the wall between culture and Christianity which post-Reformation traditions had built. In that sense, it is appropriate that we conclude with him. That is not to say that his views represent some universal philosophical consensus, but rather that they are engaged in a central problem for the philosophy of religion. If religious thought is to keep faith with itself, it cannot ignore the truth-question or bury it in an appeal to some authoritative revelation which provides a point of departure for religious reflection. Any philosophy of religion which takes its commitment to truth seriously must be able to articulate the meaning of its affirmations about transcendent truth to those who may not hold those beliefs. In that sense, religious philosophy is always concerned to communicate with secular culture. And that, of course, is one of the purposes of this book.

PART I

The Logic of Theological Inquiry

1

Grounds for Believing in God's Existence

CHARLES HARTSHORNE

I HOLD THAT THERE are rational grounds for theism, or the assertion of the existence of God, if the word *God* is suitably defined. However, there are four qualifications.

(1) A suitable definition of God (or the name for the reality worthy of worship) must be compatible with what I call the principle of dual transcendence. The definitions given in classical theology throughout the Middle Ages and down to and including Kant do not conform to this requirement. The definition implied by Hume's Cleanthes comes closer to conforming to it but does not clearly do so. Dual transcendence holds that God surpasses other beings, not by being sheerly absolute, infinite, independent, necessary, eternal, immutable, but by being both absolute, infinite, independent, and so forth, and also, in uniquely excellent fashion, relative, finite, dependent, contingent, and temporal. This combination of traits is not contradictory, since there is a distinction of respects in which the two sets of adjectives apply to God. Moreover, to describe deity as in every respect absolute or infinite is either to empty the idea of any definite and consistent meaning or to make it a mere abstraction. Concrete actuality cannot be in every respect infinite, independent, or necessary. Hence to deny any and every sort of finitude, relativity, or contingency to God is not to exalt God. Classical theism is for me false a priori, a tragic error.

(2) Valid reasons for theism cannot be empirical in the strong

17

sense that some conceivable experiences would be incompatible with its truth. I hold with Popper that not all significant beliefs are empirical in this strong sense; and I take theism to be one of the exceptions. Insofar I agree with Hume and Kant that there are no valid empirical arguments for or (here agreeing with Kant) against theism. I do not agree with either writer that the ontological argument is a mere fallacy, and I hold that there are a number of arguments other than the ontological which are equally a priori. None is a mere formal fallacy.

(3) I do not claim that any argument for theism is so evidently cogent that there can be no reasonable ground for rejecting it. Rather, I see room for intelligent disagreement in this matter. But (in my *Creative Synthesis and Philosophic Method*) I have formulated arguments which, taken together, convince me and which I think are free from obvious fallacy.

(4) A formal agreement is a set of options claiming to be exhaustive. If p entails q, then the options are: accept q or reject p. But merely rejecting p is negative and rather vague as to what the rejection positively imports. Hence, in my formulation of the six arguments, this blanket negation, *not p*, where p is theism, is analyzed as a disjunction of the possible, more or less positive forms the negation could take. If the disjunction is finite and exhaustive, then one must either accept the negative disjunction as a whole or accept the theistic conclusion — unless one chooses to take no stand, to be merely agnostic.

I try to arrange the disjuncts making up the nontheistic position in an order or increasing likeness to theism. Thus, consider the following options using the concept of cosmic order. Symbolize atheism by A and theism by T. Then we have the following positions.

(A') There is no cosmic order, even approximate or probabilistic.

(A'') There is cosmic order, but no cosmic ordering power.

(A''') There is cosmic order, and an ordering power, but the power is not divine.

(T) There is cosmic order, and an ordering power, and the power is divine.

A' is scarcely attractive to anyone, I should think.

A'' is not obviously false but suggests a mystery. We know that order can be at least partly brought about by an ordering power, as in political affairs. I also hold that a waking human consciousness partly orders the behavior of its human body. In deep sleep the bodily cells as ordering agents, and still simpler entities under the cosmic power, take over.

Concerning A''': I can give reasons, cogent to me, for thinking that what gives an ordering power its capacity to order is some intrinsic merit or value. Even Hitler and Stalin were not totally without merit or value. I see the same principle in the mind-body relation. In the case of cosmic order, this principle takes its supreme form.

Divine in this argument, and in general as I use the word, means: maximal in value in every respect logically permitting such a maximum; and in those respects of value (and there are some) that do not permit a maximum, it means unsurpassable except by itself. Or, God is the all-surpassing, self-surpassing being, exalted beyond all possible rivalry and capable of increase in value only in those dimensions, or according to those criteria (for example, intensity and complexity) that logically exclude an absolute maximum. This definition differs subtly but definitely from Anselm's "that than which no greater can be conceived" (as he interpreted this formula), also from Kant's *ens realissimum*, the Aristotelian-Thomistic "pure actuality," and Descartes's "Perfect Being." Arguing about existence with respect to the new definition is another matter than arguing about the existence of the classically defined deity. It is one thing to criticize a concept which theologians are steadily moving away from (even Karl Barth illustrates this) and another to criticize the concept which they are increasingly adopting. Using the latest, most sophisticated techniques to attack an obsolescent doctrine is a form of cultural lag that has diminished steadily in my lifetime and that will, I trust, continue to diminish long after my death. If theism is to be relevantly evaluated, should it not be in the form the doctrine is now taking, not in that which it had in the time of Hume or Kant?

It is clear that the decision to reject or accept the atheistic disjuncts depends finally upon informal rather than formal logic.

I find all three atheistic options conceptually, intrinsically incredible and, therefore, find it rational to accept theism. But anyone who can believe one of the options will find the arguments from cosmic order unconvincing.

Is the argument empirical? I think not. Any cosmic order would present the problem, and as for the idea of a merely chaotic world, I find that a confused notion. Any world in which the theistic or any other question could arise would have an order. I see as absurd the notion that a function of empirical inquiry is to find out whether reality is or is not merely chaotic. Some order or other is a presupposition of inquiry and of all thinking.

I view in the same way the notion that there might have been nothing. Any experience would be other than nothing, and the question, "Why is there something rather than nothing?" seems without empirical meaning. Experience cannot be of nothing. Contingency does not mean that instead of X there might have been nothing, but rather that instead of X there might have been some Y the actuality of which would have excluded that of X. Each of us, merely by existing at a given moment, occupies some place and takes some role that something else could have occupied or taken had we not existed. Existence is contingent because it is competitive, and there is no competition with mere nothing.

If the world is cosmically and divinely ordered, why is there suffering and evil? Here dual transcendence comes in. In the classical tradition God was, in relation to the world, sheer cause, in no way effect; influencing, indeed determining, everything, uninfluenced by anything. Neoclassical or dual-transcendence theism holds that God excels just as much in capacity to be influenced as in capacity to influence. The creatures must have some initiative in relation to God and one another. They partly decide details of the world. Creative freedom — or what Peirce called spontaneity and Bergson, Berdyaev, and Whitehead, creativity — is a strictly universal concept, what the Scholastics would have called a transcendental, applicable to all beings, divine or otherwise. The creatures are lesser creators. The logical consequence is that, although sheer chaos is not a possibility, an element or aspect of the chaotic is quite real. No one agent, divine or otherwise, can fully determine what happens. Actuality is in principle a joint product and involves aspects of chance. This is not because God is weak, but because, according to this philosophy, the idea of power as a sheer monopoly is nonsensical. It would be power over nothing. Classical theism reduces the creatures, unwittingly, to nothings. They decide nothing; God decides everything. But the everything would be empty, meaningless. Hence the existence of evil in various forms is compatible with the divine existence, goodness, and power.

I shall explain two other arguments. One is a revised version of the ontological argument, and its main value is not to justify belief but to discredit the idea that the theistic question is an empirical or contingent one. Here in simplest form is the revised ontological argument.

Given either the classical or the dual-transcendence definition of God, there are the following options:

(A') The definition lacks definite and consistent meaning.

(A'') The definition has definite, consistent meaning; but it is compatible with this meaning that what is defined may not exist.

(T) The definition has definite and consistent meaning; and it is incompatible with the meaning that what is defined could fail to exist.

Formalizing:

"MT" for "theism is logically possible," where *logically* means taking into account certain meaning postulates about God and about the relation between logical and ontological modalities. "$\sim$" for not, negation.

Options		Argument		
(A') $\sim MT$		Premise	(1)	MT
(A'') $MT \,\&\, M \sim T$			(2)	$\sim MT \quad V \sim M \sim T$
(T) $MT \,\&\, \sim M \sim T$				$\sim M \sim T$
				T

Neither of the premises is derivable from logical constants alone. They can be justified only by informal logic, the logic of ideas outside formal logic as now constituted. They are metaphysical principles. (The comparison of them with the axioms of set theory might be worth exploring.)

The usual opinion has been that premise (2) (which I call Anselm's Principle) is the more doubtful one. I find premise (1) to be much more difficult to justify. Consistency is not easily judged where, as here, the claim to have an actual case would beg the question. We know from the Russellian and other paradoxes how easily a verbal formula can conceal a contradiction. Without the premise of consistency, no ontological argument can prove its conclusion. But this does not mean that it then proves nothing. For, if the argument is rejected because of the possible or actual falsity of premise (1), the implication is that the theistic question may, or must, be nonempirical. Empirical evidence adjudicates among logically possible proposals and is irrelevant to logically impossible ones. If the theistic question is not empirical, the classical atheistic argument from observed evils is unacceptable on this ground also.

Premise (2), or Anselm's Principle, is convincing to me as it has been to Anselm and many others. It is implied by Aristotle's dictum that "with eternal things, to be possible and to be are the same" ($MT = T$). Aristotle, followed later by Peirce and this writer, thought that contingency is inseparable from the productive process by which ordinary things come to be and also pass away. Aristotle said, too, that it was necessary that eternal things be necessary, also necessary that noneternal things be contingent. It is no accident that in time accidents happen; but in eternity there can be no accidents.[1]

I am strongly convinced that Aristotle was doubly right in all this. Peirce's dictum, "Time is a species of objective modality" (meaning that the past is actual and necessary, given the present; but the future is a mixture of chance and necessity, a matter of approximate or probabilistic implication, given the present) is (as he knew) close to Aristotle.[2] I see no coherent meaning for the idea of deity as possibly existent and possibly nonexistent; and I see no consistent way to reject theism except by rejecting its logical possibility or coherent conceivability. Atheists can do this, and only some other argument than the ontological can be used against their doing it.

It remains that the program of monolithic empiricism, regarding even God's existence as a contingent, empirical matter, can be maintained by nontheists only if they reject premise (2), and this in my judgment is to misunderstand the meaning of any suitable definition of deity. God could not just happen to exist, or just happen not to exist. This is an incoherent idea.

The following diagram may help to bring out the difference between the neoclassical version of the ontological argument and traditional ones.

"*VF*" for verbal formula, definition;

"Essence" for coherent idea expressed by the definition;

"Existence" (of the Essence) for somehow actualized or instantiated;

"Actuality" for how or in what concrete form, if at all, the Essence is actualized.

Transitions	1		2		3
T or Temporal things	*VF* ? Essence	<	Existence	<	Actuality
E or Eternal things	*VF* ? Essence	=	Existence	<	Actuality

The following transitions are contingent or nondeductive: *T2*, *T3*, *E3*. Transitions *T1* and *E1* (given meanings for the words in *VF*) are not contingent, but may be difficult to see as necessary (or impossible). Consistency is hard to judge, apart from actual instances, which in the theological case would beg the question. Transition *E2* is deductive, an equivalence, and Aristotle, Anselm, and many others have believed that they understood it as such. This was the strong point in Anselm's *Proslogium*. Others had virtually seen the equivalence before him, and Aquinas in a fashion agreed with Anselm on this point. I say "in a fashion" because the Thomistic distinction between merely conceptual and real existence could be construed as a way of almost seeing the difference between existence and full actuality. Thomas and Gaunilo were strongest in challenging the obviousness of the step *E1*. Do we really have a coherent, consistent idea of God? This is not immediately evident.

When Kant said that existence is never a predicate, he

would have been right had he distinguished "existence" from "actuality" and made his negative statement about actuality. From any essence or definable idea, how that idea is actualized or given existence, in what concrete form, is always contingent and non-deducible. This holds even of the divine essence.

The reason actuality must be contingent was first clearly hinted at, though not quite stated, by John Findlay. Any definition is abstract, and from the abstract, nothing less abstract can follow. From the logically weaker the logically stronger cannot be deduced. Abstractions exist (Aristotle) only in the concrete. What form this concretization takes cannot be entailed by the essence. Nevertheless, that there is some such concretization can in certain cases be entailed. The reason is that "somehow actualized" is in these cases no less abstract than the definition of the essence. God's possible, mutually exclusive or competitive, forms of actualization are as unbounded as the possible competitive forms of actuality in general. Thus God may exist knowing your or my existence, if you or I exist, or knowing our nonexistence if we do not exist. Infallible knowledge is potentially as multiform as possible states of reality. Like other abstractions, "omniscience" has a variety of possible forms of actualization; but in this case the variety is maximal, and since contingency is always some set of possibilities other than maximal, in competition with other such sets, contingency here loses its meaning. The same is true, I hold, of possible forms of *world*, where this means "concrete reality other than God." But this meaning of world is extremely indefinite and unindividual and does not connote an eternal rival to God. It only means that God could not be merely potentially, but must be actually, creative, or have some creatures or other.

If I am right, no classical defender and no classical critic of Anselm's argument have clearly seen the conceptual problems involved. All have missed the distinction between abstract and concrete, or mere existence of a defined essence and the concrete how of this existence. The distinction is valid not only of God but of ordinary and contingent beings. That Jimmy Carter exists now means that what makes him Jimmy Carter, the individual whose career began with a certain birth to certain parents, with identifying qualities and relations already actual when he was baptized and even earlier, the Jimmy Carter essence, is now still somehow actualized. It may be that he is awake or asleep, in good health or with a bad cold; still he is Jimmy Carter. Only a Leibnizian or one who, like Quine, spatializes time or eternalizes all truth needs to deny the distinction I am making. Common sense and ordinary language are, I believe, on my side in this. But philosophers have fallen in love with the too simple dichotomy, essence-existence. Like so many dichotomies it conceals a distinction as important as the one it makes.

The sense in which "the present king of France" is a Russellian definite description differs logically from that in which the definition of God is such a description. Ordinarily an essence is one thing, and the existence of that essence is another and additional thing or truth. This is because ordinary beings are produced by the creative process, which, as Bergson said, "is reality itself." And production is always partly contingent, might go this way or that way. The actuality is how it goes. In the case of God, the being itself, as identified by its essence, could not be produced but is defined as eternal. This means that it is essential to the creative process rather than one of its conceivable products. Insofar contingency does not apply. But the noncontingency of an essence only means that there can be no such thing as the essence simply unactualized. Either the divine essence is eternally somehow actualized, or the supposed idea fails to make sense and could not be actualized. Yet how, or in what concrete form, it is actualized can only be contingent. There can be wholly necessary yet fully actual reality.

Classical theism was like belief in the class of all classes. But it was never the God of religion that classical theism defined, as I and others have tried, during the past three and one-half centuries, to show. It is a glaring example of human fallibility that two thousand years were required to fully uncover the mistake. The "unmoved mover" of Aristotle is not the God of religion, not simply because of Aristotle's denial that God creates, knows, or loves the creatures (Aristotle was only being consistent in that), but because no simply unmoved being could create, know, or love concrete actualities, or be itself concrete or actual.

Anselm's proposal that "we can conceive God as such that

his nonexistence cannot be conceived" can be justified (assuming *MT*, or theism is possible) not only by the consideration that contingency has its ontological basis in the creativity of becoming as productive of noneternal things, but also by the principle already mentioned that contingent things are competitive in their existence. Each new baby implies a new claimant for room in the world, for food, drinkable water, breathable air, and so on. But God makes no such competitive claims merely by existing. God could conceivably exist no matter what else does. This does not mean that God's full actuality excludes nothing otherwise possible. To say that would imply that God is powerless, a mere empty abstraction. But, as we have seen, God's actuality is contingent, being not merely that the divine essence is actualized but precisely how or in what concrete form it is actualized. Only in concrete form is God competitive or contingent. But thus God is not powerless. It is only the existence of God, not the actuality of God, that is like the existence of a number, which neither knows nor creates.

In addition to the new argument from order, which is neither identical with nor unrelated to the old argument from design, and the ontological argument, which again must be revised from any of the older forms, there are four readily distinguished reasons for belief. One is a revision of the old cosmological argument; it is closely related to the ontological but starts from the idea of reality in general. It is not empirical, for any conceivable experience would present the problem.

Three additional arguments, which I call normative, turn on ideas of value: value first as aesthetic goodness or beauty, second as ethical goodness or rightness, and third as cognitive goodness or truth. I shall present only the ethical argument, which is most nearly anticipated by, but is significantly different from, Kant's reasoning about the *summum bonum*, which the good person tries to promote or bring about. It answers the question, "What is the ultimate aim or master purpose an ethical being should adopt, by which to judge all more specific aims?" Popular discussions about the possible "meaninglessness" of life bear some relation to this question.

The argument can be stated in various ways, using the format of atheistic disjuncts. Thus:

(*A'*) There is no meaning (or supreme purpose).

(*A''*) There is a meaning, and it is only the happiness, welfare, or goodness of oneself.

(*A'''*) There is a meaning, and it is only the welfare of some group of society, or the species, or all sentient beings (excluding God), either as in this life alone, or also in some posthumous mode of existence.

(*T*) There is a meaning, and it is the happiness or welfare of the creatures, whether (as I think) in this life alone, or as, in some cases at least, individually immortal, but all as somehow permanently enriching the divine life and its happiness.

For me, at least, A' is totally unacceptable. I find what Camus and Sartre, or Bertrand Russell, say about this to be contradicted by their behavior, and indeed by living at all.

A'': this merely egocentric notion I find as obviously false as any belief I know. No one can fully and consistently live by it. (The Buddhists saw this long ago, more clearly than most Christians have.) It also has the disadvantage that one must either postulate personal immortality or see one's life as destined to lose all its value in death. Rational purpose takes the future into account; but mortality means that self-centered purposes or valuations are, from an ultimate perspective, only short-term ones. A'' has not, since I reached the age of 20, been a living option for me.

A''' is in principle open to the second of the two objections just considered. Life on this earth, human or otherwise, shows no sign of being immortal, though, if we are wise, it may last a long time. In addition, what we can do for posterity is no adequate measure of what we feel is the value of our lives as we live them.

In this argument T is incomparably more credible to me than the atheistic options. It is clear that this was one of Whitehead's arguments for theism. Indeed all of the six arguments except the ontological can be read into his discussions. Nor do I have difficulty in sympathizing with his neglect of the ontological argument as he knew it.

The theistic arguments, which — as exhaustive sets of options — can be found in only one of my books, *Creative Synthesis and Philosophic Method*, are all ways of trying to show that the theistic view of life and reality makes better sense than any nontheistic view. Unintentionally, the French existentialists furnish a neat way of expressing the point. Their formula "Since God does not exist, life is absurd," can *modus tollens* be converted into, "Since life is not absurd, God exists." The deduction is just as valid, and the premise of the converted form can more plausibly claim to be intuitive. However, this claim is weak if the old idea of monopolistic power is allowed to define deity. Dual transcendence gives religious intuitions a new chance to achieve philosophical intelligibility. The nasty classical form of the problem of evil has always been the basis of a formidable argument against the divine existence. But the premise of theological determinism used in the argument never was in harmony with religious belief at its best.

It is time that theologians should cease giving away their case by playing fast and loose with the idea of freedom. Either we genuinely decide something and God (taken as existent and actual) does not decide everything, or we decide nothing and God decides everything. The second option was assumed as the meaning of belief by the French existentialists, and they were right to reject it. It was implicitly nonsensical. Unless we are genuinely creative in some degree, we cannot give meaning to the idea of supreme or eminent creativity as a property of deity. *Creative* here means settling what no antecedent or eternal cause or truth fully determines or is sufficient condition for. It means that while all occurrences, including instances of decision-making, have necessary conditions, they do not, in their concrete definiteness, have sufficient conditions. For the concrete there are only approximately or probabilistically sufficient conditions. In this view Epicurus, Aristotle, Peirce, Bergson, Whitehead, and many scientists agree, and I have long defended their doctrine in this aspect.

All careful philosophical arguments depend for their convincingness or lack of it upon a background of more or less systematized basic conceptions of life and reality. I am aware of how different this background is in my case and in that of many of my contemporaries. Take, for example, the philosophy of perhaps the most influential of living American philosophers, Willard V. Quine. He rejects any strict dichotomy of a priori and empirical, or necessary and contingent, statements, whereas my view depends on this dichotomy. Like Russell and Carnap, Ayer and Von Wright, Quine accepts Hume's view of the logical independence of events from their predecessors and treats causal connections as mere universality in the way events succeed one another. I think there are strictly necessary connections, or internal relations, holding asymmetrically between events and their predecessors. We could not have existed as we do unless our ancestors had existed as they did; we require them but they did not require us. My entire system collapses without this asymmetrical connectedness, which I take as the ontological analogy to the normal asymmetry of implication, the simple conditional as compared to the biconditional or equivalence. Hume's system is like a logic with all propositions logically independent; and Blanshard's or Spinoza's philosophy is like a logic with all propositions equivalent. My system, or Whitehead's or Peirce's (taking into account his Firstness, Secondness, and Thirdness), is like a reasonable logic with equally genuine cases of logical as well as ontological dependence and logical as well as ontological independence.

If *universal* means true regardless of time, then it is equivalent to eternal and is indeed coincident with necessary. But no amount of empirical science could establish such unrestricted universality, even as probable. Here I hold with Popper. All such questions are nonempirical, metaphysical, or modal.

Quine thinks that modal logic has no ontological bearings, whereas I hold with Peirce that time is "objective modality," and with Aristotle that all temporal existence is contingent and all eternal existence is necessary. In addition, the indeterminacy of the future and the view that becoming is essentially creative mean that, as there are new actualities each moment, there are new truths about actualities each moment. This idea conflicts sharply with Quine's doctrine of the timelessness of all truth. With James, Dewey, Bergson, Peirce, and Whitehead I hold that historical or biographical truths have not always or timelessly been true. This does not mean that before a certain time they were false, but that before a certain time there were no truths or falsehoods concerning Quine, say, or myself. With new subjects come new predicates of subjects, new possibilities of truths about the world. The idea of timeless truths about temporal things seems to me the ghost of medieval theism.

Not only are there, in my view, new truths with new individual subjects, but the final concrete subjects are not individuals enduring through changing states. Rather the subjects are the states themselves, my awareness now, for example. A moment ago there were no truths about that awareness, for there was not yet a definite entity with definite predicates having that locus in space-time. The future is irreducibly potential rather than actual, and this means in some degree, however slight, indeterminate rather than determinate. Becoming is the passage from incomplete definiteness to definiteness. It is creation.

I agree with Quine, however, that we do not need a three-valued propositional logic. This is a different issue from whether all truth can be stated in timeless terms. From the standpoint of eternity nothing concrete or particular can be seen, only eternal necessities, and these are all abstract. Assigning dates is possible only within time. The eternal is an extreme abstraction from the temporal. Definite events are all past, and, as Peirce said, one cannot look upon all time as though it were wholly past. (I grant that the relation of this to relativity physics is difficult. But so is the relation of relativity physics to quantum physics.) Nevertheless, statements about the future are all definitely true or false, provided they are properly formulated.[3] "Tomorrow X will do such and such" is true if, as things now are, X could not, causally could not, fail to do such and such. Otherwise it is false. Will and will not are inexhaustive, the third option being may-and-may-not. Or: it is now settled that X happens tomorrow; it is settled that X does not happen tomorrow; it is not settled whether X happens or does not happen tomorrow. Only one of these is true.

Like Quine I am not a phenomenalist but accept physical realism. I also agree with him that there is "no unbridgeable gulf between the mental and the physical." But this means for him that reality consists solely of a vast variety of forms of the physical, while I think, as Leibniz did, that it consists of a comparable or greater variety of forms of the mental, the physical being merely certain relational patterns exhibited primarily by low levels, or nonhuman forms, of the mental, or as I prefer to say, psychical. I am no more willing than Quine to accept a sheer dualism of sentient inextended mind and insentient extended matter. Rather, every single actuality (a stone or a tree not being single in this sense) is in its concreteness an instance of sentience, and every such actuality (even God) has a spatial aspect. Materialism is a fallacy of misplaced concreteness. What it asserts is true, but not all that it denies is false.

Another issue is that of the relation between individuals identical through change and their momentary states. I hold with all Buddhists and Whitehead that individual identity is a relative matter, that individuals are less concrete than their states or actual careers (with which Quine identifies the individual). With Peirce, Bergson, and Whitehead I hold that the future is incompletely definite, having only more or less general or unparticularized aspects, and this means that sheer nominalism is insofar false not simply because classes are real but because actuality has an irreducible aspect of indeterminate determinability as to how it will be superseded by subsequent actualities. Here, too, the "somehow" but not the "how" is necessary. Finally, I am not so far from Quine's moderate nominalistic "predilection" as Whitehead is in his eternal-objects doctrine. And I can go at least part way with Quine in his ontological relativity. For instance, whether a statement is analytic or synthetic depends partly upon how we arrange our language. However, the contrast between past events as the set of necessary conditions for a given event and the future as the partially indefinite potentialities (for the actualization of which the given event will be necessary condition) is not dependent upon language, nor is that between things that contingently come to be in time and things existing eternally and without possible alternative. If our language does not express these contrasts, then, as Peirce strongly hinted, so much the worse for our language.

I regret that I am not enough of a logician to present things with the technical precision and elegance of which Quine is a master. My favorite modern philosophers have been logicians: Leibniz, Peirce, Whitehead. James and Bergson, from whom I have learned a good deal, seem to me to suffer by their lack of logical skill and their belief in the irrelevance of logic metaphysics. Without being much of a logician, I have tried to be clear and to learn from those who were logicians. I derive some comfort from the consideration that, if my views conflict with those of some contemporary logicians, they continue a tradition to which three of the greatest logician-philosophers of all time have made central contributions: Aristotle, Peirce, and Whitehead. By contrast

Hume was no great logician, and his influence on contemporary logic I feel safe in regarding as excessive.

In three basic ways Hume begs the question against theism. He assumes that if two entities are distinguishable they are mutually independent (separable). It follows that if God and one of God's creatures are distinguishable, the creature could conceivably exist without its creator! He assumes that, though all events are mutually independent logically, they are causally completely determined by their predecessors. But then the laws of nature, which for a theist are divinely decreed, plus the past of any given creaturely act, completely determine that act. So not I, but the cosmic past and God, determine my decision. A theism that understands itself regards God as supremely free in a causally transcendent sense, supremely creative even of causal laws themselves, and regards a creature as a lesser form of such freedom. Theological determinism is a confused doctrine. The causal principle must be conceived by a theist asymmetrically as providing necessary but not in the strict sense sufficient conditions for an act. The act must be finally self-determined, in a sense *causa sui*, as Lequier, Sartre, and Whitehead say. Third, Hume assumes that all existence is contingent, so that God exists, if at all, thanks to some contingent circumstance, or else as sheer accident or miracle. As Whitehead implies, there is an important missing character in Hume's *Dialogues*.

I am not lacking in respect for Hume, and in some ways I think better of his thoughts than of Kant's. He showed with admirable clarity how certain assumptions are incompatible with theism. He also showed, in the words of Cleanthes, that classical theism was an empty abstraction logically equivalent to atheism. The case for theism cannot be rationally evaluated so long as logical atomism, classical determinism, universal contingentism, or classical theism is allowed to define the issues.

NOTES

1. For Aristotle's view on modality, see his *On the Heavens* 283b13; *On Generation and Corruption* 337b12–15; 337.34–338a3; *Metaphysics* 10.10; *Physics* 203b30.

2. For Peirce's doctrine of Objective Modality, see his *Collected Papers*, ed. Charles Hartshorne and Paul Weiss, 6 vols. (Cambridge, Mass.: Harvard University Press, 1931–1935), 5.453–63; 1.22, 173, 211, 300, 403.

3. See my essay, "The Meaning of 'Is going to be,'" *Mind* 74 (January 1965): 46–58.

2

Verification in Matters Religious

DAVID B. BURRELL

IN WHAT FOLLOWS I shall be offering a constructive thesis on ways of verifying religious statements — statements like "God created the heavens and the earth."[1] Over the past ten years, I have been concerned with avoiding that issue, concentrating rather on finding acceptable ways to parse the statement itself. But my philosophical colleagues have joined forces with the philosopher in me to bring me around to meet the issue of truth after all. Yet the face of the issue has undergone several changes as I would encounter it inadvertently while trying to elude it — so many, in fact, that I am willing to recommend my decade-long strategy as one of prudence rather than cowardice.

It was a strategy in part taken, and in part dictated. It was taken in reaction to the fruitless (yet not pointless) efforts to establish an acceptable procedure for verifying questionable statements — or at least for falsifying them, or for confirming the theories in which they function. While profiting a great deal from these discussions, as one may be able to detect, I found that they tended to presume a relatively unexamined notion of what it would be like for a statement to be true. In the wake of Wittgenstein's unsettling questions, and provoked by J. L. Austin's suggestion that "true" might on scrutiny bear at least as many senses as "good," I was persuaded that we cannot hope to proceed to verify statements like "God created heaven and earth" unless we make a concerted effort to understand what those who use them intend them to mean.[2] A crucial turn in the confirmation discussion guided me here: we in fact seldom set out directly to confirm a theory; we are rather concerned to show one to be better than another. That we exercise and develop our criteria of assessment in this way — comparatively rather than absolutely — says something about the role theories play in the continuing interpretative enterprise of scientific understanding, as well as in addressing the point of the moments of assessment.

I was forced to attend in a similar fashion to actual practice when I assumed (over the same decade) the chair of a faculty of theology. While administrative chores distract, the task itself can serve quite powerfully to concentrate the mind — a function Samuel Johnson ascribed to the prospect of death! In my case, I was brought to appreciate the intellectual skills required to elucidate a religious tradition and was confirmed in my suspicion that philosophers characteristically tend to raise the truth question too quickly, presuming they can summarize a theological position (like the one encapsulated in the creedal statement "God created the heavens and the earth") in a clear string of assertions.

This practice, in fact, bears a disappointing resemblance to a tactic employed by papal condemnations in the early decades of this century, wherein summary documents created the "heresies" of modernism and of Americanism. In this latter case, moreover, the philosophically suspect character of the procedure served those whose writings were purportedly condemned, for they were invariably able to contest the summary identification of their own position. Given the more directly speculative aim of a philosophical representation, however, everything turns on an accurate delineation of the specific theological account before asking how it might be said to be true. How can that be facilitated, if not assured?

My guide here will be Aristotle, who encourages us to think of intellectual capacities organized into relevant skills, and who warns us "never to expect more precision in the treatment of any subject than the nature of that subject permits" (*Nicomachean Ethics* 1.3 [1094b25]). Such intellectual tact is, he avers, "a mark of the trained mind." In a similar vein, Bernard Lonergan has suggested how we might differentiate the manifold skills relevant to theological inquiry into functionally distinct disciplines, much as he worked to develop in his students the capacities needed to perform so discriminating a task.[3]

My own attempt to understand what classical theologians were up to has confirmed this approach: by attending to their specific mode of argumentation, we can discern what they are trying to do, and only then can we hope to offer a summary at once accurate and helpful.[4] The sorry caricature "classical theism," often brought forward to motivate an entirely fresh start in philosophical theology, offers a negative illustration of this same contention.[5] My own preoccupation with theological education at all levels over most of the past decade has convinced me how much learning anything at all is a matter of acquiring the requisite skills. Consciously attained and exercised, they allow us to say what we mean, and so mean what we say.[6]

One more preliminary remark before proceeding to my thesis. I suspect that the outlook manifested in my proposal is congenially, if not characteristically, Catholic. For the particular arguments presume an unfolding context of inquiry, each stage of which contains critical features appropriate to it. Conscious of the continuing need for reform, and particularly grateful for the radical prodding of the Reformation, it does not, however, identify the beginning of "true religion" with that set of events, nor does it credit the complementary intellectual movement of the Enlightenment with initiating us into critical thought. The outlook orienting my proposal both permits and requires us to recover classical thinkers as contributing to our own self-understanding. In short, it stands within a tradition which embodies an active "handing on" (traditio) as illuminating in its continuities as in its innovations.

In fact, continuity must claim logical priority, for sheer grammatical consistency. Innovations have normally forced theologians to a more sharply critical stance, but no period can lay exclusive claim to that honorific title. Furthermore, it is my experience among theologians which has helped to bring this perspective into clearer view, as it has introduced me to many who would espouse a similar outlook without being themselves Catholic in a denominational sense. In deliberately addressing the issue of truth in religious matters, I shall try to bring what I can of that experience to bear on the elusive questions involved.

Verification of judgment

First of all, I shall presume that a religious affirmation is made in faith, and reflects a faith-understanding. This particular mode of understanding and affirming will show itself in the ways in which believers employ the language of faith. Our scrutiny of some characteristic uses will allow us to ascertain what might count as evidence for or against any claims which may be made. The assertion "God created the heavens and the earth" will offer a recurring instance, although Thomas's confession in John 20, "My Lord and my God!" will provide, with its narrative context, the paradigm for my account. Paul's second-level reflection on wisdom in I Corinthians 1–2 will offer a New Testament precursor of the account I shall propose.

It is crucial to this account that a faith-understanding, with its concomitant faith-assertion, be irreducible to other modes of understanding and asserting. It will involve them, to be sure, but no combination of historical conclusions or philosophical apprehensions can suffice to warrant my believing that God created the heavens and the earth. Yet this grammatical observation, however crucial, cannot be construed to allow us to avoid the issue of truth. For in believing God to be the creator, I am presupposing that what I believe in fact obtains. My confession, "I believe in God the . . . creator of heaven and earth," at once unites me with a community of believers who assert God to be creator. The fact that we are conscious of holding what we affirm by faith neither keeps us from asserting it, nor *a fortiori* restricts us to asserting merely that such is what we hold.[7]

I belabor this point to counter the pejoratively subjective connotations that inevitably accrue to that act of confessing one's faith, and do so because of the peculiarity of this understanding-cum-assertion: its being underdetermined, as it were, by the evidence.[8] Hence the apologetic arguments designed to bring me to believe that God created the universe are usually directed toward showing that I might believe so global a proposition responsibly. This indirect approach is called for precisely because the argument which would immediately warrant me to believe it — that such a claim is true — is not directly available. If it were, divine creation would not be an article of faith (except in a provisional sense). Yet such an indirect hold on a statement does not preclude my asserting it, so long as indirection remains consciously part of my act of asserting.[9]

It is this curious feature of faith-statements which makes them remind us that verification always involves a judgment: the judgment, in fact, that the evidence we have suffices to warrant asserting p. Only in highly restricted situations, bounded already by a complex set of judgments about proper procedures, can verifying a statement simply amount to a procedure, or even (as in the limiting case of calculation) to checking. The legal institution has established rules of evidence to circumscribe so far as possible the arena of judgment, and witnesses are regularly subjected to cross-examination to see if their testimony holds up.

If this be the case, then bringing a judgment to bear presupposes a linguistic field, even when the stipulations are so exacting as to be clearly ostensive. Take the ones announced by Thomas in the celebrated passage from John 20: "Unless I see the holes that the nails made in his hands and can put my fingers into the holes they made, and unless I can put my hand into his side, I refuse to believe." The procedure minutely described would presumably verify that the one who appeared to the disciples was indeed the same Jesus who had been crucified. But is that what is presented in the Gospel of John for us to believe?

In part, no doubt, but only in small part, that is what the story relates. For eight days later, when Jesus comes in through closed doors, he greets them: "Peace be with you," then speaks to Thomas: "Put your finger here; look, here are my hands. Give me your hand; put it into my side. Doubt no longer but believe." Thomas replied, "My Lord and my God!" Thomas's affirmation far exceeds what one might conclude from executing those procedures, and furthermore, the literary structure of the narrative presumes that Thomas had no need to go through with them. What takes place instead is a complete reorientation of his religious framework regarding the Holy One of Israel: in a flash of recognition, this moment brings Jesus' extended teaching, set in the background of the Scriptures, to a penetrating focus. Thomas confesses Jesus to be the Lord.

And as if it were not enough to show, as he has, the disproportion of a faith-assertion to what would normally count as evidence, John has Jesus go on to make explicit the connection of this event with those who would hear it recounted. To Thomas he says: "You believe because you can see me. Happy [blessed] are those who have not seen and yet believe." Thomas did not need to carry out his laboratory check, but he did see Jesus and then confess him to be the Lord. No one hearing the episode had even that possibility; all that is known is the extended story. Yet such ones are said to be happy — blessed, as in a particularly favorable relationship to the Lord, the creator of heaven and earth.

The point of the interpretative statement — "blessed are those who have not seen and yet believe" — is obviously to deflect any suspicion that first-generation witnesses are closer to the evidence for assenting to the grounding assertion of Christianity — Jesus is Lord — than later hearers of the word. John would forcibly remind us that is is not the signs by themselves which constitute evidence sufficient for believing; it is rather the way in which they have been organized in the gospel format which leads us to "believe that Jesus is the Christ, the Son of God, and that believing this you may have life in his name" (John 20:31).

The structure of John's gospel, moreover, is said to parallel the sacramental structure of initiation into a Christian way of life. That interpretive scheme would support my contention that verification — especially in matters religious — involves knowing one's way about that arena. And knowing our way about involves practices, linguistic and otherwise. Kierkegaard puckishly describes participating in religious practices as "making the movements," and recommends that an inquirer do just that. In fact, initiation into any field involves engaging in a complex of practices, many of which embody the norms for testing proper use of the key terms which they also implicitly define.[10] If such be the normal situation, how can we hope to set out the procedures for assessing adequacy of religious assertions without attending to the ways in which such practices manifest and qualify the linguistic fields germane to such statements?

In short, verifying involves many intellectual virtues which conspire both to discriminate valid entailments from others and to discern in what adequacy consists. As I try to articulate these virtues, I shall also respond to the observation that practices can be perverse as well as benign. How do we discriminate among them? How do we judge some to be more authentic than others?

Constructive thesis

The thesis I am proposing is at once descriptive and normative: we count a revelation to be true as it (a) confirms in a discriminating manner those aspirations which set one seeking, and (b) continues to realize them in a supereminent way. The first part of the thesis is designed to remind us that one cannot speak coherently simply of satisfying religious needs, since such needs invariably turn out to be aspirations. Indeed they involve one's aspiring to be related to oneself and to the universe in a way which is truthful — to become the sort of individual who can live with the truth of oneself as that relates one to others and to the world. Since the shape of such an individual will inevitably alter as one self-deception after another is exposed, the aspirations will invariably be described differently as well. (One may begin by wishing to be successful, go on to reject that goal, and, yet further on, reformulate success). A revelation will be adjudged to be true in the measure that it assists rather than hinders this process, discriminating among specific ideals yet in the process confirming the direction which the aspiring continues to take.[11]

The second part of the thesis focuses on this process of discrimination by requiring that the aspirations be realized in a supereminent way. The phrasing of this requirement is deliberately ambiguous: part of our counting a revelation as true will be its having been realized in the rather paradoxical fashion I shall describe, first in others and then in ourselves. This insistence attends specifically to the communal dimension of religious belief, and intends to incorporate the role which exemplary individuals, such as saints, play in forming and in transforming such communities and in eliciting our assent to those beliefs that the community deems essential.[12]

The way in which a religious revelation realizes specific aspirations will not be simply to satisfy them, but will always contain a transforming element or dimension as well. And, as Wittgenstein was fond of saying, "that is a grammatical remark."[13] For it has to do with what we countenance to be appropriate as religious revelations and aspirations, as well as the ways they interact to effect relevant transformations.[14] Hence Jesus works untiringly — notably in Mark's account — to avoid the title of Messiah, and Paul summarizes the entire trajectory as showing forth "God's foolishness," which is nonetheless "wiser than human wisdom" (1 Cor. 1:25). Yet the original aspirations will be restored in being so made over: this wisdom of God which can only be foolishness to us nevertheless is a wisdom (1 Cor. 2:6–9), and charity, as Aquinas points out, becomes in the saints the form of all the virtues, elevating the Aristotelian synthesis to unsuspected heights.[15]

This last instance affords a useful example of the process I have called transformation. For the introduction of charity—"not our love for God but God's love for us" (1 John 4:10) — not only bridges the great gulf which Aristotle observed "between God and man [making] friendship . . . impossible" (*Nicomachean Ethics* 8.7 [1159a5]), but also forces a new reading of the *Nicomachean Ethics*. If we replace what appears to be Aristotle's ideal, the "magnanimous man" (4.3), with Augustine's intimate friend of God, then we are led to accord to the later books of the *Ethics* on friendship a more central place than the original organization of the text would suggest. That is, of course, the sort of recasting which Aquinas worked time and again on Aristotle, whom he regarded as having fairly represented the human situation addressed by the revelation of God in Jesus.

The pattern is illuminating: one accepts the aspirations as delineated, yet shows how they can be realized in unsuspected ways. This sort of discourse logically presupposes a personal identification with the original description, together with some actual acquaintance with the diverse ways such aspirations may be realized, so that we can appreciate even the more paradoxical embodiments as extending the range of aspiration which originally claimed our energies. Such a pattern displays and embodies the structure of analogous discourse, which mode of speech finds its clearest examples among aspiration expressions. For we are led to distinguish a class of expressions as analogous when we notice how their range remains open to expansion, and does so notably through the challenge of exemplary individuals.

Aristotle seemed always to have Socrates in mind when he spoke of "the just man," for virtue cannot be spelled out without instancing individuals (*Nicomachean Ethics* 2.6 [1107a1]). So we speak as well of "the compassionate Buddha," of Gandhi as opening our hearts and minds to the possibilities of nonviolence, and of Jesus as "the way, the truth, and the life." These individuals are judged to be exemplary in that they embody what we have been looking for, yet do so in such a way as to confirm that original quest by giving yet more determinate sense to those aspirations.

So we are invited, by a quite spontaneous process of emulation, to model our lives after them. Nor is this call simply an ethical one. It has to do with understanding as well. We sense that we must venture after them if we would continue to use the language we now want to use fully, with the range and the harmonics it intimates. We can now formulate an appropriate meaning for verification in matters religious: the sense of discovery and progressive authentication which attends the way in which the practices of worship and of service lead us to a fresh understanding of what is good, beautiful, and true — and do so in an unsuspected manner. So Paul, in the midst of contrasting our wisdom with God's, can nonetheless affirm: "Still we have a wisdom to offer those who have reached maturity" (1 Cor. 2:6).

One need not, of course, agree with Paul's conclusion of the unique truth of God's revelation in Jesus. It would in fact betray the sense of his paradoxical treatment in 1 Corinthians to presume the evidence to be so compelling. My proposal is algebraic; it offers a way of proceeding. What it argues substantively is that the procedures include exercise in dealing with the realities to which our aspirations direct us. Worship and service are paradigmatic terms to describe the movements involved. Neither of these should be undertaken mindlessly. Critical intelligence need be no stranger to the pathways of the heart; yet it is a cultural fact of our times that it will tend to remain so unless we first venture to follow those aspirations usually identified as religious. It was Augustine who asserted, in the opening lines of his *Confessions*, "Our hearts find no peace until they rest in you"; yet this asseveration was only possible after the progressive discrimination among successive aspirations of his own heart so painstakingly recorded in that work.

Indeed, this way of addressing verification in religious questions reserves a central role for documents like Augustine's *Confessions*. For the sense of discovery and progressive authentication referred to are not matters for public review. Nor are they private, either, any more than our aspirations to what is good, beautiful, and true. The aspirations are shared, as Augustine's chance encounter with the poor yet happy beggar (Book 6) reminds us. On the strength of what we have come to know of ourselves from following the sinuous lead of those aspirations, he will recount the ways in which he was led to acknowledge — with Paul — how, "by God's doing [this Jesus] has become our wisdom, and our virtue, and our holiness, and our freedom" (1 Cor. 1:30). Even if we cannot match Augustine's stride, we can nonetheless comprehend the stages as he recounts them in retrospect. For we can recognize them as successive transformations of the original shared aspirations.

That is all Augustine could hope to achieve, and all that is required to claim his work as a classic. Anything more must — on his own testimony — be the work of God himself. Yet our purposes need nothing more; it suffices that efforts like his can attenuate strong claims to seal off religious from nonreligious language, or to make special claims for a knowledge reserved to insiders. There is indeed a progressive growth in understanding available to one who ventures to pursue, as he did, the pathways to a discriminating grasp of the claims of religious understanding. Yet the very effort of composing the *Confessions* presumes that this dynamic can at least in part be communicated. The relative success lies in the way the work itself solicits, not our agreement, but our undisputed attention. That feature, shared by classics generally, becomes in autobiographical religious writing a way of publicizing the procedures I have identified as verifying religious issues.

On a more austerely philosophical note, it will help to test this proposal against a recent essay of Kai Nielsen, who has continued to alert philosophers of religion to the issue of verification, and whose progression on this question has proved most illuminating to me.[16] In an essay inelegantly entitled "On the Rationality of Radical Theological Nonnaturalism," he expressly resumes his earlier contention "that nonanthropomorphic conceptions of God do not make sense."[17] In so speaking, he has a particular collection of recent writers on religion in mind, but what he says would certainly address classical theological formulations as well. As he notes specifically, "I mean that we do not have sound grounds for believing that the central truth-claims of Christianity are genuine truth-claims and that we do not have a religiously viable concept of God."[18]

He argues this familiar contention in predictable ways:

> (1) While purporting to be factual assertions, central bits of God-talk, e.g. "God exists" and "God loves mankind," are not even in principle verifiable [in being linked to] experienceable states of affairs . . . which would make their assertion or denial more or less probably true.

> (2) Personal predicates, e.g. "loves," "creates," . . . suffer from such attenuation of meaning . . . in religious linguistic environments . . . that we do not understand what we are asserting or denying when we utter "God loves mankind" or "God created the heavens and the earth." . . .

> (3) When we make well-formed assertions . . . we should be able successfully to identify the subject of that putative statement so that we can understand what it is that we are talking about. . . . But . . . we have no tolerably clear idea how God, an infinite individual, occupying no particular place or existing at no particular time, and being utterly transcendent to the world, can be identified.[19]

Given what has been noted here, one can insist that (1) central doctrinal claims must be linked with human experience, albeit indirectly through the practices of worship and of service which such claims both demand and legitimize. Indeed, the modes of service and of worship help us distinguish among divinities. If statements of the sort which Kai Nielsen singles out—"God exists,"

"God loves us," and "God created the heavens and the earth"—are not directly verifiable, that is because of the complex of roles such statements play in grounding religious life and practice.[20] Not that they are any less factual as foundational; it is rather that we can only understand the way they assert what they do assert by attending to the role those assertions play in founding the relevant religious practices. Certainly they do not so differ from other assertions that we are dispensed from monitoring their use in our desire to ascertain their meaning. In the case of religious assertions, this strategy shifts our attention and the demand for verification from the statements themselves to the practices they ostensibly ground—as the narrative of Augustine exemplifies so well.

Here we can notice an illustrative ambiguity in the very notion of a "foundational" statement. While it is true that "God created the heavens and the earth" serves to ground certain practices regarding the cosmos and humankind's relations with it, it is equally true that we are often drawn to affirm creation as we note the difference it can make in the ways a community can relate to the world. If the creedal statement is offered as warrant for the practices, the perceived rightness of the practices, especially by contrast with current alternatives, can warrant one's assenting to the statement. In an archaeological sense, the statement grounds the practices; in a constructive sense, the practices ground the statement. And since we often want to use "foundational" in both senses, it can be helpful to distinguish among them in each case.[21]

With regard to (2) personal predicates like "loves" or "creates," one must note how they also enjoy an enrichment of meaning when they are connected with human experience via the practices of service and worship which they legitimate and stimulate. Jesus' rebuke to his disciples discussing who would be first encapsulates this point:

> You know that among the pagans their so-called rulers lord it over them, and their great men make their authority felt. This is not to happen among you. No; anyone who wants to become great among you must be your servant . . . for the Son of Man himself did not come to be served but to serve . . . (Mark 10:42–45).

By his characteristic behavior, Jesus confirms a reading of the Scriptures which would offset the penchant to turn the God of Israel into a pagan god. Again, it is the comportment of the rulers, in the name of their god, which conveys better than sacred writings a sense of divinity.

Finally, with regard to (3), identifying the subject "God," one can respond by noting how carefully Christian theologians have been compelled to elaborate conceptions of divinity that display uniqueness. Augustine's own record of his continuing inability to "free [himself] from the thought that [God was] some kind of bodily substance extended in space" (*Confessions* 7.1), followed by his subsequent use of the Platonism of his own day to break through this limitation, offers a conceptual and existential way of conceiving a transcendent divinity nonetheless linked to our intellectual activity of judging things to be more or less true, as well as to our human need for understanding forgiveness.[22] Aquinas, more steeped in logic and speculative grammar, offers a syntactical formula designed to display perspicuously God's uniqueness — "to be God is to be" — and goes on to indicate how this status also generates the parameters for assuring the appropriate transcendence to every statement we can make about God.[23]

In each case, of course, I have offered a new twist. To Kai Nielsen's demands that (1) religious claims be linked to human experience, I have countered (2) the observation that the meaning of personal predicates is attenuated with the claim that their sense can in fact be enhanced, and I have suggested (3) conceptual and syntactical ways of identifying the subject of a sentence. These maneuvers do not reply in detail to Kai Nielsen's contentions so much as they indicate ways in which the discussion can be continued. More significantly, they endorse the point of this insistence that we must show how religious claims can be verified, without relinquishing the peculiar character which religious assertions display when they are permitted their functioning habitat.

I have tried, in delineating this constructive proposal, to do justice at once to philosophers' demands for verification and to theologians' insistence on the inherent mystery that is God.[24] An obvious objection to my proposal should appear from the way in which I was compelled to handle Kai Nielsen's mode of argument. By shifting the ground the way I did, I might be charged with circularity. By refusing to countenance the sense of "experienceable state of affairs" or of "identify" implicitly operative in Nielsen's arguments, I have subtly introduced new norms for judgment. I do not regard this as reprehensible, needless to say, since I have been trying all along to show how religious practices can refine our aspirations. So I can respond that I am not challenging logical norms so much as conventionally secular ones — a contention which Kai Nielsen himself recognizes in a recent review of Anthony Flew's *Presumption of Atheism*.[25]

In that illuminating essay, Nielsen challenges Flew's arguments that the burden of proof rests with the believer, and does so on logical and epistemological grounds. Logically, he finds Flew merely *assuming* "that an uncommitted stance on matters of grave import where there is a paucity of universally acceptable reasons or evidence is always morally superior."[26] Nielsen asks "whether reason commits us to any such thing" and further remarks that "Flew must give us, to make his position convincing, good reasons for believing that we have a common conception of rationality with strong enough criteria to give us grounds for assessing the comparative rationality of the commitments of believers and skeptics."[27]

If I am not mistaken, just such a presumption animated much of Nielsen's writing over the past decade, and if he finds it questionable now, that is because he has been impressed with the analyses of belief offered by Donald Evans and Diogenes Allen, and the vein of reflection inspired by Wittgenstein's *On Certainty*.[28] It is these epistemological reflections which lead him to question Flew's "Rationalist Principle," countering that it is "actually an unreasonable demand to require that all one's reasonable believing must have grounds and that the strength of our belief should be proportional to our evidence for that belief."[29] His authorities are Wittgenstein and Peirce, and it is reflections of this sort which make a timely treatise of Newman's *Grammar of Assent*. The precise point which is not governable by rule is that point where independent lines of argument do or do not converge to bring one to assent or to dissent to the question at issue: whether or not to believe in God.

Finally, I would like to conclude by pulling together observations throughout this inquiry pertaining to the skills requisite for discernments of the sort that Newman identifies. Reminding myself and others that practices always introduce us into accepted ways of identifying objects or of countenancing experiences, I have been arguing that religious practices demand commensurate attention. In fact, religious communities have developed keen capacities for discernment — criteria not unlike those to which Jesus alluded in the conversation with the anxious and ambitious disciples. These norms have been honed by practice into working sets of skills, often associated with programs of renewal. In these situations, the grounding religious norms are used to carry out a continuing critique of ideological positions — especially those which the religious group itself so naturally spawns.

By challenging any use of key normative expressions that close off a new perspective or curtail self-criticism, a religious community will evidence its vitality. Hence both Juan Luis Segundo and John Paul II warn against identifying liberation with a specific political program.[30] It is the relative success of procedures of this sort, which are identifiable and recognizable to a participant-observer, that allows us to discriminate among religious communities. If we judge some to be more authentic than others, and still others to be perverse, it is by their capacity to release the critical force and enhancing power latent in their key creedal statements that one can know them.

My own proposal to carry this program forward is to adopt an explicitly cross-cultural strategy. By examining the ways in which Islam has both formed and criticized the culture that it continues to inform, I would hope to gain some purchase on a similar assessment of Christianity: so identified with the dominant Western mindset, how has it and how can it also function to criticize the ways that mindset becomes an ideology? Such a comparative study promises to indicate — in the interstices, if you will — the strengths and weaknesses of each in offering an antidote to the pervasive human penchant to make an idol of one's own cultural arrangements.[31] One can also hope through studies of this sort to develop the intellectual virtues required of someone in our age to begin to verify a religious doctrine-in-practice. For religious matters are so intertwined with matters cultural, and hence with our very own skin, that our best chance to discriminate as well as to avoid presupposing the matter under examination seems to lie in an intercultural inquiry.

Furthermore, philosophers have met nothing but disappointment in their search for general criteria of meaning and truth from which to assess the sense and truthfulness of religious statements. By undertaking the effort to understand another tradition, however, one invariably gains critical purchase on one's own. Such a perspective may be the closest we can hope to come to the touted "universal viewpoint" to which we cannot help aspiring.[32] And the tactic explicitly incorporates the leading insight from philosophy of science regarding confirmation of theories to which I alluded at the outset. In any case, this promissory epilogue is offered in the hope that I will be able better to meet the challenge of this topic after actively exploring for a year or two the perspectives which emerge from such a study.

NOTES

1. The statement chosen exemplifies a creedal statement. In his "Metaphysics and Verification Revisited," *Southwestern Journal of Philosophy* 6 (1975): 91, see also pp. 75–93, Kai Nielsen offers it as an example, in tandem with another: "The soul sinks into the Ur-One once it leaves behind the consciousness of anything." By deliberately remarking that the one chosen is a creedal statement, I wish to remind the reader how embedded it is in a tradition of practice as well as of theological inquiry. In that respect, the two statements are hardly parallel.

2. John Langshaw Austin, *Philosophical Papers* (Oxford: Clarendon Press, 1961), pp. 97–100.

3. Bernard J. F. Lonergan, *Method in Theology* (New York: Herder and Herder, 1972).

4. David B. Burrell, *Exercises in Religious Understanding* (Notre Dame, Ind.: University of Notre Dame Press, 1974).

5. Cf. chap. 5 in my *Aquinas: God and Action* (Notre Dame, Ind.: University of Notre Dame Press, 1978), for a critical appraisal of the polemical starting points generally assumed by "process theology."

6. Cf. "From System to Story: An Alternative Pattern for Rationality in Ethics," in Stanley Hauerwas, *Truthfulness and Tragedy*

(Notre Dame, Ind.: University of Notre Dame Press, 1977), pp. 15–39.

7. John Henry Newman's *Grammar of Assent* has recently been reissued by the University of Notre Dame Press (1979) with an introduction by Nicholas Lash which displays how contemporary a work this has become. Wilfred Cantwell Smith's recent *Faith and Belief* (Princeton, N.J.: Princeton University Press, 1979) shows how a reflective historian of religions must confront current philosophical paradigms for religious assent as quite inadequate to the cross-cultural situations which in fact obtain.

8. This fact troubles theologians of a classical liberal persuasion as well. Their tactic will minimize the differences among particular religious faiths by seeking for a universal human trait which can be shown, by transcendental argument, to presuppose the existence of a God. They are *theologians*, then, in the sense in which Aristotle gives that name to those who do constructive metaphysics (*Metaphysics* 983a6–11).

9. It is worth recalling that we can only use analogous expressions properly when we remind ourselves how they are made to allow for "improper" use. See my *Analogy and Philosophical Language* (New Haven, Conn.: Yale University Press, 1973), chap. 9.

10. I am indebted here to an illuminating address by James Redfield entitled "Classics and Anthropology," in which he noted how the humanities and social sciences can be seen diverging precisely in the character of the exercises and hurdles these two paradigmatic disciplines design for their graduate students to negotiate.

11. Alastair McKinnon, in his *Falsification and Belief* (The Hague: Mouton, 1970), pp. 75–81, offers a schematic account of this process with respect to a believer's progressive use of "God is loving."

12. For a provocative account of this process, see Patrick J. Sherry, "Philosophy and the Saints," *Heythrop Journal* 18 (1977): 23–37.

13. Ludwig Wittgenstein, *Zettel* (Berkeley: University of California Press, 1967), #717. The entire remark is worth noting: "'You can't hear God speak to someone else, you can hear him only if you are being addressed'. — That is a grammatical remark."

14. Rosemary Haughton's study of paradigm situations — *Transformation of Man* (London: Geoffrey Chapman, 1967) — exemplifies this contention in an illuminating fashion.

15. *Summa Theologiae* 1–2.65.3: "Manifestum est autem quod caritas, inquantum ordinat hominem ad finem ultimum, est principium omnium bonorum operum quae in dinem ultimem ordinari possunt."

16. Nielsen's bibliography on this question is extensive. Besides

the essay cited in note 1, see "On the Rationality of Radical Theological Nonnaturalism," *Religious Studies* 14 (1978):193–204, and his review of Anthony Flew's *Presumption of Atheism* in *Religious Studies Review* 3 (1977):144–50.

17. Nielsen, "Rationality of Radical Theological Nonnaturalism," p. 193.

18. Ibid.

19. Ibid.

20. The burden of Alastair McKinnon's *Falsification and Belief* (see note 11) is to remind us of the various roles which creedal statements can play, and to suggest how one might discriminate among them. His schematic delineation offers some useful guidance to those intent on tracking foundations.

21. I have explored the parallel senses of justification in "Religious Belief and Rationality," in *Rationality and Religious Belief*, ed. C. F. Delaney (Notre Dame, Ind.: University of Notre Dame Press, 1979).

22. See my essay on Augustine in *Exercises*, pp. 23–27.

23. See my *Aquinas* study, chaps. 2–3.

24. Karl Rahner's treatment of God as "absolute mystery" offers the key to his theology, as well as to his recent *Foundations of Christian Faith* (New York: Seabury Press, 1978), chap. 2.

25. Nielsen's review of Flew's *Presumption of Atheism*, pp. 144–50.

26. Ibid., p. 146.

27. Ibid., p. 147.

28. Donald Evans, "A Reply to Flew's *Presumption of Atheism*," *Canadian Journal of Philosophy* 2 (1972):47–50; Diogenes Allen, *Reasonableness of Faith* (Washington, D.C.: Corpus Books, 1968); Ludwig Wittgenstein, *On Certainty* (New York: J. and J. Harper, 1969).

29. Nielsen's review of Flew's *Presumption of Atheism*, p. 148.

30. This is the burden of Juan Luis Segundo's *Liberation of Theology* (Maryknoll, N.Y.: Orbis Press, 1976), as well as John Paul II's address to the Conference of Latin American Bishops at Puebla.

31. This is the point of Peter Winch's much discussed essay, "Understanding a Primitive Society," *American Philosophical Quarterly* 1 (1964), reprinted in Bryan Wilson, ed., *Rationality* (Oxford: Clarendon Press, 1970).

32. See Jean Ladrière's summary remarks: "Le Rencontre avec L'Islam," *Revue Philosophique de Louvain* 77 (1979):143–59.

3

Hegel and Schleiermacher
on Theological Truth

ROBERT R. WILLIAMS

In 1822 AFTER THE appearance of the first half of Schleiermacher's *Glaubenslehre*, Hegel launched an attack that soon became highly influential. In this attack Hegel's sarcastic invective produced a notorious caricature of Schleiermacher's thought that continues to haunt Schleiermacher-interpretation: "If religion in man is based only on a feeling, then the nature of that feeling can be none other than the feeling of his dependence, and so a dog would be the best Christian, for it possesses this [feeling] in the highest degree. . . ."[1] Then, as if to anticipate the argument of the second part of the *Glaubenslehre* which had not yet appeared, Hegel continued: "The dog also has feelings of deliverance when its hunger is satisfied by a bone."[2] Beneath the sarcasm and polemic there is a serious point: Schleiermacher's definition of religion as a feeling of dependence appears to signal a retreat of theology from its traditional doctrines and truth-claims into mere private feeling and subjectivity. To Hegel Schleiermacher appears as a theologian who has lost his theological nerve, who seeks to make peace with modern critical consciousness by adopting a noncognitive or emotivist interpretation of faith or religious consciousness. Religion and theology are thus to be rendered compatible with the modern mind by surrendering all truth-claims. Such a theological retreat achieves only a superficial barren peace, for, on the one hand, faith has lost all substantial content, and all that is left is the empty husk of subjective feelings. On the other hand, critical reason and philosophy have renounced all claims to speculative truth, and so the human spirit is left with only appearances and feelings for its sustenance.[3]

The controversy between Hegel and Schleiermacher was one-sided; Schleiermacher maintained public silence, although privately he indicated that he thought himself untouched by Hegel's barrage. His silence is thus best construed to convey the point that Hegel's remarks were such obvious and gross distortions of his thought that no response or rebuttal was necessary. To defend himself against Hegel would be to admit that some of the charges had struck home. I believe that Schleiermacher was correct. Yet there has been much ink spilled on and about this controversy, most of it in favor of Hegel. Thus Hegel begat Feuerbach, who in turn begat Barth. The result was and is that Schleiermacher's theological agenda was virtually pre-empted by the Hegelian criticism and Barth's program. Moreover, now that Hegel is being rediscovered, Hegel's interpretation of his period and contemporaries tends to be accepted uncritically. His caricature of Schleiermacher, for example, is completely accepted by an otherwise careful interpreter who writes that "Schleiermacher's mature stance could only be conceived as a theology of feeling" and that "the main thrust of Hegel's case against allowing feeling to be normative needs no comment."[4] On the contrary!

What follows is an attempt to sort out the confusions and to identify the real issues in the controversy. In the first section I shall show that Hegel's portrayal of the feeling of utter dependence as a noncognitive animal-like dependence is an irresponsible caricature and a bogus issue. Hegel himself knows better, as we shall show. In the second, I shall point out some significant differences between Schleiermacher and Hegel in respect to their understanding of the phenomenological and hermeneutic moment of theological reflection, differences that result in different interpretations of the meaning and truth of Christianity. As will become clear, the real issues are still with us.

FEELING: MEDIUM OR OBJECT OF RELIGION?

There is a striking ambiguity pervading Hegel's discussions of *feeling*. In his attack on Schleiermacher Hegel takes feeling to

mean a mere subjective sentiment or sensation void of content
and thus incapable of supporting doctrine, and also a wholly private, solipsistic subjectivity incapable of community and thus unable to support institutionalization. However, this is not Hegel's
final word about feeling. It has not been sufficiently recognized
that Hegel presents a quite different assessment of feeling in his
Lectures on the Philosophy of Religion, one which closely approximates that of Schleiermacher. Hegel claims that feeling is the
original and immediate apprehension of all that is true:

> All that is true begins in its appearance, i.e., in its being in
> the form of immediacy.[5] . . . First it exists as intuition,
> faith, feeling, as the felt flash-like witness of the Spirit . . .
> and thus it must be developed from the . . . interiority of
> feeling into the mode of representation.[6]

It appears as a paradox that feeling in Schleiermacher should
mean mere blind emotion, private subjective sentiment, and that
feeling in Hegel's thought should appear as the original and pri-
mordial apprehension of reality and truth.

Hegel exploits an ambiguity in the term feeling to portray
Schleiermacher in the worst possible light. As Lewis White Beck
has observed, the term feeling (*Gefühl*) is susceptible of two interpretations. It can mean (1) a merely subjective sentiment of
sensation, something like the English sense data, and (2) the general openness and receptivity of the human being toward the
world, in which case it is "a cognitive faculty of great complexity."[7] In the former sense feeling is sensation (*Empfindung,*) and
it derives its philosophical ancestry from Locke. The function of
the sensation is to be the unit of experience which mediates between the so-called external world and the private interior of a
worldless, solipsistic subjectivity. Thus, as is well known, Hegel
has no difficulty in refuting the claim of sense certainty to be immediate; sensation itself is a mediated, derivative theoretical
reconstruction of perceptual experience, which comes to us originally in the form of little bits which come to be ordered and associated by the mind. In his attack on Schleiermacher, Hegel would
have us believe that Schleiermacher seeks to determine religion as
feeling in this subjectivist, solipsistic sense. He takes Schleier-

macher to task for seeking to "*base* religion on a feeling," to make feeling the source of the divine, and for seeking to "establish Christian doctrine on the basis of feelings," to "make feeling the seat and the *source* of the True. . . ."[8] Feeling as sensation (*Empfindung*) is the lowest form of sentience, a capacity shared by humanity and animals. Hence a dog would possess an *Empfindung* of dependence in the highest degree, and be the most religious being.

Yet even in the heat of his polemics against Schleiermacher, Hegel is mindful of the other more important sense of feeling as original medium of apprehension of truth and reality. He observes that it is one thing to say that the meanings of God, truth, and freedom are merely felt, that they are supposed to have their warrant in feeling, and quite another to say that "such an objective content possesses its own inherent validity before it enters into one's heart and feeling, so that the character, correction, and warrant of feeling derive from that content. Everything turns on this difference of attitude."[9] Elsewhere Hegel comments on the issue in the following way: "Feeling *as such* is not rejected by philosophy. The question is only whether the *content* of feeling is the truth and can prove itself to be true in thought."[10] This nonsubjective, nonpsychologizing sense of feeling as general perceptual consciousness open toward the world is accepted by Hegel himself. Further, it should be noted that Hegel claims that religion and philosophy have the same content: "In both the object is the truth, in that supreme sense in which God is the truth."[11] In fact, Hegel is quite close to Schleiermacher in claiming that religion apprehends the truth immediately in feeling, while philosophy is a reflective, speculative comprehension of that same truth. Hegel even concedes Schleiermacher's point that feeling is the original, primary form of apprehension of ultimate truth, while doctrines are secondary and derivative: "Religion can exist without philosophy. But philosophy cannot exist without religion. For it encompasses religion."[12] Philosophy or speculative thought does not create or invent the truth; rather it depends on the prior givenness of truth to religious consciousness. Hence philosophy depends upon religion for its content. And the encompassing of religion by speculative thought is supposed to alter only the form but not the content of religious and theological truth.

In fact, Schleiermacher holds the precise concept of feeling as general perceptual consciousness that Hegel defends. Further, that this is Schleiermacher's meaning is evident in the first half of the first edition of the *Glaubenslehre* which Hegel read. In view of the previously noted ambiguity of the term feeling, Schleiermacher's declaration is extremely important: "I do not want to be drawn into controversy with the respected theologian who recently said that nobody in his right mind would make feeling the ground [basis] of religion. I only assert that feeling is the locus of piety."[13] In his lectures on *Dialektik* (1822) Schleiermacher drew a clear and sharp distinction between *Gefühl* and *Empfindung*.[14] The latter term signifies the private, subjective sensation or sentiments. *Gefühl* signifies consciousness as such, which on the one hand is open toward the world and on the other hand mediates, underlies, and accompanies all forms of human praxis and cognition. Schleiermacher's assignment of primacy to *Gefühl* as general intentional consciousness is his version of the primacy of perception: "What I understand by feeling does not at all proceed from a representation, but rather feeling is the original expression of an immediate existential relation."[15] Like the later Husserl, Heidegger, and Merleau-Ponty, Schleiermacher breaks with the Cartesian version of consciousness as purely rational, self-transparent, and cut off from the world and embodiment. In designating consciousness as feeling, Schleiermacher seeks to call attention to its pretheoretical existential dimension, which is not a consciousness directed at itself but rather one that bypasses itself toward the world and is "immersed" in the life-world. Thus the two basic modalizations of *Gefühl*—the feeling of freedom and the feeling of dependence—are essentially mundane and reflect the self in reciprocal relation with the life-world. Schleiermacher's break with Cartesianism is further evident when he indicates that the basic contrast structuring experience is not the logical or epistemological contrast between subject and object, but rather the personal-existential contrast between I and Thou.[16] *Gefühl* is inherently social and intersubjective; the world in which it is immediately immersed is a cultural and social world, structured by reciprocity.

Consequently, Schleiermacher's enterprise is far from a misguided effort to base religion on merely subjective, animal-like *Empfindung*. There is no need to respond to this gross caricature! However, Schleiermacher is not even contending that religion is synonymous with *Gefühl* or consciousness as such. To be sure, he thinks that persons are essentially religious (as does Hegel). But religion is not simply identified with *Gefühl*; rather religion is a distinctive modification and determination of *Gefühl*, with a distinctive intentional object and intentional structure. In short, *Gefühl* per se is not the ground, basis, or object of religion. Rather *Gefühl* becomes religious when it undergoes modification, when it becomes a *Gefühl* of utter dependence. The feeling of utter dependence is constituted on the one hand by the recognition of the finitude and contingency of both self and world (coexisting in mutual reciprocity), and on the other by reference to the transcendent Whence of both self and world. Elsewhere I have sought to show that Schleiermacher's phenomenology of religious consciousness amounts to an existential version of the ontological argument.[17] His point is similar to Hegel's discussion of the theological proofs as expressing an underlying pretheoretical elevation of the mind to God. The common point is that the proofs are secondary theoretical articulations of a pretheoretical religious sense for the infinite or God-consciousness. It is crucial to see that the feeling of utter dependence in its reference toward the Transcendent presupposes the constitution of the social and cultural world and the recognition of full human freedom. In other words, a being incapable of having a social and cultural world and of relatively transcending the world in freedom, would not be capable of the feeling of utter dependence. Moreover, since the feeling of utter dependence presupposes the constitution of the social world and freedom, it never occurs all by itself. Hence it is always expressed concretely and determinately in images and terms drawn from a particular historical, sociocultural world.

For this reason there is no such thing as a feeling of utter dependence, understood in a subjective sense as a discrete, purely private experience (*Empfindung*). The term *feeling of utter dependence* designates an intentional structure common or generic to religious consciousness. This terminology is the result of eidetic and intentional analysis, of reflection on actual religious communions. Schleiermacher's phenomenological reflection uncovers the feeling of utter dependence as the depth dimension or noetic structure in correlation with the Transcendent, and constitutive of actual religious experience. Its abstract character is evident from Schleiermacher's emphatic statement that there is no absolutely general consciousness of utter dependence or God-consciousness; rather, it is always as a particular person determined in a particular historical-sociocultural way that one is conscious of being in relation with God. For example, in Christianity fellowship with God is mediated by redemption through Christ. Christians are concretely conscious of sin and grace, redemption, and so forth. But the feeling of utter dependence is co-present as a depth dimension of these more concrete intendings, and occurs in concrete modified form. Hence the discussion of the feeling of utter dependence is meant as an eidetic of religious consciousness in deliberate abstraction from concrete historical determinacy. For this reason the feeling of utter dependence is not offered as a natural theology; Schleiermacher rejects natural religion and theology as abstractions.

There is no real dispute between Hegel and Schleiermacher on the question of the primacy of perception. Both agree that the so-called turn to the subject need not be executed in a psychologizing way, which leads to subjectivism and solipsism. The turn to the subject is actually meant as a phenomenological recovery of the things themselves, a return to the life-world and religious praxis as a distinctive region of the life-world. However, there is real disagreement concerning the meaning and execution of this move. Hegel indicates that feeling as such is not rejected by philosophy; the only question is whether the content of feeling is the truth and can prove itself true in thought. In other words, although theological reflection depends on concrete religious consciousness and praxis for its content and thus must begin with the life-world, it does not have to stay at home. The truth-question is not settled at the concrete life-world level of the perceptual origins of religion; rather, it is settled at the speculative level, at the point of discernment whether the immediate content of faith can prove itself true in thought. The issue can therefore be reformulated in somewhat more contemporary terms, namely, how does the symbol give rise to thought?

HOW DOES THE SYMBOL GIVE RISE TO THOUGHT?

Schleiermacher's identification of feeling as the locus of piety in human experience represents an important corrective to the one-sided abstract intellectualism and formalism dominant in the tradition, according to which religion is essentially doctrine, and measured by assent to doctrines. In identifying feeling as the locus of piety, Schleiermacher is claiming against Cartesian intellectualism that consciousness is not fully self-transparent, that it feels itself rather than sees itself through purely rational intuition. Here Schleiermacher makes common cause with existential phenomenology. Further, the language in which religious consciousness originally expresses itself is not doctrine, but rather concrete poetic images, symbols, and myths. Consequently, self-knowledge is not given at the outset (save in purely formal and abstract terms); rather, it must be recovered through a hermeneutic reflection on the poetic images, myth, and story put forth by the faith-community. Here Schleiermacher makes common cause with hermeneutic phenomenology: the full, concrete self-consciousness must be recovered from the world-understanding and orientation toward the Transcendent present in the concrete images and symbols. Therefore Schleiermacher distinguishes three forms of theological propositions. The first and most basic form consists in an existential phenomenology of Christian religious consciousness and a hermeneutic phenomenology of its direct expressions. Thus the first form of proposition is a description of God and world as coconstitutive of the self-consciousness of sin and grace. Doctrines are meant as secondary and derivative expressions of the Christian consciousness; thus nothing should appear in doctrine not previously found in or expressly meant by Christian consciousness. The second and third forms of theological propositions move at the abstract level of anthropology, cosmology, and rational theology; they are legitimate only if they can show derivation from the first form.

Therefore the slogan "the symbol gives rise to thought" has the following meaning.[18] The language of feeling already possesses intrinsic meaning and truth prior to reflection. It is this meaning which must be recovered through phenomenological reflection and must be given to thought. The symbol donates significance to thought; it gives to thought something to think about. Second, the meaning that the symbol donates to thought is irreducible to thought. Thought is dependent on the symbol for this specific content. If the symbol donates concepts, these concepts are indirect — as, for example, original sin, the servile will, redemption. This means that the symbol has already said everything enigmatically that thought can say clearly. Thought may clarify the meaning of the symbol, but it does not entirely replace or substitute for it. Schleiermacher stresses this point when he says that "a proposition which had originally proceeded from the speculative activity, however similar it might be to our proposition in content, would not be a theological proposition."[19] Thus reflection cannot bypass or substitute the symbolic meanings. The task is not to invent new meanings or to impose them on an inchoate religious experience, but rather to uncover, clarify, and criticize the pretheoretical meaning of faith.

There are two ways which the above hermeneutic principle can be violated. The first is to interpret symbols literally as revelations of a separate, supersensible, supernatural realm. This occurs in dogmatic mythology (such as Gnosticism) and in supernaturalism.[20] In this interpretation the symbols become heteronomous. In Schleiermacher's language, they represent Docetic and Manichaean distortions of Christianity. The second way is to interpret the symbols as merely imaginative trappings and decorations of a purely rational truth. This amounts to allegory: once the veil of imagery has been stripped away, the inner rational kernel shines forth and is directly accessible. The symbolic mode of expression is then dispensable in principle; the meaning can be better expressed in another form. This amounts to a complete demythologizing of the meaning of faith; its symbols are interpreted as expressions of rational autonomy. In Schleiermacher's language, the result would be a purely rationalistic interpretation of Christianity (formalism) closely related to the natural heresies of Pelagianism and Ebionitism. Against both reductive interpretations, there is an opacity to the symbols which makes it impossible to reduce them to rational thought; hence complete demythologizing is impossible. Reflective thought remains dependent on the symbol for its concrete determinate sense. However, this dependence is not heteronomous as in Gnosticism and supernaturalism, for the symbol discloses the concrete existential condition of humanity in relation to the Transcendent. It is this existential condition that must be reflected in the *Glaubenslehre*, and for this reason the system can never be finished or complete; not can it be wholly speculative.

Although Hegel would agree that pretheoretical religious consciousness and its symbols are the starting points of theological reflection, such priority is not logical but merely chronological. If theological thought begins with the life-world and the corresponding pretheoretical modes of expression, thought does not have to remain at home. Indeed, thought is here in a foreign medium. Hence the symbol must be elevated to the level of thought. The immediate form of truth must be sublated (*aufgehoben*) so that the meaning of truth can be properly expressed. Within the immediate life-world modes of expression, this meaning cannot be fully, properly, or adequately expressed. To be sure, the meaning is there in the symbol, but in confused form, a form inadequate to the content. Hence, "the symbol gives rise to thought" means that the symbolic mode of expression can be replaced by a more exact concept. The concept is a more adequate form of religious truth. Hegel thus runs the risk of reducing feeling and its symbols to primitive and confused expressions of speculative thought. For example, Hegel tells us that "this content [of feeling] is *in its essence* no sensuous idea . . . it does not exist for the imagination, but only for thought; God is Spirit, and only for pure Spirit, that is, for thought."[21] Despite his polemics against Jacobi's faith-philosophy, Hegel claims that thought itself is intuitive, and this means "an intellectual intuition of God; in short . . . how belief and intuition, when transferred to these higher regions, differ from thought, it is impossible for any one to say."[22]

But if speculative thought itself is intuitive, then it does not essentially depend upon symbols and indirect concepts yielded by symbols for access to otherwise hidden depth dimensions of existence (the servile will) or to the relation between humanity and God. Thought can dispense with symbols and directly grasp the realities themselves. Thus a reversal of the dependent relation of thought upon symbol takes place; "feeling . . . receives through philosophy its true content."[23] Once the meaning of the symbol has been rationally comprehended and put in proper conceptual form, the symbol is dispensable; the meaning and truth of the symbol can be generated directly out of the concept itself, which sublates and replaces the symbol.

Hegel's version of "the symbol gives rise to thought" arises out of his reading of the process of doctrinalization of Christian theology, and his interpretation of Christianity as containing the speculative principle itself, namely, the unity of infinite and finite, or the Incarnation as the idea of God-human. The process of doctrinalization is a process of translating the immediate faith-utterances and symbols into doctrines and concepts. This involves a process of stripping away the merely figurative and positive elements to uncover the inner speculative principle, which is evidenced in the replacement of Scriptures by doctrines or concepts. In contrast to the regressive procedure (*Rückfragen*) of hermeneutic and transcendental phenomenology (which seeks to ground and clarify language in lived experience) Hegel's hermeneutics is governed by the principle that the pretheoretical meaning of religious faith is to be found not in the original symbols, but rather in the results, for example, in the doctrines of historic Christianity. For this reason Hegel virtually identifies Christianity with its classical orthodox doctrines. He does not seek to question back behind these doctrines to Christian consciousness; the traditional doctrinal package, including particularly the Trinity and the Incarnation, is accepted as an adequate representation of Christian consciousness. The problems Christianity encounters in light of modern historical consciousness are not due to the speculative substance of its doctrines; these are the truth, and always will be. Rather, the problems are due to the precritical form in which the speculative truth and principle are expressed.

In short, the process of rational articulation and explication, stripping away the positive and mythical elements and translation into universal form, has not been carried far enough. Hegel claims to be bringing the process of rational explication and articulation of the meaning of Christianity, already begun in the historical doctrines, to its conclusion by formulating the speculative substance in a form adequate to its content. Hegel believes that

Christianity itself authorizes the speculative ascent to the absolute standpoint, and thus authorizes Hegel's speculative logic. Consequently Hegel regards himself as the champion of theological orthodoxy against the revisionist theologian of his day, namely, Schleiermacher: "It is now philosophy that is essentially orthodox; the propositions that have always been valid, the basic truths of Christianity, are maintained and preserved by it."[24]

Of course Hegel champions not theological orthodoxy per se, but rather the speculative truth and significance implicit in the doctrines. It is this truth that must be speculatively re-enacted. Hegel's speculative re-enactment and transfiguration do for the orthodox doctrines what they had previously done for the pretheoretical expressions of feeling; namely, they correct the deficiencies of form and translate the meaning into a more adequate universal conceptual scheme. Fackenheim describes this transfiguration as follows: "Thought and speculation will grasp as one single activity what in faith and representation [that is, doctrine] remains double. How is this possible? Religious spirit . . . exists on the human side of the divine-human relationship. Philosophic spirit — speculative thought — rises to its divine side."[25] The intellectual intuition of God which makes symbols dispensable also means that speculative thought can "rise above time to the Deity dwelling in eternity."[26] What to faith and doctrine (as immediate and representational forms of truth respectively) remains distinct and separate, becomes a unity in the speculative form of thought: "God is God only insofar as he knows himself. His self-knowledge . . . is a self-consciousness in man and man's knowledge of God, which proceeds to man's self-knowledge in God."[27] Fackenheim explains: "For the speculative thought which reenacts Divinity, the human other is a divine self-othering; the diremption between the Divine and the human a divine self-diremption; and the divine reconciliation with the human a divine self-reconciliation."[28]

The existence of the Right Hegelians on the one side, and the Left Hegelians on the other, attests that the exact meaning of Hegel's thought is extraordinarily difficult to determine, much less assess. Hegel's claim is that the speculative re-enactment alters the form but not the content of theological truth. This assertion suggests that there must be some equivalence between the theological doctrines and their speculative transfiguration. Further, the fact that religion can exist without philosophy implies that the religious consciousness and its secondary expression in doctrines are true apart from and independent of the speculative re-enactment. Yet the actual meaning and truth of religion are not fully comprehended until they are put in final, adequate form, which is the speculative. As Hegel says, feeling receives through philosophy its true content. Thus, not only does speculative thought transfigure Christianity, it is also the final measure of all previous forms of truth. Hence one cannot appeal to the prespeculative forms of expression of religious truth as criteria of adequacy to measure the speculative transfiguration without challenging Hegel's claim concerning the supremacy and finality of speculative thought and logic. Here the lines are drawn: Hegel may locate and preserve some speculative significance in the orthodox doctrines of Christianity, but he does so only by abandoning the concrete life-world essence of Christianity.

TOWARD A REDEFINITION
AND REASSESSMENT OF THE DISPUTE

There are some real issues at stake, but these are not the issues in terms of which the historical controversy was carried on. Two major issues can be identified: (1) What is the essence of Christianity and where is it to be located? (2) Is the life-world the foundation of all praxis, the subsoil of truth and validity, or can it be replaced by a "more adequate" conceptual scheme?

The essence of Christianity

As Troeltsch has pointed out, Schleiermacher's introduction of the concept or motif of the essence of Christianity (*Wesen des Christentum*) marks a fundamental change in the theological situation and theological method. Classical Christianity would never have used this term; it would have spoken of the faith of the church or the Word of God. The very term *essence of Christianity* signals an attempt to describe and portray Christianity as a historical form of religious life. Thus Schleiermacher breaks with the intellectualism and provincialism of the tradition according to which religion is assent to doctrines and propositions. Rather, the essence is to be sought beneath the intellectual doctrinal formulations in the concrete historical-existential configuration of Christian consciousness, in Christianity as a historical-cultural form of life. Such a move is necessary in view of the discrediting of traditional theological authorities (such as an infallible Scripture, an infallible magisterium, the eclipse of metaphysical natural theology) by historical consciousness. The essence is synonymous neither with the traditional doctrines of historic Christianity nor with the traditional theological authorities. Hence Schleiermacher's identification of piety as a modification of feeling rather than a knowing (intellectual assent to doctrines) or a doing (postulates of moral faith).

To grasp the essence it is necessary to penetrate beneath the doctrines to a more basic level. The essence is recovered through a phenomenological description of the total configuration of actual Christian consciousness — the feeling of utter dependence as a general cultural and communal dimension of human life, as concretely shaped and modified by redemption. The essence thus becomes the new theological norm determining the basic sense of Christianity, its historical development, its doctrines and ontological interpretation. Doctrines, philosophical theologies, and so forth, are not the essence but derivative accounts and explications of the essence. Such interpretations and elaborations of the meaning of Christianity are limited by its natural heresies as distortions of the essence: the Manichaean-Docetic-supernaturalist distortion, and the Pelagian-Ebionite-rationalist distortion. The crucial point is that the essence itself is not doctrine or ontology, but prior to such; moreover, it is not primarily speculative, although it obviously has ontological and doctrinal implications.

Hegel tends to identify Christianity with its historic doctrines. To be sure, Hegel is not theologically conservative; what interests him is not the underlying concrete historical sense, but rather the speculative truth implicit in the orthodox doctrines. The doctrines of the Trinity and the Incarnation portray the unity of God and humanity in the form of imaginative representation. Hegel's philosophical enterprise is a transfiguration of this speculative principle. But in his identification of Christianity with its historical doctrinal package and his reading of this as fundamentally speculative, Hegel misreads Christianity. Kierkegaard aptly framed the issue: "If speculative philosophy is asked what Christianity is, it replies at once: Christianity is the speculative interpretation of Christianity."[29] Speculative thought commits the fallacy of misplaced concreteness. In light of Schleiermacher's introduction of the motif of the essence of Christianity, it can be questioned whether the traditional doctrinal package is an adequate account of Christianity. Schleiermacher specifically questions whether the classical doctrines of the Trinity and the Incarnation are essential to Christianity. In his interpretation of such doctrines, Hegel picks out precisely the speculative aspects and terminology which Schleiermacher is willing to jettison. It is not sufficient to turn to historic Christianity to determine what Christianity is. The question of the essence takes priority because the essence serves as the principle of historic as well as contemporary Christianity. The point is not that historic Christianity is a mistake (although that might be established by theological criticism); the point is rather that the question of the essence is prior to the attempt to determine the speculative ontological significance of Christianity, historic or contemporary. Schleiermacher's question is prior to Hegel's speculative re-enactment.

The question of the primacy of the life-world

Hegel in effect concedes that religious feeling is the original mode of apprehension of theological truth. However, such a form of apprehension enjoys only a chronological priority; it is only the point of departure, not a foundation. Thought is not dependent on the symbol; the symbol per se is dispensable. To be sure, feeling is not rejected; the question is whether the content of feeling can prove itself to be true in thought. Feeling is the poorest form of truth; the full significance of its content is not apparent until it has been put in proper form. This means that the images and symbols of faith must be replaced by concepts and more adequate forms. According to Hegel, the great representative of the intellectualist tradition, speculative philosophy is the final arbiter of truth. It is through philosophy that feeling receives its true content. Seen from this perspective, Schleiermacher appears as the modern theological sophist. He locates and bases religion in feeling, the poorest form of truth; he declares the doctrines to be secondary derivative expressions of feeling; and he seeks to pry Christianity loose from its speculative moorings. Thus Hegel derides Schleiermacher's position as "a theology which only describes feeling [and] does not get beyond the empirical, historical and . . . contingent particulars, and has not yet to do with thoughts that have a content."[30] In short, Schleiermacher surrenders the truth question. However, Hegel's interpretation can be sustained only if it is true that the life-world and its forms of expression can be replaced by better, more adequate concepts.

Schleiermacher would side with Husserl on the above question. The life-world is not merely the dispensable starting point, but the foundation of logical and rational thought. Far from surrendering the truth question as formal intellectualism claims, the regress to the life-world is a way of radicalizing it. Beneath truth in the sense of correspondence and conceptual analysis and refinement lies truth in the sense of disclosure. The latter is an a priori condition of the former; therefore Husserl considers the life-world the concrete a priori presupposition of all forms of praxis, including the theoretical and scientific. Similarly, Schleiermacher considers religion, a modification of feeling or life-world consciousness, to be the underlying foundation of science and culture, and shows that science and culture have inevitable existential-religious dimensions and presuppositions. Consequently, the truth question is not introduced into religion or theology by the arrival of philosophical reflection. Faith or immediate consciousness is an essential aspect of the life-world a priori. Faith is already a comprehension of self and world vis-à-vis the Transcendent. Hence religious faith is already struggling with truth questions such as sin, idolatry, evil, and flight. To be sure, speculative philosophy can clarify and seek to communicate these pretheoretical truths; but it would be madness to think that speculation can replace and dispense with the original life-world forms of existence and their sense. This exclusive preoccupation with speculation would turn Christianity into a doctrine which must be understood, while ignoring what the doctrine is about. If the speculative re-enactment of symbol and doctrine is true, it is true about the life-world and must refer to the life-world a priori. This reference and aboutness are not themselves speculative or theoretical; they are a condition of seeing that anything, including speculative theories, is true. To lose sight of or to forget this fact is to become comic. Schleiermacher admitted that he was a dilettante as a speculative philosopher; however, no one has accused him of being merely comic.

NOTES

1. G. W. F. Hegel, Foreword to H. Fr. Hinrichs's *Die Religion in inneren Verhältnisse zur Wissenschaft* (1822), trans. A. V. Miller, in *Beyond Epistemology: New Studies in the Philosophy of Hegel*, ed. F. G. Weiss (The Hague: Martinus Nijhoff, 1974), p. 238. Hereafter cited as Foreword.

2. Ibid.

3. Ibid.

4. Merold Westphal, in *Beyond Epistemology*, Appendix, p. 222.

5. G. W. F. Hegel, *The Christian Religion*, pt. 3 of the *Lectures on the Philosophy of Religion*, ed. and trans. Peter C. Hodgson (Missoula, Mont.: Scholars Press, American Academy of Religion Texts and Translations Series No. 2. 1979), p. 241.

6. Ibid., p. 263; cf. also p. 255.

7. Lewis White Beck, *Early German Philosophy* (Cambridge, Mass.: Harvard University Press, 1969), p. 416.

8. Hegel, Foreword, pp. 238–239. The same misrepresentation of Schleiermacher is to be found in the *Lectures on the Philosophy of Religion*, 3 vols., trans. E. B. Speirs and J. B. Sanderson (New York: Humanities Press, 1962), pp. 119, 125, 137.

9. Hegel, Foreword, p. 240.

10. Hegel, *Christian Religion*, p. 292.

11. Hegel, *The Logic of Hegel*, trans. from the *Encyclopedia of Philosophical Sciences* by W. Wallace (London: Oxford University Press, 1959), p. 2.

12. Hegel, 2nd Preface to the *Encyclopedia*, cited in Emil Fack-

enheim, *The Religious Dimension of Hegel's Thought* (Bloomington: Indiana University Press, 1967), p. 116.

13. Friedrich Schleiermacher, *Der Christliche Glaube* (Reutilingen 1828) #8 Anmerkung 'b'.

14. See Rudolf Obebrecht, *Friedrich Schleiermachers Dialektik* (Leipzig: J. C. Hinrichs, 1942), p. 287. Schleiermacher expressly says that *Empfindung* is *post*-subject-object, and hence theoretically mediated, while *Gefühl* refers to global self-consciousness at the pretheoretical level, prior to the theoretical construction of experience as subject-object. Hegel makes the same point in the *Phenomenology*, in his critique of sense-certainty.

15. Schleiermacher, *Sendschreiben an Luecke*, ed. Hermann Mulert (Giessen: Topëlmann, 1908), p. 15.

16. See my *Schleiermacher, the Theologian* (Philadelphia: Fortress Press, 1978), chap. 1.

17. Ibid.; see also my "Schleiermacher versus Feuerbach on the Intentionality of Religious Consciousness," *Journal of Religion* 53 (October 1973).

18. See Paul Ricoeur, "The Hermeneutics of Symbols and Philosophical Reflection," in *The Philosophy of Paul Ricoeur*, ed. Charles Reagan and David Steward (Boston: Beacon Press, 1978).

19. Schleiermacher, *Glaube*, 2nd ed. #16 Postscript.

20. Schleiermacher, *Glaube*, 2nd ed. #22; see also Ricoeur, "Hermeneutics of Symbols."

21. Hegel, *Lectures on the Proofs for the Existence of God*, in *Lectures on the Philosophy of Religion*, 3:164. Italics are mine.

22. Hegel, *Encyclopedia*, pp. 124–25.

23. Hegel, *Christian Religion*, pp. 292–93.

24. Ibid., p. 25.

25. Fackenheim, *Religious Dimension of Hegel's Thought*, pp. 190–91.

26. Ibid., p. 151.

27. Hegel, *Encyclopedia* #564; from *Hegel's Philosophy of Mind*, being pt. 3 of the *Encyclopedia of the Philosophical Sciences*, trans. W. Wallace (Oxford: Clarendon Press, 1973), p. 298.

28. Fackenheim, *Religious Dimension of Hegel's Thought*, p. 203.

29. Soren Kierkegaard, *A Concluding Unscientific Postscript*, trans. D. F. Swenson and Walter Lowrie (Princeton, N.J.: Princeton University Press, 1968), p. 335.

30. Hegel, *Proofs for Existence of God*, in *Lectures on the Philosophy of Religion*, 1:134.

4

The Status of *Vorstellung* in Hegel's Philosophy of Religion

PAUL RICOEUR

THE AIM OF THIS ESSAY is twofold: historical and critical. On the
one hand, I want to stress the central position of *Vorstellung* in
Hegel's philosophy of religion. On the other, I want to question
the relevance of this problem for a modern hermeneutics of religious discourse.

First, a word about the term itself. It makes sense within the
pair of opposites: *Vorstellung* and *Begriff*, and not, as in Kant, as
a synonym for the phenomenon opposed to the thing in itself
(*Ding an Sich*). Therefore, it should not be translated as "idea,"
but as "figurative thinking." "Representation" is acceptable, to
the extent that this translation underscores the breadth of the Hegelian use of *Vorstellung*. It covers not only stories and symbols —
images, if you will — but also such highly refined conceptualized
expressions as Trinity, Creation, Fall, Incarnation, and Salvation, not only in religious but also in theological discourse. Hegel's
claim is precisely that, regardless of how rationalized this discourse may be, it is not yet conceptual, in the most cogent sense of
the word, but still pictorial or figurative, in a way that it is now
our task to delineate.

Two main issues are at stake here: first, the broad characterization of religious discourse — including the theological one — as
figurative; secondly, the status of figurative language vis-à-vis
conceptual. Only the second issue remains controversial: it is difficult to say to what extent the conceptual abolishes the figurative,

70

and, if it does not, to what extent the conceptual still needs the support of the figurative to assert itself and to remain meaningful.

I

   Concerning the characterization of religious discourse as figurative, there is little change from the *Early Theological Writings*, edited by Nohl in 1907, to the Berlin *Lectures on the Philosophy of Religion*, given four times, in 1821, 1824, 1827, and 1831. At the beginning, the problem arises under another name, that of the "positivity" of religion. This term is intended to underline the cultural status of religion as a body of beliefs relying on founding events, embodied in distinctive symbols, and transmitted by highly institutionalized communities. By calling religion positive, Hegel wants to assert that there is no such thing as a rational or natural religion, as Kant and the thinkers of the Enlightenment would like to have it. Consequently, the mode of thinking proper to religion is indispensable. It is inherently constitutive of religion as such. Therefore, there is nothing disparaging in the characterization of religion as intrinsically positive and not natural or rational.

   Nor is its characterization as figurative, in the *Phenomenology of the Spirit*, meant to be disparaging. The main reason for this appreciative recognition is the basic conviction which rules the whole Hegelian hermeneutics: that figurative thought, in spite of all the shortcomings that we shall consider later, is the closest to philosophical thinking. It is potentially speculative. This statement drastically distinguishes the Hegelian approach to religious discourse from the Kantian one. For Kant, and in general in a philosophy of limit, there is no room for a self-presentation, a *Selbst-Darstellung*, of the Absolute. The theoretical task of philosophy is achieved and complete with the unmasking of transcendental illusions and the imposition of limits to such claims as, for example, the claim of phenomenal thought to equate itself with absolute being. The only permissible extension of transcendental claims is practical reason. Religion, then, belongs in one way or the other to this sphere of practice.

For Hegel, on the contrary, religion foreshadows speculation, rather than enhancing practice. Religion therefore must
show how it is already speculative, though still figurative. This
ambiguous status of the *Vorstellung* defines its place in the system: close to the end, but inadequate to the end. Close to the end?
In the *Phenomenology*, it comes after the whole survey of the
stages and configurations of the cultural world and before the
chapter on absolute knowledge; in the *Encyclopedia*, it comes in
the midst of the theory of absolute spirit, between art and philosophy proper. Inadequate to the end? This is the controversial
question that we shall come to grips with in the second part of the
paper.

Let us proceed a step further in what I called the appreciative recognition of figurative thought. The figurative component
of religion is not only attracted forward by the speculative moment of philosophy, it is related backward to all the cultural
"shapes" (*Gestalten*) or configurations which precede it along the
journey of the human spirit from nature to culture, and from culture to the self-disclosure of the Absolute.

Figurative thought could not fulfill its task with regard to
speculative thought if it were not rooted in the world-spirits. It
recapitulates the cultural determinations (*Bestimmungen*) that
precede it — if not historically, at least logically. These moorings
of religion in culture imply that religion assumes the historical peculiarities of each *Volksgeist*. This cultural tie between religion
and the world-views of peoples explains the proximity between
art and religion. Hegel underscores this proximity by the treatment of Greek religion as art-religion in the *Phenomenology;* by
placing religion between art and philosophy in the *Encyclopedia;*
and by the high ranking of Greek religion still evident in the Berlin *Lectures*, where it competes with the Hebraic religion as the
proper preparation to revealed or absolute religion. But, above
all, the capacity of religious representation to recapitulate previous cultural shapes or determinations is mirrored in the very
structure of the figurative thought of religion, which repeats the
divisions of the Spirit in "consciousness," "self-consciousness,"
"reason."

A dialectic of *Vorstellung* is made possible by this retrieval, within the sphere of figurative thought, of the self-structuring of the Spirit in all the spheres of its manifestations. This transfer of structure from culture to religion witnesses is a fundamental trait of the whole Hegelian mode of philosophizing: it belongs to the meaning of the Spirit that it does not proceed in an additive way, part after part, as happens in nature, but that it is present as a whole in each of its moments. The whole process of philosophy consists in the progressive recognition of the immanence of the whole to its part. This is why the figurative thought of religion is not added in an extrinsic way to the fabric of culture, but retrieves the determinations that have already appeared at the crucial moment of the return of the Absolute to itself.

This last remark leads us to the threshold of the most decisive trait of figurative thought in religion, its inner dynamism. It is precisely this trait which will raise the critical question of the final assessment of figurative thought by Hegel. To say that religion and philosophy have the same speculative content, but that religion grasps it only in the figurative mode and philosophy grasps it in the conceptual mode, is not a way of putting them side by side. The speculative mode is not extrinsic to the figurative mode, but generates the inner dialectic of the representational mode itself. Religious representations are not inert contents, but processes traversed by an inner dynamism pointing toward the speculative mode. It is therefore the description of the inner dynamism of the figurative mode that constitutes the Hegelian hermeneutics of religion.

With this leading thread, Hegel is able to fulfill three tasks which after him will become independent, if not mutually exclusive, but which he was both the first and the last to attempt to conceive and to achieve as an indivisible enterprise. These three tasks correspond to three questions:

What is religion in general?

What are the different types or kinds of religions?

What is the basic meaning of Christianity?

For us these three questions have fallen in three different fields: cultural anthropology, comparative history of religions, biblical theology. For Hegel, to answer the first question is to move to the second, and to solve the second is to raise the third.

Since religion in general is nothing else than the inner dynamism of *Vorstellung*, the rationale of this dynamism has to be disclosed by the very shapes of the different religions. And if these shapes may be ordered along a scale, according to the degree of opacity and transparency of the shapes, then religions have not only to be compared, but graded. And if this grading leads to the conclusion that the figurative element raised in Christianity is both the ultimate degree of transparency that religious symbolism may offer and the ultimate resistance of its residual opacity, then the philosophy of religion achieves and exhausts its task in the philosophical reinterpretation of Christian dogmatics. And this reinterpretation in turn, in virtue of a kind of feedback, brings back the general meaning of religion, since it leads the phenomenology of representation to the point where the difference between representation and concept fades away and where the anticipation of the end at the beginning of the inquiry becomes the end of the inquiry and the end of its topic: "The completion of religion consists in the two forms becoming identical with each other."

I am unable to give even a hint of the grandiose scheme of this overarching process which consists in the "differentiating and self-returning" of the individual moments of religion. To do that I would have to show how the rational structure which organizes the shapes of the *Vorstellung* repeats the basic structures of the phenomenology as a whole—consciousness, self-consciousness, reason, spirit—and therefore makes the *Vorstellung* recapitulate all the previous stages of the process according to the most fundamental insight of Hegel's thought: namely, that the Spirit is present as a whole at each of its phases and that it proceeds not by external additions, but by inner development and in a cumulative manner.

I prefer to select two significant moments, two "shapes" which represent critical turns in the whole dialectic and allow us to pinpoint Hegel's own ambivalent attitude concerning the inadequacy of religious *Vorstellung* and the prospect of its disappearance for the sake of conceptual thought. Those are the death of the Greek gods at the turning point from art-religion to revealed religion; and the death and Resurrection of Christ at the turning point, within revealed religion, from Christology to ecclesiology.

Greek religion finds its first expression in the plastic arts: the statue of the god expresses the return of the externality of nature to the interiority of self-consciousness. The statue, in turn, has to be relocated within its appropriate setting: namely, the whole cultic situation, where the surrender of the worshipper's own will rejoins the descent of the god in the realm of actuality. Then the meaning of this aesthetical-ethical concept of religion is brought to language through the epic, tragic, and comic modes of speech, which together constitute the spiritual work of art. This is, roughly, the shape of Greek religion: from statue, through cult, to speech. It is the dissolution of this last stage which will occupy us for a while.

At this last stage, embodied in comedy, the interiorization of the Absolute in the reflective self resumes the main traits of the unhappy consciousness and its culmination in skepticism.[1] Comedy brings to language the ironic distancing of a self which may dare "drop the mask just because it wants to be something genuine" (*Phenomenology* #744). We may already wonder whether this apology for ironic distancing (#745) does not reveal something of Hegel's strategy concerning not only Greek religion but religion as such. The question is so puzzling that we may wonder whether the irony of comedy is still religion. "The individual self is the negative power through which and in which the gods, as also their moments, viz. existent Nature and the thoughts of their specific characters, vanish" (#747). The discreet admiration of Hegel cannot be ignored. "This self-certainty is a state of spiritual well-being and of repose therein, such as is not to be found anywhere outside of this Comedy" (#747).

Unhappy consciousness, returning in the midst of the phenomenology of religion, is redescribed as "the knowledge of the total loss" (#753) of the ethical world and of the religion of that world. And what is most puzzling is that Hegel transfers to this loss of the Greek idols the Lutheran hymn for Good Friday: "God is dead": "It is the consciousness of the loss of all *essential* being in this *certainty of itself*, and of the loss even of this knowledge about itself — the loss of substance as well as of the self, it is the grief which expresses itself in the hard saying that 'God is dead'" (#752).

The question will be whether a similar grief and a similar

conversion of worship into remembrance — *Erinnerung* — does not return in the philosophical hermeneutics of Christianity with the theme of the Resurrection of Christ in the midst of the spirit of the community. Or, to put it in more telling terms: whether *Erinnerung*, beyond the death of the contextual setting of any symbolic systems, is not a universal constraint in the hermeneutics of religious symbolism *überhaupt*. I shall return to this point in Part II.

If we stick to the letter of Hegel's philosophy of religion, it is not the paradigmatic character of the death of the pagan gods that he underscores but its significance as the necessary transition to revealed religion. Very cautiously Hegel has not linked his praise of Greek comedy and the death of the gods to the highly rhetorical passage about the mourning over the death of the idols, and the conversion of that mourning into *Erinnerung*. He preferred to use it as an introduction to his account of revealed religion, that is, of Christianity.[2] The reason he thought that this sense of total loss should be encompassed within the framework of revealed religion is that only this sense may prevent revealed religion from falling back to natural religion by reinstating "substance" in the place of "subject."

In order to be the revelation of the Spirit, absolute religion — as it is also called — must include within its own symbolic structure the emergence of self-consciousness. This absolute subjectivity is secured by "the knowledge of the total loss" of the ethical world. The same reason may explain why, in the last Berlin *Lectures*, Hegel spoke of Greek religion on an even higher level than Jewish religion. In this sense the function of *Erinnerung* is not only to conclude the Greek cycle of religious symbols but to establish revealed religion itself at the level of interiorized remembrance. Such is the thesis that the Hegelian interpretation of the Cross and Resurrection confirms and expands.

It is of course with Christianity, according to Hegel, that the inner dynamism of *Vorstellung* reaches its climax. On the one hand, its primacy in the field of symbolic discourse arises from the near transparency of its figurative shapes, to the extent that its basic symbol is a self, the very self of Christ, the shape of self-consciousness par excellence. On the other hand, its residual inadequacy constitutes the most formidable resistance to the transposition of figurative thought into conceptual thought, because of its links with historical events, pictorial contents, and sedimented traditions. Let us put aside for a moment this negative assessment of *Vorstellung* in absolute religion and ponder on its inner dynamism.

If Christian figurative thought has a unique significance it is because the Absolute has equated itself with actuality, with presence. Hegel is unequivocal on that point: "That absolute Spirit has given itself *implicitly* the shape of self-consciousness, and therefore has also given it for its *consciousness*—this now appears as the *belief of the world* that Spirit is *immediately present* as a self-conscious Being, i.e. as an *actual* man, that the believer is immediately certain of Spirit, *sees, feels,* and *hears* this divinity. Thus this self-consciousness is not imagination, but is actual in the believer. Consciousness, then, does not start from *its* inner life, from thought, and unite within itself the thought of God with existence; on the contrary, it starts from an existence that is immediately present and recognizes God therein" (#758), and further: "This incarnation of the divine Being, or the fact that it essentially and directly has the shape of self-consciousness, is the simple content of the absolute religion" (#759). No philosopher before Hegel has ever spoken, as philosopher, in such terms of Incarnation. Absolute knowledge is possible because there the Absolute has made itself known. In that sense, absolute religion is a synonym for revealed religion, *geoffenbarte Religion.*

To express this ultimate immediacy in the dialectical terms of Hegel's system, the two propositions—the self is absolute being and the absolute being is the self—have to be equated in the speculative proposition which rules the exchange between subject and predicate. That equation may be understood as an anticipated answer to Feuerbach. If only the human self relinquishes itself to offer itself up to the Absolute it is because the Absolute does the same thing. The Incarnation is a double *kenosis:* "Spirit has in it the two sides which are presented above as two converse propositions: one is this, that substance alienates itself from itself and becomes self-consciousness; the other is the converse, that self-consciousness alienates itself from itself and gives itself the nature of a Thing, or makes itself a universal Self. Both sides have in this way encountered each other, and through this encounter their true union has come into being" (#755). A one-sided *kenosis*, the one Feuerbach considers, would generate only a mere fanciful spiritual life: "Spirit," Hegel says (#756), "is in this way only *imagined* into existence (*eingebildet*)". The immediacy of absolute religion relies on the actuality of Incarnation (#757).

At first glance, this assertion of the immediacy pertaining to revealed religion seems to be the most nonhermeneutic assertion. If there is a place in space and a moment in time where and when the Absolute coincides with actuality, does not the intuition of this sameness and this abolition of otherness put an end to interpretation or rather prevent it from ever starting? It seems to me that the great originality of Hegel's hermeneutic and its permanent value resides in the following dialectical situation: far from blocking the process of interpretation at its beginning, it is this very assertion of sameness, this immediacy of the "being there" of the Absolute which generates the whole process of interpretation. But the converse is no less true: there would be nothing to interpret if there were not, as at the beginning of the *Phenomenology*, an absolute presence, a substantial given, which calls for mediation. Because there is revelation, because there is this seemingly nonhermeneutical moment of sameness between Absolute and immediacy, an infinite process of mediation is launched. The problem of *Vorstellung* in Christianity finds its rooting in this process: "This Notion of Spirit that knows itself as Spirit is itself the immediate Notion and is not yet developed. Absolute Being is Spirit, i.e. it has appeared, it is revealed; this first revelation is itself *immediate;* but the immediacy is equally pure mediation or thought, and it must therefore exhibit this in its own sphere as such" (#762).

A hidden split occurs between "*this individual* self-consciousness" — the historical Jesus — and "universal self-consciousness" (ibid.). This split generates the whole process of figurative thought in the midst of the community of believers and interpreters. What Hegel has clearly seen is that the display of figurative thought is borne by the community. This community is both generated by the immediate presence of the Absolute and delivered to its interpretive role by the subsequent disappearance of the Absolute.

This disappearance of the Absolute is the turning point between immediacy and mediation, therefore between visible presence and figurative interpretation. [The historical Jesus] "is the *immediately* present God; consequently, his 'being' passes over into 'having been'. . . . Or, in other words, just as formerly He rose up for consciousness as a *sensuous existence*, now He has arisen *in Spirit*" (#763). This disappearance of the immediate is the very condition of the universalization of the appearance itself: pastness and distance — "remoteness in time and space" (#764) — are forever inherently constitutive of the figurative mediation characteristic of historical Christianity: "This *form of picture-thinking* constitutes the specific mode in which Spirit, in this community, becomes aware of itself" (#765).

There is no doubt that the Hegelian interpretation of Cross and Resurrection is contained *in nuce* in these last lines. For Hegel — anticipating to a large extent Rudolf Bultmann — the Resurrection occurs in the community. The short Christology which occupies a few pages in the *Phenomenology* (#778ff.), by comparison with the lengthy developments of the Berlin *Lectures*, confirms this surmise. As Saint John before him, Hegel sees only one event: the Cross as the elevation of the Lord. Pictorial thought distinguishes two moments: first, the "spontaneous act" of self-consciousness alienating itself from itself and yielding to death; then the resurrection from the dead. Hegel sees this self-relinquishing as the elevation itself: "This death is, therefore, its resurrection as Spirit" (#779). The meaning of Resurrection is this *Aufhebung* of the immediacy in universal self-consciousness. This universal consciousness is what dwells in the community of interpretation and projects it toward the pure universality of conceptual thinking (#780).

Ecclesiology, then, absorbs Christology. This dissolution of the immediacy of historical presence in the spiritual life of the community is the equivalent of the *Erinnerung* which concluded the dialectic of the art-religion. This tentative comparison leads us to the threshold of the critical question that kept arising all along our previous analysis. The question is the following: to what extent is Hegel's hermeneutic a recognition or a dissolution of the specificity of religious language? The discussion of the possible answers to this question will be our next concern.

II

Roughly speaking, I tend to think that Hegel has so cleverly built his argument that he manages to discard the either/or — either recognition or dissolution — in order to keep both interpretations competing together: recognition and dissolution. But I want to qualify this global assessment by saying that between the *Phenomenology* and the Berlin *Lectures* there is a very significant shift. Whereas the *Phenomenology* does not conceal the impatience of Hegel with the resistance of figurative thought to its "sublation" in and by conceptual thought, the Berlin *Lectures* underline more and more the convergence between the two modes of discourse. At the end of this essay I shall try to go beyond the mere historical account of the evolution which occurred in the thought of Hegel, and to sketch a possible explanation drawing on some potential developments of the Hegelian system.

In the *Phenomenology*, the prevailing trend is a continuous and sometimes harsh critique of *Vorstellung* as the focus of resistance to the very process of *Aufhebung*. I have given several hints about the inadequacy of pictorial thought as regards conceptual thought. But I have emphasized the positive implication of this inadequacy, the inner dynamism that this inadequacy generates, and the process-character of the symbolism generated by this inner dynamism. Religious discourse, under the pressure of conceptual thought inherent in the pictorial mode, is a process of self-*Aufhebung*. But, by the same token, an impossible task is assigned to religious discourse, that of approximating speculative thinking with inadequate means.

Now, why must *Vorstellung* remain thus inadequate?

The answer has to be found in the *Preface* to the *Phenomenology*, which links unequivocally the fate of *Vorstellung* to the peculiarity of the unfolding of the Spirit that Hegel calls "determinateness" (*Bestimmung* or *Bestimmtheit*), meaning the constraint of proceeding from one "shape" to another. It appears that the problem of *Vorstellung* goes much further than the hermeneutics of religious discourse. It is a structural constraint of the dialectic itself.

In this *Preface*, more strongly than anywhere else, Hegel fights against any conception of the Absolute which would "lack the seriousness, the suffering, the patience, and the labour of the negative" (#19). Any nondeveloped, nonmediated, nonupheld position of a principle remains an empty claim. The Absolute calls for development, mediation, reflection. Now it is this very need for mediation which entails the dialectic between determinate shapes, the identifiable patterns, and the flux which shatters all fixed forms. We have both to dwell in determinate shapes and also accompany their dissolution into further different shapes. That is the law and the fate of all educative process (#29). But this necessary sojourn among shapes gives rise to a tendency to abide in these forms which have become an acquired custom of the Spirit. ". . . This acquired property still has the same character of uncomprehended immediacy as existence itself; existence has thus merely passed over into *figurative representation*" (#30). Such is figurative representation: because it spares us the toil of the Spirit, and stores for us the sedimentation of the life of the Spirit, it transforms the determinate into the frozen and the dead. Figurative representation, then, becomes the focus of the resistance to the process of "sublation" (*Aufhebung*) as "the tremendous power of the negative" (#32). So, *Vorstellung* tends to be equated with aborted *Aufhebung* in the context of the *Preface*. "But the life of Spirit is not the life that shrinks from death and keeps itself untouched by devastation, but rather the life that endures it and maintains itself in it. It wins its truth only when, in utter dismemberment, it finds itself. It is this power, not as something positive, which closes its eyes to the negative, as when we say of something that it is nothing or is false, and then, having done with it, turn away and pass on to something else; on the contrary, Spirit is this power only by looking the negative in the face, and tarrying with it. This tarrying with the negative is the magical power that converts it into being" (#32).

You may have noticed that this treacherous side of the representation is not specifically linked to religious symbolism. It threatens all the stages of the dialectical process, to the extent that this process requires determinateness for each of its shapes.

"God, Nature, understanding, sensibility and so on, are uncritically taken for granted as familiar, established as valid, and made into fixed points for starting and stopping" (#31). To this process of sedimentation, Hegel opposes the "magical power" (*die Zauberkraft*) that converts the negative into being. A last word concerning the grandiose opening of the *Preface:* the problem of *Vorstellung* is not only broader than that of religious symbolism, but even of mere pictorial thinking. Toward the end of the *Preface*, the fixity of representative thinking is already coupled with that of ratiocinative thinking. "The habit of picture-thinking, when it is interrupted by the *Begriff,* finds it just as irksome as does formalistic thinking that argues back and forth in thoughts that have no actuality" (#58). Together they have to be seen as "the abnormal inhibition (*Hemmung*) of thought" (#63).

Let me conclude this quick incursion into the *Preface* of the *Phenomenology* by stating two facts: (1) We find Hegel fighting on two fronts: against the romanticist appeal to the inarticulate and the abysmal, he pleads for determinacy and shape. Against the dogmatic claim for fixed symbolism, he pleads for the dissolution of all fixed forms in the flux of thinking. (2) The problem of *Vorstellung* arises at the intersection of these two pleas.

In the *Phenomenology* Hegel lays the main accent on the inhibiting side of the *Vorstellung.* This explains why (in chapter 7 on religion) he is more impatient with religious symbolism than in the Berlin *Lectures.* The negative account of the figurative function of religious discourse in the *Phenomenology of Spirit* may be perceived at the very beginning of the chapter on religion. After having said that religion and philosophy have the same subject matter and that religion owes this sameness of content to a potential transparency, Hegel hastens to underscore the inadequacy of the figurative mode to its own content: "The reality it contains is shut up (or enclosed) and superseded (or transcended, or sublated) in it in just the same way as when we speak of 'all reality'; it is universal reality as *thought*" (#677). The next paragraph is still stronger. Philosophy is "Spirit in its own world," whereas religion remains in the sphere of consciousness,[3] tied to sensible contents that are at the same time stripped from their own right (#678). Hegel suggests thereby that *Vorstellung* entails a double betrayal: a betrayal of sensible reality which it allegorizes[4] and a betrayal of the subject matter that it fails to grasp. The same critique returns with still more acuteness in the section devoted to revealed religion and culminating in the interpretation of Resurrection.

After having acknowledged picture-thinking as the specific mode of religious discourse (#765), Hegel adds immediately: "This form is not yet Spirit's self-consciousness, that has advanced to its *Begriff* qua *Begriff:* the mediation is still incomplete" (ibid.). The remaining part of chapter 7 betrays an increasing suspicion concerning the capacity of figurative thinking to overcome its trend to abide in fixed and frozen determinations. The resistance to conceptual transfer has its sources in the trend of the religious community to confuse the "origin," *die Ursprung,* of this thrust with the first historical appearance, of which the "representations of the primitive imperfect community" (#766) convey the memory. In other words, the community tends always to historicize the origin. Philosophical hermeneutics henceforth will have to come to grips with this resistance of the historical to the conceptual. It is this very wrestling which brings us back to our previous question: to what extent is this reduction of the historicity, say, of the life of Jesus, compatible with the claim that the Absolute has been revealed in "this" man? How can the immediacy that generates the whole hermeneutical process be preserved if the historical dimension is cancelled? Hegel would certainly send us back to his statement concerning the "being there" of the Absolute. We may have overlooked the repeated reference to the believer in this statement. Let us once more read #758 by underscoring the insistence on the unbreakable link between presence and belief. Revelation, as immediate as it may be, requires a believer, a witness. It is never a brute fact, open to public observation and description. Modern historical criticism would certainly vindicate Hegel on this point and even suggest that the presence to the believer cannot be isolated from the first interpretations given of this eschatological event by the community. In that sense, thought is at work not only in the process of interpretation but in the witnessing to the appearance of the Absolute. This implication of the believer in the initial appearance lays the burden of interpretation on the community from the beginning to the end of the whole process. The consciousness of the community is the place where the content of the *Vorstellung* is both rooted in the actual appearance and directed toward its return to the self-consciousness of the Spirit. We may even suspect that the consciousness of the community *is* the revelation, its figurative rendering and its philosophical reinterpretation.

The general tone of the *Phenomenology* concerning the openness of figurative thought to its "sublation" in conceptual thought seems therefore that of suspicion and mistrust. Dealing with the Lutheran doctrine of atonement understood as the reconciliation between the goodness pertaining to Christ's self-denial and the satisfaction of God's justice concerning evil, Hegel contends that for us philosophers, the self-centeredness, the *Insichgehen*, which is the root of evil, is an essential moment in the life of the Absolute. Redemption, then, is the equivalent, for picture-thinking, of the dialectical identity between self-centeredness and true self-denial. Hegel concludes this complex argument by saying: "It is this spiritual unity, or the unity in which the differences are present only as moments or as suspended, which has become explicit for the *picture-thinking* consciousness in that reconciliation spoken of above; and since this unity is the universality of self-consciousness, self-consciousness has ceased to think in pictures: the movement has returned into self-consciousness" (#780). By saying self-consciousness, Hegel means the community, being itself the movement of overcoming its historical limitations for the sake of the universality which is its speculative horizon.

But is it possible for a human mind to "cease to think in pictures" and to keep for philosophy the inner thrust which projects figurative thinking toward speculative thought?

Such is the quandary that the philosophy of religion of the *Phenomenology* left unsolved and that the Berlin *Lectures* attempted to solve by following a less antagonistic stance as regards picture-thinking. Hegel could attenuate the dilemma evolving from the ambiguity of *Vorstellung* by definitely displacing the axis of *Vorstellung* itself. In the Berlin *Lectures*, it is not so much the narrative and symbolic kernel of religious discourse that captures his attention as the trinitarian framework inherited from the Greek and Latin Fathers, the Scholastics, and the Reformers. His hermeneutics, I should say, is less and less a biblical hermeneutics and more and more hermeneutics of Christian dogmatics. In other words, philosophy has to deal with a religious discourse that theology has already brought to its dialectical expression. Between the trinitarian expression of Christian thought and the high dialectic of conceptual thinking there is a homology that exceeds the shortcomings of pictorial thinking. The realm of the Father, the realm of the Son, and the realm of the Spirit constitute together a systematic ordering of representations which mediate between the purely narrative-symbolic level of picture-thinking and the ultimate level of conceptual thinking.

III

In conclusion, I should like to offer some personal suggestions concerning the permanent value of the Hegelian hermeneutic of religious discourse. These suggestions may at the same time help to reconcile the impatience of the *Phenomenology* and the patience of the Berlin *Lectures* concerning the inability of religious representation to transgress the boundaries of its figurative mode.

My first suggestion concerns the status of speculative thought to which picture-thinking is measured. Three traits tend to give to speculative thought an epistemological status which requires the indefinite support of picture-thinking.

First, as we already said, speculative thought has the same subject matter as picture-thinking. This equivalence may be read both ways and not only on behalf of speculative thought. In this sense, Feuerbach and Marx could rightly claim that philosophy is religion in thought. They correctly forecast that the collapse of religion would entail the collapse of philosophy as its speculative transcription.

Secondly, absolute knowledge, as the last chapter of *Phenomenology* suggests and the concluding section of *Encyclopedia* states explicitly, does not constitute one more level of knowledge. It is not like a supplement of science, extrinsic to the whole process of thought. It is the ability to recapitulate the process itself in the eternal present of time. This *Wiederholung* does not abolish, but legitimates, all the shapes that lead to this ultimate stage. This implies that the cultural disappearance of pictorial-thinking would also make the repetition pointless. I understand the last pages of the 1831 Berlin *Lectures* in this sense: becoming more and more aware of the mutual reliance of religion and philosophy, Hegel had to overcome his own distrust for picture-thinking in order to secure the future of philosophy itself.

Finally, absolute knowledge affords no supplement of thought, but it is no less and no more than the conceptual light within which each cultural context, and finally each religious representation, thinks itself. For my part, I tend to interpret absolute thought less as a final stage than as the process thanks to which all shapes and all stages remain thoughtful. Absolute knowledge, consequently, is the thoughtfulness of picture-thinking.[5]

Absolute knowledge, therefore, is not a supplement of knowledge, but the thoughtfulness of all the modes that generate it. As a result, we have the possibility of reinterpreting the hermeneutics of religious thinking as an endless process thanks to which representative and speculative thought keep generating one another. This suggestion sends us back to the inner dynamism which keeps directing figurative thought toward speculative thought, without ever abolishing the narrative and symbolic features of the figurative mode.

Following this line of thought, I should like to schematize in the following way a modern hermeneutics of religious representation that would be consonant with the Hegelian philosophy of religion.

This hermeneutics connects together three components: immediacy, figurative mediation, and conceptualization.

Immediacy

(a) There is a hermeneutics of religious representation because there is a revelation. This nonhermeneutical moment generates the whole further dialectic. But without this initial sameness between the Absolute and its immediate presence there would be no otherness and no process of interpretation.

(b) This nucleus is common to figurative and to speculative thought.

(c) Within Christianity this moment of immediacy is secured by the appearance of Jesus as a historical figure.

Figurative mediation

(a) This individual Jesus is no longer accessible, except through past and distance. Disappearance and negativity are the conditions of the appropriation of the meaning of the Event.

(b) Religion proceeds to this appropriation under the principle of *Vorstellung*, or figurative thought, through narrative and symbolic representations.

(c) The process of interpretation that figurative thought generates is carried on by the confessing community. This community is gathered by the *Erinnerung* of the immediate presence, the remembrance and the interiorization of the mediated immediacy.

Conceptualization

(a) The dynamism of representation is secured by the thrust of figurative thought toward speculative thought.

(b) The concept is the endless death of the representation.

(c) The concept is nothing without the dying process of the representation; it is the ability to recapitulate thoughtfully the inner dynamism of the representation.

In this sense, a hermeneutics of religious discourse consonant with Hegel's philosophy of religion is the circular process which:

(1) keeps starting from, and returning to, the moment of immediacy of religion, be it called religious experience, Word-Event, or kerygmatic moment;

(2) keeps generating stories, symbols, and interpretations applied to them in the midst of a confessing and interpreting community;

(3) keeps aiming at conceptual thought, without losing its rooting in the initial immediacy of religion or in the mediating shapes of figurative thought.

A hermeneutics which would "follow Hegel rather than Schleiermacher"[6] could be defined by its claim to keep together the three moments of manifestation, interpretation, and conceptualization without losing the force of any of these equally necessary components.

NOTES

1. Actually this dissolution was foreshadowed from the start. The *Kairos* of Greek religion is not so much the moment of triumph as that of decline of the ethical substance, the "withdrawal (*Zurückgehen*) from its truth into the pure knowledge of itself" (#701). This is why, in the whole Hegelian scheme, Greek religion, for all Hegel's admiration for it, is basically transitional. The artist is depicted at the very beginning as "the vessel of [Spirit's] sorrow" (#704). All quotations and paragraph citations refer to: G. W. F. Hegel, *Phenomenology of Spirit*, trans. A. V. Miller (Oxford: Oxford University Press, 1977).

2. This famous paragraph (#753) is crucial, especially its concluding words: "And all this we do, not in order to enter into their very life but only to possess an idea of them in our imagination" (*sondern nur um sie in sich vorzustellen*).

3. The reference to consciousness, in the sense of chapter 1 of *Phenomenology*, where Spirit is understood as having a world of objects other than itself, without knowing itself, is obliquely implied in the definition of religion as "the Spirit represented as an object."

4. This argument could be read as a pre-Nietzschean attack on religion as denial of life.

5. This last suggestion seems to me to be in agreement with Gadamer's assessment of Hegel's "absolute mediation" in Hans-Georg Gadamer, *Truth and Method*, trans. Garrett Barden and John Cumming (New York: Seabury Press, 1975), pp. 305–10.

6. Ibid., p. 153.

PART II

Religious Belief and Social Process

5

The Origins of Process Theology

JOHN B. COBB, JR.

THE ROOTS OF PROCESS theology extend back to Heraclitus in the West, to Buddhist philosophy in India, and to Chinese and Hebrew thinking in general. In the nineteenth century, Hegel represents the most important expressions of processive modes of thinking in philosophy, and Darwin, the most influential in science. There is no doubt that both Hegel and Darwin have exercised a powerful influence upon the history of process theology and that many other developments in nineteenth-century thought have also affected its origins and development. But what is surprising is not that this twentieth-century movement arose out of nineteenth-century antecedents but rather how little process theology has consciously derived its emphases from these antecedents.

There are two channels through which we could trace the sources of process theology most fruitfully. The first is through Alfred North Whitehead who, today, exercises dominant influence on process theology. Whitehead devotes a great deal of attention to the historical sources of his thought. For example, in *Science and the Modern World* he traces the conjunction of intellectual and cultural movements which gave rise to modern science and which, together with science, now pose the task for fresh philosophical reflection.[1] This book contains a chapter on the nineteenth century. But unlike preceding chapters, this one does not deal with any philosopher of the period it treats. The reason, of

I am grateful to Bernard Meland for his help in revising this lecture for publication.

course, is that Whitehead's concern was to develop an understanding of reality appropriate to, and partially deriving from, what we have learned from science, whereas the great philosophers of the nineteenth century rejected that task.

Whitehead's chapter on the nineteenth century does mention Darwin and devotes some attention to evolutionary theory. But this is incidental to the major thrust of the chapter which prepares the way for understanding the great twentieth-century developments in physics. These are treated in the two following chapters on relativity and the quantum theory. If one wanted to find evidence in this book that Whitehead was influenced by Darwin, one would have to look to the appreciative comments made in the preface about Lloyd Morgan's *Emergent Evolution* and Alexander's *Space, Time, and Deity*.

The situation is similar in Whitehead's later writings. So far as I can discover, Darwin is not mentioned in *Process and Reality*, and even the topic, evolution, plays a very minor role. Darwin is mentioned in *Adventures of Ideas* but chiefly in connection with his negative effect on the understanding of the human soul, an understanding which Whitehead prizes.[2] The still widespread supposition that Whitehead is appropriately classified under the heading of evolutionary philosophy has small purchase in his major writings. Of course Whitehead takes for granted that there had been evolution and that a philosophy unable to account for this is inadequate. In this sense he is an evolutionist. But Whitehead was more deeply affected by developments in mathematics and physics and by the idea of living organisms as developed in biology than by specifically evolutionary motifs.

The neglect of nineteenth-century philosophers which I noted in *Science and the Modern World* also characterizes *Process and Reality* and *Adventures of Ideas*. *Process and Reality*, in its author's own words, is "based upon a recurrence to that phase of philosophic thought which began with Descartes and ended with Hume."[3] *Adventures of Ideas* correlates Whitehead's thought with that of Plato.

Whitehead's reason for neglecting the nineteenth century is made explicit in a passage from *Process and Reality*. He writes: "It had been a defect in the modern philosophies that they throw no light whatever on any scientific principles. Science should investigate particular species, and metaphysics should investigate the generic notions under which those specific principles should fall. Yet, modern realisms have had nothing to say about scientific principles; and modern idealisms have merely contributed the unhelpful suggestion that the phenomenal world is one of the inferior avocations of the Absolute."[4]

This does not mean that there are no parallels between Whitehead and Hegel. George Lucas has recently developed the similarities in *Two Views of Freedom in Process Thought: A Study of Hegel and Whitehead*. It is even possible to find a few passages in Whitehead which acknowledge these similarities. According to Lucas, on one occasion at the conclusion of extended discussion with one who knew Hegel's thought well, Whitehead exclaimed: "Well, if that is what Hegel meant, then I agree with him! My problem is, I never could understand him!"[5] But if this is evidence for similarity, it is certainly not evidence of influence.

My conclusion may be summarized as follows. Of course Whitehead was deeply influenced by the thought and world-view of the nineteenth century in which he was born and educated. Many of his ideas were in the air during formative periods of his thought, and these may be traced in part to Darwin and to Hegel. But Whitehead was much more interested in new developments in mathematical physics than in evolutionary theory or historical dialectics, and he did not find nineteenth-century philosophers wrestling explicitly with the questions that concerned him most. So he turned to the tradition from Plato to Hume in which philosophy was more directly concerned with mathematics and science. He directed his energies to the renewal of that tradition in relation to the vast changes that had taken place in science during the nineteenth and early twentieth centuries.

I have mentioned that the roots of process theology can be traced in two ways. The first of these is through the thought of the greatest philosophical influence in the present phase of this tradition: Alfred North Whitehead. I have now made some comments about him. The second channel for tracing the sources of process theology is through the origins and development of the Chicago school. I am going to turn now to this other source of process theology and deal with it in somewhat greater detail. This will lead us back to Whitehead at the point where his influence grew at Chicago, and I will conclude by considering the systematic relation of the two roots.

By the Chicago school I mean the group of scholars who constituted the faculty of the Divinity School at the University of Chicago. This faculty was the core around which the university developed in the 1890s. The first president of the university, William Rainey Harper, was himself a biblical scholar and was keenly interested in developing a strong faculty in that field.

One of Harper's early appointments was Shailer Mathews. Mathews was a historian who was appointed first to teach New Testament and subsequently became a theologian. By 1908 he became dean, a position he held until his retirement in 1933. Along with teaching, scholarly writing, and administration, he found time to produce literature for the Sunday schools and to found and edit journals in both biblical studies and public affairs. He lectured widely, and for many years he was director of religious affairs for the Chautauqua Institute. He was the single most dominant figure in the formation of the Chicago school, and it will be convenient for us to take him as typifying the first phase of its development.

Obviously the problem to which the Chicago school addressed itself was shaped by the events of the nineteenth century. Yet, with the Chicago school as with Whitehead what is striking is the limited influence of the greatest thinkers of the nineteenth century upon its faculty. Neither Kant nor Hegel, for example, appears to have directly affected the intellectual problem as it was experienced by those who founded the school.

This statement is exaggerated. The influence of Albrecht Ritschl was widespread in the United States at the time, and it was felt by some of the Chicago faculty, for example, George Burman Foster. But it is not clear that the Kantian philosophy which underlay Ritschl's thought came through in an effective way at Chicago. Similarly, Troeltsch was recognized as an influential force, but those very features of Troeltsch which are most Hegelian were least appreciated.

The philosophical climate at Chicago was stamped by John

Dewey. Dewey was chair of the Department of Philosophy and head of the School of Education from 1894 to 1904. Dewey had himself been trained in absolute idealism, but he had turned against it. Of course his rejection of what he understood to be Hegel in favor of a pragmatic naturalism itself bears witness to the influence of Hegel. Insofar as the Divinity School faculty attended to philosophical questions, they associated philosophy with the kind of work that Dewey was doing. Accordingly, if one wishes, one could trace some roots of the school through Dewey to British absolute idealism, and through that to Hegel. But little light is thrown on the distinctive character of the Chicago school by such a procedure.

Perhaps the conclusion to draw is that the Chicago Divinity School faculty was, on the whole, philosophically naïve. Certainly they did not look to philosophy as the major conversation partner. They looked more to the sciences, especially to sociology, and shared in the optimism that a generally empirical style of inquiry would provide the needed understanding. Rather than adopt a position of the issues raised by Hume and the solution provided by Kant, most of them went about the business of understanding the world on the naïvely realistic assumption that it was there to be investigated in a quite unproblematic way. Even later, when more philosophically rigorous scholars joined the faculty, the distinctive philosophical position of the German idealists did not become a serious option. Down to the present day the whole school has formulated its philosophical issues in the context of realist and naturalist assumptions.

My point thus far is that although the interest in social process could have derived from the influence of Hegel, that influence was quite indirect and vague and was little recognized. Nineteenth-century developments in the natural sciences and especially in biology were more directly and consciously appropriated as sources. Here, of course, Darwin and all that Darwin represents were central.

Even so, it would be an overstatement to assert that Darwin or Darwinianism was a major source for the Chicago school, though there was a movement of American thought concurrent with the rise of the Chicago school for which that would be true.

Men like Fiske were rethinking the doctrine of God and the relation of God to the world in light of biological evolution. A new evolutionary theism was emerging in the English-speaking world which later flowered in the work of William Temple and F. R. Tennant in England and Robert Calhoun and Peter Bertocci in the United States. Some members of the Chicago school took a friendly interest in these developments, and there were points of contact in the late twenties. But the Chicago school was not a part of this evolutionary school of theology.

Mathews and others, knowing that theology needed to keep in touch with the natural sciences, made a special effort to keep informed about developments in biology. Nevertheless, the major influence of evolutionary theory was mediated through the cluster of new social sciences that emerged toward the end of the nineteenth century. In the study of history these shifted attention from rulers and wars and political institutions to social and cultural developments. In this context the Chicago school devoted itself to the sociohistorical method which was its chief contribution to the theological disciplines.

Indebtedness to Darwin can be traced in a second way. The controversy over Darwin's theory of evolution was a major factor in the United States in stimulating critical biblical scholarship. That scholarship was central to the Chicago school. The controversy also opened up discussion of theological questions to wider cultural influences. In his autobiography, *New Faith for Old*, Mathews devotes a page to explaining how his encounter with evolutionary thought in college introduced him to critical thinking about Christian doctrine and to "the organization of a tolerant attitude toward that which was not in current evangelicalism."[6]

This is to say little more than that the Chicago school developed in a cultural and ecclesiastical climate which had felt the impact of Darwin's theory of evolution and that it belonged to that segment of the church which welcomed this impact and appropriated it. The emphasis on process was certainly encouraged by this impact as the older image of fixed orders of creation crumbled. Already existing tendencies to see history, including religion, in developmental ways were stimulated and grounded in a larger world-view. In terms of actual influence Darwin was undoubtedly more important than Hegel. But beyond this general influence, Darwinian evolutionary theory was not a significant source or root of the early Chicago school.

These negative comments add up to the point that the faculty of the Chicago school was not greatly influenced by the major movements of process thought in the nineteenth century except in the pervasive way in which these informed the experience and consciousness of the whole period. It is time now to consider what the central interests of this school were rather than what they were not.

The Chicago school was established during the heyday of the social-gospel movement, and it clearly reflected, embodied, and expressed the spirit of this movement. The American social gospel was the response of concerned Christians to the social injustices that accompanied industrialization of the northern and midwestern cities during the decades after the Civil War. The movement originated not in doctrinal development but in an outraged conscience. Christians could much more easily declare that what was happening was a violation of justice than they could justify their concern from established theological positions. Action on behalf of the oppressed came first. Theological reflection followed. As late as 1917 Walter Rauschenbusch could begin his Taylor lectures at Yale by saying: "We have a social gospel. We need a systematic theology large enough to match it and vital enough to back it."[7] This same subordination of theology to the needs of the church's mission for justice characterized Shailer Mathews and to varying degrees other key members of the Chicago school.

Shailer Mathews's identification with the social-gospel movement was clear and conscious. In 1910 he published a book with the title, *The Social Gospel*, followed four years later by another, *The Individual and the Social Gospel*. Another half-dozen titles express this commitment only a little less directly. Mathews not only supported the movement by his publications but worked vigorously to shape institutions that could be socially effective. He was a moving spirit in the organization of the Northern Baptist Convention and the Federal Council of Churches. He served terms as presiding officer of both.

My first positive point about process theology in the Chicago school is that its roots grew in the soil of the social gospel and that it participated fully in that general movement. My second point is that within that movement it made a special contribution in the area of biblical studies. In its origins the Chicago school was primarily focused on the study of the Bible. The faculty was deeply concerned that the Bible was increasingly being experienced as irrelevant to the real issues of the time. Mathews and others were convinced that if the Bible were understood as modern critical scholarship explains it, its relevance would be manifest and its influence powerful.

The third point to make is that the two concerns — that is, the social gospel and critical biblical study — were woven together into the sociohistorical method. Eyes attuned to the contemporary social crisis read the Bible in a new way. Today we would say that the biblical scholars of the Chicago school studied the Bible with a social hermeneutic that is very similar to the political hermeneutic which is now called for by political theologians of liberation. Instead of asking of the text questions arising from the individual quest for salvation and moral direction, the Chicago scholars asked questions about social movements and revolution.

I do not mean to say that in studying the Bible in this way the Chicago scholars were unique. They learned from the German scholarship of their time. And other proponents of the social gospel were also studying the Bible in similar ways.

Nevertheless, the sociohistorical method led to results and ways of understanding quite different from those of other leaders of the social gospel such as Rauschenbusch. Rauschenbusch knew what the church should be doing and turned to Scripture for support. He found that support in the Old Testament prophets and in Jesus. From their teaching he could move directly back to application to the class struggle of our own time.

Such procedures can be found in Mathews also. But as the sociohistorical method developed, this kind of selectiveness was abandoned. The task today is not primarily to find support in the Bible for what we need to accomplish, but to use the Bible for the reconstruction of that whole historical movement out of which our own church and faith arose. The teachings which are recorded in the Bible guided that movement in specific ways that may or may not be relevant to our needs today. That is for us to decide. Their contemporary inapplicability does not interfere with our appreciation of their function in a different time and place.

The dominant relation to the Bible, especially in Protestant-ism, is as authority for believers in all times and places. This rela-tion is expressed even in much political theology today. Herme-neutics is important because the meaning of the authoritative texts for our times is often not apparent without reflective inter-pretation. Those who reject this approach to the Bible as author-ity treat it for the most part merely as one body of ancient litera-ture alongside others. Many biblical scholars seem to alternate between these two approaches.

The sociohistorical school offers another alternative. We can understand ourselves today to be part of a movement whose ori-gins are recorded in the Bible. The Bible is decisively important for us in order that we may understand who we are and how we came to be what we are. It is not for us just one literature among many. But neither are its texts understood as having supratem-poral importance. They inform us about our origins and help us to know who we are. They do not necessarily give us appropriate guidance in dealing with the new situation in which we find our-selves. But we are not likely to respond appropriately to the chal-lenges of our time if we know nothing about how our ancestors in the faith responded to the challenges of their time. We are called to be equally creative, not to repeat their responses.

This position immediately raises questions about the identity of the Christian community through time. Mathews recognized this problem and struggled with it. In *The Faith of Modernism* he dealt with it as follows:

> Historical study enables us to recognize that the permanent element of our evolving religion resides in attitudes and con-victions rather than in doctrines. The process of making the-ology does not involve the abandonment of values and atti-tudes which outgrown patterns expressed for their authors, for these are preserved by the continuing group itself. New

patterns, however, are found which will more constructively express these loyalties under new conditions. Theology changes as banner-words change, but Christian experience, conviction, attitudes, prayer, and faith will continue. For, although group interests and consequently accepted patterns change, Christianity has bred true to itself.[8]

It seems from this passage that attitudes, convictions, loyalties, and perhaps Christian experience, prayer, and faith remain constant while only theology and banner words change. And there is no doubt that Mathews felt himself in deep continuity with the whole of the Christian movement at this level. But he recognized that such identities cannot be strictly pressed. We cannot state exactly what those attitudes and convictions are which provide continuity as doctrines change. Faithfulness today may involve rejection of features which have characterized the Christian movement from the beginning. In Mathews's words: "Modern Christianity is the descendant of the religion of the men who wrote the New Testament, but it is not identical with its ancestor."[9]

If Mathews seems at times reluctant to follow the full implications of the sociohistorical school, this is not true of his younger colleague, Shirley Jackson Case. Case saw clearly the negative consequences of every effort to identify an essence of Christianity. He wrote in 1914:

Any effort to fix upon an irreducible minimum or genuine "essence" can succeed only by setting up some quantity of experience, or belief, or practice as essential, while all other features are denominated unessential. But this is a doubtful procedure. In the first place, instead of defining Christianity comprehensively, attention is centered upon certain restricted phases of the whole. Even if it were possible to ascertain with perfect certainty a given sum of items possessed in common by all Christians, it would still be quite unfair to neglect all other features which may have been equally important and essential at certain periods and with particular circles. To affirm, for example, that the essential elements of Christianity in the first century were only those items which believers of that day have in common with the "liberal" theologian of the twentieth century, is to eliminate as unessential to first-century believers their realistic eschatology, their belief in demons and angels, their vivid supernaturalism, their sacramentalism, their notion of the miraculous content of religious experience, and various other features of similar importance. Certainly primitive Christianity cannot be perfectly understood without taking full account of all these items, and one may fairly question the legitimacy of any interpretation which does not make them even "essential" to Christianity's existence in the first century.[10]

The practitioners of the sociohistorical method were quite aware that this was a point which separated them from most other Christian scholars. Ernst Troeltsch was the German scholar with whom they had most in common. But they saw that in Troeltsch there remained a sense that Christianity must have an essence. Case noted that "Troeltsch can speak of an 'essential' Christianity in whose history the fundamental 'ideal' is being realized through progress toward the 'absolute goal'."[11] Case, on the other hand, knew nothing of such an essence or goal. In Troeltsch's latest writings this difference is softened if not erased, but for Troeltsch this failure to establish an essence of Christianity seemed almost a violation of Christian faith, whereas for the Chicago school it could be affirmed enthusiastically as the ground for contemporary Christian vitality.

In this vision the study of theology is subordinated to the study of Christianity as a total sociohistorical movement. Doctrines are developed according to the need of the movement and in terms of the concepts available and convincing at a particular time and place. These doctrines do and should change. Such change is found already within the Bible itself and continues throughout the history of the church. A vital church today will be engaged in developing doctrines that are suitable to its needs and intellectual context.

After teaching New Testament for twelve years Mathews shifted to a chair of theology. In a series of books on such topics as God, the atonement, and immortality, we can find his suggestions as to how an understanding of the church's past doctrinal formulations can help us in our task today. A brief summary of his suggestions about the doctrine of God will illustrate the mode of theology that is called for by the sociohistorical school.

Mathews wrote in 1931: "All the various conceptions of the object of worship . . . are relative to the conscious needs and the dominant social mindsets of various times and civilizations. The meaning of the word God is found in the history of its usage in religious behavior."[12] However, this does not mean for Mathews that the object of worship is simply a human projection. He knew, what Tillich pointed out later, that "projection is projection *on* something."[13] Mathews was convinced that the something in question was "the personality-evolving and personally responsive elements of our cosmic environment with which we are organically related."[14] That there are such elements, Mathews believed, is indicated as much by our modern knowledge as it has ever been.

Our theological task is not, for Mathews, the careful scientific analysis of these elements. The theological task is to image or conceive them appropriately for our time. The appropriate concept will be one that fits our modern ways of thinking and guides us into responses that are socially positive and adequate. If we apply this approach to our present situation today, we can consider whether it is now appropriate to call God "Our Father." We might decide that this language is too personalistic to carry conviction in our time, or that it supports male dominance in society, or that it projects masculine stereotypes on God. If we decided any of these things, the fact that Jesus said "Father" would not be any obstacle to change; for, again, our task is not to repeat the patterns of the past but to respond creatively in our different situation.

The idea that Christianity as a sociohistorical movement has no essence is not inherently startling. Sociohistorical movements in general do not have essences. For example, there is no essence to the Democratic party. There may be some distinctive characteristics which it has had continuously from its inception to the present day, but these might change without the loss of the recognizable historical continuity in terms of which we in fact identify it.

Movements which reverence a particular leader or text are more likely to think of themselves as having an essence. Marxists, for example, are likely to think that Marxism has an essence, and at present they can make their case somewhat more plausible than Christians can in arguing for an essence of Christianity. But this is only because their history is shorter. Already an adequate understanding of Marxism must be historical rather than systematic. That is, we must understand the development of various forms of Marxism in differing contexts. It is already difficult to identify either a common doctrine or a common mode of relation to Marx among all committed Marxists.

The lack of an essence in no way means that a sociohistorical movement lacks vitality. The contrary is nearer to the truth. A community of people who conscientiously repeat past forms through changing circumstances may preserve defining characteristics which can be called an essence. But they do so precisely at the cost of life. Such communities do not become historical movements, because they do not move. In their static sameness, they are dead.

In a living movement the question is not how to preserve an unchanging core but how to respond faithfully to new situations. Such response is always a change. The question is whether a movement changes in the right or the wrong way.

An outsider cannot determine in advance what change is right for a movement. This is because there are no unchanging principles of right change. Such principles are also caught up in change. Which change to make is a matter of wisdom, not an application of rules. Only those who are parts of the living movement, sharing in its faith, shaped by its history, can judge. And of course they are likely to disagree strongly among themselves. That, too, can be a mark of vitality. Only time can tell what the outcome of a choice will be.

It is understandable that those who find themselves responsible for decision prefer to think in terms of essences. One can be more comfortable about one's choice if one believes that it is required by faithfulness to an essence than if one recognizes it as based on one's own judgment. But belief in an essence only serves to shift the debate to diverse views of the essence and to increase the danger of intolerance toward those with whom one disagrees.

Except in a quite formal sense this does not mean that Christians will decide about how to change in the same way that Democrats or Marxists do. On the contrary, Christians will decide as those who are immersed in that community of faith whose origins are found through the study of the Old and New Testaments. They will decide as those who know themselves to be shaped by nineteen centuries of Christian history. But nothing about this vast and varied background provides advance clarity as to how to respond to new challenges such as those of feminism and Zen Buddhism. No one set of fixed criteria are simply provided for our use. On the contrary we must discuss these questions as faithful Christians shaping our criteria and our conclusions at once.

I noted that Mathews pointed to the personality-making forces of the universe as that reality to which the symbol *God* refers. He was much more interested in exploring the history of the images of God and their role in directing the mission of the church than in pursuing the question of the objective nature of those forces. Yet he recognized that such inquiries, too, may have their place. Hence we can see why Mathews's theology was in principle open to the work of those who were reconsidering cosmology in the light of new developments in science and also analyzing more carefully the processes through which human personality develops. These interests were vigorously pursued by Gerald Birney Smith, and during the late twenties they began to compete with sociohistorical inquiries in the Divinity School. By the thirties the focus of attention among the students of systematic theology had shifted to empirical and philosophical questions.

The individual who best typifies this new stage of the Chicago school is Henry Nelson Wieman. For him the all-important question was the question of God, and that was the question of who or what God really is. We can image God correctly, on this view, only when we know clearly what it is that we are imaging. That means that philosophy takes precedence. Instead of beginning with the church's mission and developing a theology that is appropriate to and supportive of that, Wieman would have us begin with a philosophical grasp of what God is and develop a theology and a practice appropriate to that.

For Wieman this meant careful empirical analysis of the personality-making forces of the universe, or, since this was not his language, of the source of human good. He found this source in a particular process of interchange among human beings, and it is that creative event that he identified as God. As we understand God better, we can give ourselves to God in trust and be transformed by God.

Charles Hartshorne joined the philosophy faculty at Chicago two years after Wieman came to the Divinity School. Many of the Divinity School students studied with him. His focus was also on the true nature of God. He employed rational rather than empirical methods of inquiry. For him, too, clarification of God's nature was primary, and the history of ways in which this has been imaged by the church was of secondary interest.

Although Chicago remained a bastion of defense against the neo-orthodox movements from central Europe, still it is appropriate to note that these too emphasized the truth of God as primary and derived their understanding of mission from what could be known of God. For them this knowledge was given in supernatural revelation rather than empirically or rationally. But the general concern to begin with what is known of God and only move subsequently to what we are thereby called to be and do was reinforced by these movements and their critique of the social gospel. The tendency in Wieman, Hartshorne, and neo-orthodoxy is to seek a knowledge of God which is not caught up in the relativities of historical experience. This is a clear and somewhat abrupt reversal of the sociohistorical approach to theology.

Within the Chicago school this tendency was countered by Daniel Day Williams who emphasized that all thinking, and especially all theology, is perspectival. But even Williams did not develop this point in such a way as to continue the tradition of the sociohistorical approach. The sociohistorical approach virtually died out in the systematic theological faculty.

The sociohistorical method has a longer history in the biblical department. Harold Willoughby and Allen Wikgren were schooled in this method and continued to work with it in some isolation from both the new European currents in New Testament scholarship and what was occurring among the Chicago theologians. Amos Wilder brought to Chicago a congenial understanding of Christianity as a cultural movement and developed this in conscious relation to the theological developments there. Even after he left Chicago for Harvard, he maintained a certain continuity with the Chicago school, insisting against the Barthians on the importance of historical-cultural factors in the New Testament and, against the Bultmannians, that these cannot be stripped away to reveal a kerygmatic kernel. William Beardslee studied with Wilder, and through his years of teaching at Emory University he continued this tradition in biblical scholarship. In the 1960s he began self-consciously to relate himself to process theology as the heir of the approach in which he had been schooled.

During the 1950s and 1960s most of those professors who were aware of continuing and developing earlier Chicago traditions left. They were replaced by persons who did not see themselves as heirs of that heritage. Hence there gradually ceased to be a Chicago school in the sense of a group of colleagues with distinctive shared assumptions and methods. However, some of the distinctive features of the Chicago school were continued at various institutions by former teachers at Chicago and by some of its graduates. The term *process theology* has come increasingly to the fore as a way of identifying this group of thinkers in terms of their shared interests.

There is a marked tendency to trace the origins of this process theology to Wieman and Hartshorne. This is in part because the best-known feature of process theology is its doctrine of God as participating in process. Such considerations about God play no important role in the early stage of the Chicago school, since Mathews and his colleagues had little interest in philosophical reflection about God. Nevertheless, there is irony in this dating. In many respects the idea of process is more pervasive in the early Chicago school than in Wieman and Hartshorne. Certainly the church, Christian faith, and theology are understood in more processive ways. Even the term *process* is more conspicuous. Among Mathews's book titles can be found *Christianity and Social Process*, *The Atonement and the Social Process*, and *Immortality and the Cosmic Process*. Unless process theology is supposed to be identified only by a philosophical doctrine of God, there is no reason to think of it as beginning as late as 1930!

The tendency to trace the sources of process theology only to the early 1930s may be due in larger measure to the close association of process theology with Whitehead. The leaders of the sociohistorical school were aware of Whitehead in the 1920s and impressed by his work, but they did not assimilate it. It was Wieman and Hartshorne who brought Whitehead's influence strongly into the Chicago scene. Williams and Meland also appealed to aspects of Whitehead's thought. Thus, in spite of the qualifications these last two introduced, Whitehead's philosophy was associated with the quest to establish a doctrine of God beyond the relativities of cultural history. Hence the influence of Whitehead functioned to help bring an end to the sociohistorical school as the theological position at Chicago.

There is irony in this effect, too. Whitehead's own position is as favorable to the sociohistorical school as to either Wieman or Hartshorne. An adequate theological program implied by his work would introduce sociohistorical considerations as strongly as empirical and rational ones. The time has come for process theology under the influence of Whitehead to recover the achievements of this stage of the Chicago school and to develop them in a wider context.

Whitehead would have viewed the effort to attain a doctrine of God that could in any way be considered final as misdirected. This did not mean that thought is purely relative. For him philosophy could advance when it related itself to science because it could benefit from the advances of science. It could advance also through achieving more adequate concepts for the analysis of its own problems. But Whitehead believed that the present stage of insight attained by both science and philosophy is still quite superficial. It is incumbent upon us to press rational inquiry as far as possible. It is equally incumbent upon us to realize how preliminary are our results.

Whitehead laid far more emphasis than did either Wieman or Hartshorne upon the role of social factors in shaping thought. However, he went much further than Mathews in tracing the relatively independent role of ideas. In *Science and the Modern World* he shows how important for the rise of science was a climate of ideas. In *Adventures of Ideas* he shows how the idea of the human soul was born in the slave society of Greece and could

only have its full effect in establishing the idea of a free society after technology had freed civilization from the need of slaves.
Against both the sociohistorical school and contemporary political theology he would encourage theologians to engage in the
quest for truth somewhat independently of immediate relevance.

Nevertheless, Whitehead is not properly understood as an
intellectualist. In *Science and the Modern World* he wrote:

> We cannot think first and act afterwards. From the moment
> of birth we are immersed in action, and can only fitfully
> guide it by taking thought. We have, therefore, in various
> spheres of experience to adopt those ideas which seem to
> work within those spheres. We cannot even keep before our
> minds the whole evidence except under the guise of doc-
> trines which are incompletely harmonized. We cannot think
> in terms of an indefinite multiplicity of detail; our evidence
> can acquire its importance only if it comes before us mar-
> shalled by general ideas. These ideas we inherit — they form
> the tradition of our civilization. Such traditional ideas are
> never static. They are either fading into meaningless formu-
> las, or are gaining power by the new lights thrown by a more
> delicate apprehension. . . . One fact is certain, you cannot
> keep them still. No generation can merely reproduce its an-
> cestors. You may preserve the life in a flux of form, or pre-
> serve the form amid an ebb of life. But you cannot perma-
> nently enclose the same life in the same mold.[15]

The clear implication for Christian theologians is close to
that developed in the sociohistorical school. Our task is not to re-
produce our ancestors, nor is it to preserve forms. It is to preserve
the life in a flux of forms.

Even so, process theologians are called to a task still larger
than that recognized in the sociohistorical school. According to
that school the task of theology was to find images and concepts
convincing in the intellectual climate of the day which would
guide and motivate appropriate response to pressing problems.
There is little suggestion that theology should confront or challenge the dominant intellectual climate. But such a challenge is
the heart of Whitehead's work, and process theology recognizes

in that challenge an expression of its own calling. We have learned from him that much of our current scientific thinking is as inappropriate to the facts as is much of our Christian thinking. We will not gain our ends by adapting ourselves to outdated science. Instead we need to work together with those scientists who are willing to venture toward new ways of thinking that are both more appropriate to the scientific data and more fruitful for fresh Christian thinking.

Under the influence of Whitehead, process theology must distinguish itself from the older Chicago school in another, related way. That school included scholars with an interest in the natural world, but it was dominated by the sociohistorical method which focused attention on human history and society. Insofar as this method was controlling, the sociohistorical school shared with the whole nineteenth century a strong tendency toward anthropocentrism and toward viewing nature as no more than the stage for the drama of human action. In contrast, Whitehead has taught us that nonhuman nature is part of the play. If we would renew the sociohistorical method today, it must be the eco-sociohistorical method through which such renewal takes place.

Finally, Whitehead has taught us to discern the working of God in the total process in a way that is undeveloped in the sociohistorical school. The sociohistorical method as such tends to deal not with God but with ideas of God. When Mathews undertakes to tell us about God, he identifies God with the personality-producing forces of the universe, but he does not employ that idea in the account of what has occurred in history. By giving a rich metaphysical account of these forces — or better, of this activity that permeates all things — Whitehead provides us a vision of God whose work can be traced in all nature and in all history. As yet we have hardly dared to propose a theistic reading of the historical process, but this is more the measure of our cowardice than of our lack of opportunity. Pannenberg's renewal of a theology of history in his book *Human Nature, Election, and History*, points a way which any renewal by process theology of its sociohistorical heritage should follow.

I was asked to write about the roots of process theology in

the nineteenth century. This is a historical question, and I have too little historical knowledge to pursue an answer responsibly. I have argued instead that the nineteenth-century roots are quite shallow, at least in terms of the leading intellectual movements of that century.

I have shifted my attention to a question that interests me more. As a systematic theologian in the tradition of process theology, I want to know the relation between the two main roots of process theology in the early twentieth century: Whitehead's philosophy and the sociohistorical school of the University of Chicago. This question has peculiar importance for process theology today as it is confronted by the challenge of political theology and liberation theology.

Must we choose between cosmological interests, attention to nature, and a philosophical doctrine of God, on the one side, and involvement in the struggle for liberation of the oppressed, on the other? Critics of process theology from the side of liberation theology seem to think we must and that process theology is committed to the wrong choice. They certainly have much justification for their judgment in the relative silence of recent process theology on social issues. But this is a choice I for one do not want to make, and in considering how process theology came to appear so remote from the concrete issues of social justice I have been forced to turn to its history. There I find that the views of Shailer Mathews, which typify the first three decades or more of the development of the Chicago school, are quite similar to those of contemporary political and liberation theology. Did, then, the influence of Whitehead necessitate the turn away from these concerns for justice and liberation? Or did this shift reflect other factors in the sociohistorical situation of the thirties and forties?

Because these questions are important for me, I have let them direct the course of my inquiry. My conclusion is that, indeed, the sociohistorical approach to theology has an important contribution to make to process theology today. It is my belief that here, as in so many other places, Whitehead has in fact succeeded in encompassing disparate elements in a way that few twentieth-century thinkers have matched. Unfortunately, process theologians have not yet learned to follow him in this respect.

NOTES

1. Alfred North Whitehead, *Science and the Modern World* (New York: Free Press, 1967).

2. Alfred North Whitehead, *Adventures of Ideas* (New York: Macmillan, 1933).

3. Alfred North Whitehead, *Process and Reality: An Essay in Cosmology* (corrected edition ed. David Ray Griffin and Donald W. Sherburne) (New York: Free Press, 1978), p. xi.

4. Ibid., p. 116.

5. George R. Lucas, Jr., *Two Views of Freedom in Process Thought: A Study of Hegel and Whitehead* (Missoula, Mont.: Scholars Press, 1979), p. 123.

6. Shailer Mathews, *New Faith for Old: An Autobiography* (New York: Macmillan, 1936), p. 18.

7. Walter Rauschenbusch, *A Theology for the Social Gospel* (New York: Abingdon Press, 1917), p. 1.

8. Shailer Mathews, *The Faith of Modernism* (New York: Macmillan, 1924), p. 76.

9. Shailer Mathews, *Is God Emeritus?* (New York: Macmillan, 1940), p. 71.

10. Shirley Jackson Case, *The Evolution of Early Christianity: A Genetic Study of First-Century Christianity in Relation to Its Religious Environment* (Chicago: University of Chicago Press, 1914), pp. 22–23.

11. Ibid., p. 14.

12. Shailer Mathews, *The Growth of the Idea of God* (New York: Macmillan, 1931), p. 210.

13. Paul Tillich, *Systematic Theology*, 3 vols. (Chicago: University of Chicago Press, 1951–1963), 1:212.

14. Mathews, *Growth*, p. 226.

15. Whitehead, *Science and the Modern World*, pp. 187–88.

6

Weber Revisited:
Sociology of Knowledge
and the Historical Reconstruction
of Christianity

HOWARD CLARK KEE

I

FOR MORE THAN A half-century before Max Weber's birth in 1864,
historians were in disagreement among themselves as to whether
the nature and goal of their work was an art or a science. Were
their primary resources data or intuitions? Was the essence of history in human particularities or in an ideal, self-realizing
schema? Talcott Parsons assigned the blame for this dichotomous
state to Kant, whose dualistic view of human beings represented
them as at once inhabitants of the materialistic, biological phenomenal world and as spiritual beings at home in the noumenal
sphere.[1] The problem as to whether human history was to be analyzed by the methods of the natural sciences or by the "spiritual
sciences" plagued those plying the craft in the nineteenth century,
as it has down to the present day.

The difficulty was compounded by Hegel's method of treating history. As Parsons noted, what to the idealistic philosopher
was interesting about humanity — human action and culture —
was radically excluded by Hegel from the phenomenal realm.
The intellectual result was a bifurcation of the historical undertaking: (1) history was defined as a recording of human actions
and their effects, viewed in their concrete wholeness; (2) the es-

sence of history was philosophical analysis, with the focus on the realization of spirit, by which the whole was unified and ultimately fulfilled. Although Hegel perceived human life and history as a unity, he nevertheless was able to account for uniqueness in historical epochs and culture through his dialectical method, which did leave room for qualitative differences in the self-realization of the *Weltgeist*.

The empiricist response to Kant likewise left two groups in opposing camps analogous to those just sketched: the idealistic empiricists who regarded humans as unique and understandable only in terms of concrete detail; and the positivistic empiricists who reified the theoretical system, treating history as determined by a fixed pattern.[2]

Of all the historiographical dilemmas pointed out by Parsons, perhaps the most significant for our purposes (in our reexamination of the contribution of Max Weber) is the contrast between the positivistic and the idealistic strands. On the one hand the positivist in history sees norms, operative and leading to certain results, in spite of a seemingly voluntaristic system; the prime concern is to demonstrate intrinsic causal relationships. On the other hand, the idealistic strand seeks to disclose the relationships of meaning. Clearly Weber was faced with these alternatives, but he was also drawn simultaneously by the appeal of a unified idealistic system and by the historicist's sense of obligation to adduce masses of empirical data. Ranke and Mommsen exemplified the historian's task conceived as the exhaustive accumulation of objective evidence. Dilthey, however, ranged widely in his effort to display meaning in history. These conflicting historical strategies directly affected Weber. Before turning to an analysis of certain aspects of his thought, however, it may be useful to ask why, sixty years after his untimely death, a historian of Christian origins would belatedly come around to assessing Weber's present and potential significance for his field of inquiry.

II

As W. G. Kümmel has demonstrated and documented in his history of the interpretation of the New Testament, there never has been a time when the historical and hermeneutical approaches to the New Testament and other early Christian literature have not been affected directly by the cultural context of the interpreter-historian.[3] This was as evident in the platonizing perspectives of Clement and Origen of Alexandria in the second and third centuries as it has been in the post-Enlightenment period, with the Kantian, Hegelian, positivist, and other philosophical influences. In the nineteenth century, historians became self-conscious and intentional about the correlation of culture and historical interpretations. Pioneer and paradigm of the synthetic undertaking to reconstruct early Christianity by methods and norms derived from a dynamic force within the current culture was Ferdinand Christian Baur (1792–1860), who is rightly regarded as the founder of historical theology. Yet the impact of Baur's work goes far beyond the task of historical theology as such, since it had important bearing on the rise of historical-critical methods in general.

David Friedrich Strauss (1808–1874), in his *Das Leben Jesu kritisch bearbeitet* (1836), undertook a comprehensive analysis of the Gospel accounts of Jesus in which at every point he played off rationalist interpretations against those of the conservatives, showing ultimately that both were untenable. He fancied that he could replace this historical rubble with his own mythical reconstruction of the life of Jesus, based on a bare outline that survived his critical demolition. Strauss's radical criticism was intellectually vulnerable because it failed to build on a critical analysis of sources (the Gospels) and offered no coherent picture of the historical rise of Christianity based on those and other sources.[4] F. C. Baur undertook this pair of tasks. By 1833 Baur was wholly under the influence of Hegel, with respect to both his broad view of history (the self-unfolding of the spirit is the idea of history) and the process by which history moves (thesis, antithesis, synthesis). Thus Paul is seen by Baur as the mediating point between the synoptic Gospels and John; the conflict between Peter (representing Jewish Christianity) and Paul (representing Gentile, law-free Christianity) is overcome in the emergence of Catholic Christianity with its stress on unity.[5]

One of Baur's last students, Otto Pfleiderer, moved the discussion of Christian origins behind the evident pattern of conceptual conflict to examine in detail the cultural influences that shaped the incipient movement, especially the popular philosophies and religions of the hellenistic world in which Christianity had to compete for adherents.[6] That search was aided by concurrent studies in classical philology, best represented by Erwin Rohde's monumental work, *Psyche*, on the Greek cult of souls and the belief in immortality, which provided material in depth for demonstrating links between early Christianity and the Greco-Roman world.[7] The romantic mood in the culture of the late nineteenth century encouraged the steady stream of discoveries and publications of religious documents from the world of late antiquity. How were historians of early Christianity to cope with this surfeit of new information and insight? We can in this essay look at only two responses, but each epitomizes one of the opposing reactions to this historical challenge. Paul Wendland's survey, *Die hellenistisch-römische Kultur*, takes the route of religious syncretism. The author declares that "already in early Christian literature . . . borrowings of pagan ideas and motifs, reminiscences of, and relationships to the hellenistic conceptual world [increase] with the progressive stages in its development. . . . As a religion of redemption, Christianity is to be understood only against the background of purely pagan mysticism."[8]

On the opposing side, Harnack marshaled his formidable forces of erudition to defend the position that Jesus was not influenced significantly by contemporary Judaism or hellenism, that Paul was affected only by Jewish beliefs and practices, and that the Christian religion was not to be analyzed alongside other religions, since in its pure form Christianity was *the* religion. The "hellenic spirit" does dominate later development of Christian dogma, but it is absent from the original phases of Christianity, even though neo-romantic scholars would like to find it there. Though he did not quote Wordsworth, Harnack dismisses the philhellenes in a manner that implies their sympathy with the poetic lament,

> Great God! I'd rather be a pagan
> Suckled in a creed outworn.
> So might I, standing on this pleasant lea
> Have glimpses that would make me less forlorn. . . .[9]

What Harnack did constructively was to distill from the great mass of information accumulated in his researches the essence of religion, which just happened to conform in detail with the liberal theology:

> The fact that the whole of Jesus' message may be reduced to these two heads — God as the Father, and the human soul so ennobled that it can and does unite with him — shows us that the Gospel is in no way a positive religion like the rest; that it contains no statutory or particularistic elements; *that it is, therefore, religion itself.*[10]

A similar reductionist retreat — different in substance but nearly identical in strategy — appeared in the first half of this century in the work of Rudolf Bultmann. Forced to come to terms with the literary problem of the relatively late, composite nature of the Gospels, with the theological problem (posed most sharply by Albert Schweitzer) of Jesus' expectation of an imminent end of the age, and by the contextual-historical problem (posed for him chiefly by his teacher, Richard Reitzenstein, in his theory of the pre-Christian Gnostic redeemer myth to which Paul allegedly conformed his picture of Jesus), Bultmann sought solace and stability in the existentialist adaptation of Christianity. According to this view, the essence of all the New Testament writers and of Jesus himself was the call to decision: in deciding to obey God unconditionally, one died to the old world and was granted a new life. In his slim volume on *Primitive Christianity in its Contemporary Setting,* Bultmann selects the evidence and aligns it so as to lend tacit support to these conclusions about the essence of Christianity.[11]

The second- and third-generation Bultmannians continue to employ his historical approach, even though some of its foundational features such as the Gnostic redeemer myth have been thoroughly discredited as mere scholarly constructs lacking evidential support. The quantum shift of religious studies from church-related to secular or state-supported institutions in America and Great Britain has taken place concurrently with a scholarly urge to shift from historical or theological analyses of the early Christian literature to awareness of and appreciation for the timeless patterns of religious experience that these documents share with the religious literature of the world. Once more, dominant in religion is the romantic mood evoked by Sir James Frazer and embodied both in Turner's painting and in the opening lines of the massive work with which it shares the title, *The Golden Bough.* Frazer depicts the scene as "suffused with the golden glow of imagination in which the divine mind of Turner steeped and transfigured even the fairest natural landscape. . . ."[12]

For some the romantic retreat is provided by literary criticism. For others, it is to be found through the motif researches of Mircea Eliade. For still others, the anthropological writings of Claude Lévi-Strauss, with the claim to be able to discern in the human mind the universal structures and patterns that underlie the vast diversities of human phenomena, provide a sanctuary safe from historical relativities. Clifford Geertz, in a series of devastating rhetorical questions, asks whether Lévi-Strauss has pointed the way for future study of religious and cultural phenomena, or whether he is merely "like some uprooted neolithic intelligence cast away on a reservation, shuffling the debris of old tradition in a vain attempt to revivify a primitive faith whose moral beauty is still apparent but from which relevance and credibility have long since departed."[13]

Eliade has been quite explicit that his study of patterns and motifs, with its aim "to uncover the structures of transconsciousness,"[14] is his way of escaping the tyranny of history. He rejects methods which interpret evidence in historical context or subject theories about *homo religiosus* to empirical testing, "since to demonstrate the historicity of an event will not free men from the terror of a history which leads to death."[15] For Eliade, the history of religion is an ahistorical study of religious language, language that is textualized in myth and repeated timelessly through ritual enactment linked with the myth. As one critic has aptly phrased it, Eliade's decontextualization of myth points to "an epiphany of the flesh made word."[16]

III

The historiographical problems confronted by historians of religion in the late nineteenth and early twentieth centuries—that is to say, during the academic career of Max Weber — are accordingly still with us today, obvious or thinly disguised. Since Weber set himself to the task of dealing with these problems, and in the process produced an enormous corpus of scholarly writings, much of which is still widely read in translation in this country, the question comes to mind, What impact did Weber's work have on, and what value might it yet have for, historical study of Christian origins? It is significant that in the more than 500 pages and 500 footnotes of Kümmel's history of New Testament interpretation, the name of Weber never appears. The irony is increased by the fact that, not only was Weber working at historical issues identical with those of his colleagues in the theological faculties, but he was also planning to write a history of early Christianity, similar in scope and method to his studies of the religions of China, India, and ancient Judaism. Although he never undertook that project, the methods he developed and the concepts he formulated had and still have great importance for the interpretation of Christian origins.

Fortunately, there are some signs that the rich resources offered in Weber's writings are being drawn upon for the reconstruction of primitive Christianity. John Gager's book, *Kingdom and Community: The Social World of Early Christianity*, has succeeded to a commendable degree in analyzing the social dynamics and leadership roles in the early stages of the Christian movement, and has done so by employing models and insights from the sociological writings of Max Weber.[17] In Germany, Gerd Theissen has written fresh, illuminating studies on the sociological factors discernible in a variety of early Christian situations, ranging from the roles of itinerant charismatics in southern Syria[18] to the mix of social strata represented in the church at Corinth as reflected in Paul's Corinthian correspondence.[19] From Australia have come the studies of social dynamics and configurations in early Christianity by the historian E. A. Judge, whose *Social Pattern of the Christian Groups in the First Century*[20] is particularly penetrating. A similar contribution to our field of inquiry has been made from across a neighboring collegial fence in classicist R. A. MacMullen's work on *Roman Social Relations* and *Enemies of the Roman Order*.[21] Fruitful as many of the recent studies in social aspects of early Christianity are, the results are offered for the most part as data concerning strictly social features of the early church, with little attention given to the questions and aims and methods that should give structure and direction to the undertaking. What are the contributions that Max Weber's work may yet make to the task of reconstructing early Christianity?

We shall propose answers in four different categories: (1) methodological, (2) conceptual, (3) epistemological, (4) hermeneutical. Let us examine these in sequence, offering first a description in Weber's own terms of a facet of his thought under each, and then exploring how his insights and methods, whether directly or in subsequent development, may contribute to the historical study of Christian origins.

(1) Methodologically, Weber's major contribution was in the development and refinement of his notion of ideal types. As Karl Jaspers has correctly noted, Weber did not set out to be a philosopher of history in the tradition of Hegel, or to be largely a narrator like Ranke, or a portrait painter of great figures like Burckhardt; nor did he vainly suppose he could write a history of the world, either in detail or in grandiose schemata. His aim, impressive though it was in scope, was comparison: to see how phenomena in various times and cultures produce similar developments, while at the same time recognizing that contrasts appear when, from among the range of possibilities, different results emerge.[22] As Gerth and Mills note, Weber's ideal type was an attempt to construct a logically precise conception of reality rather than to posit an inexorable ideal force in the Hegelian tradition.[23] Weber's own description of this method is unambiguous: "The ideal type is a conceptual construct which is neither a historical reality nor even the 'true' reality. . . . It has the significance of a purely ideal limiting concept with which the real situation or action is compared and surveyed for the explication of certain of its significant components. . . . [The function of] the ideal type is an attempt to analyze historically unique configurations of their individual components by means of genetic concepts."[24]

Weber warned against identifying historical reality with the types, against using the types as procrustean beds in which historical data must be forced to lie, and against hypostasizing the types into the "real" forces behind the events of history. Weber's critics seriously misread him when they assert that his use of the ideal types is nonhistorical, or when they consider that, as one writer put it, the types are "unitary and almost impenetrable geometric forms." Jaspers accurately asserts that for Weber the ideal types "are not reality itself, but technical instruments by which to approach reality."[25] They are not classes of phenomena but formal patterns by means of which we measure reality in order to discern the degree to which reality does or does not conform to them. They are neither the ultimate goal of investigation nor the laws of historical process, but means by which to gain the clearest awareness of the specific characteristics of the human reality in question.

(2) The best-known concept investigated and analyzed by Weber is that of the charismatic leader, although he readily acknowledges that he did not coin the term. His familiar depiction of the charismatic is that of a natural leader, lacking official credentials or formal training, who arises in times of psychic, physical, economic, ethical, religious, or political distress. His or her gifts of body and spirit are believed to be supernatural in origin. The charismatic lacks a financial base or social status in the fixed order of society. He or she has neither abstract code nor the means of adjudication of disputes; his or her law derives rather from the leader's own personal graces and strengths, or specifically by oracle or prophetic insight. Although the original source of the charismatic's authority is seen to be supernatural, it can become institutionalized and thus serve as the basis for legitimate successors, though the mode of transmission varies with the historical situations.[26]

S. N. Eisenstadt, in the introduction to his edition of Weber's *On Charisma and Institution Building,* makes the important point that in Weber's thinking charismatic and institutional aspects of society were closely interrelated, contrary to the charge brought against him by some of his critics and the careless use of his concepts made by others. His major concern was for the process of institution building, of social transformation, and of cultural creativity flowing out of this process. In describing the charismatic as prophet, Weber differentiated between the ethical prophet, who preaches obedience as an ethical duty, and the exemplary prophet, who summons hearers to follow him or her in order to achieve salvation. If the charismatic leader makes use of discipline, its effects may survive the leader's passing, but the charisma itself becomes routine so that the values it promulgated may be preserved as tradition or in a rationally socialized form.

(3) In addition to the appeal of personal authority, the prophet conveys to hearers the conviction that there is a coherent meaning in the life of humanity and of the world, in both its social and its cosmic dimensions.[27] But that notion brings us to Weber's epistemological contribution — namely, his conception of the "image of the world," by which he meant a systematized and rational view of the world. On the basis of the world-image, for example, one could know from what deliverance might be awaited — which might range from bodily impurity, to radical evil, or enslavement in an astrologically determined universe, or imprisonment in the finite, or the cycle of rebirths. The system, Weber noted, might be more or less rational, more or less carefully thought through by intellectuals, even while resting on irrational presuppositions which have simply been accepted as given and incorporated into the image of the world. The earlier unitary views of the world tend to yield either to rational systems of cognition or of world mastery, or to mysticism.

Weber was careful to point out, however, that the specifics of a religious world-view are not a simple function of the social situation or stratum of society which serves as the characteristic bearer of that view. There is no causal link between a social stratum and ideology, nor does its religion merely reflect the ideal interest-situation of a stratum. Rather, the outlook inherent in a religious ethic, for example, "receives its stamp primarily from religious sources, and, first of all, from its annunciation and its promise."[28] Thus Weber sought to avoid the charge of his critics that religion was reducible to or caused by social factors. Instead he aimed to show that the network of assumptions about reality and about the place of human beings within the world — both in present plight and in ultimate deliverance — was the constitutive base for identity among those whose community shared any given world-view. Viewed methodologically, Weber's effort to show the

links between a prevailing psychological state, an act of perception, and the meaning of a phenomenon — and to do so with full
acknowledgment of the historical situation within which the
perception-meaning process is taking place — anticipated the rise
of what is now known as sociology of knowledge. That development, as we shall see, required assists from Husserl and Alfred
Schutz, and later from Luckmann and Berger.

(4) Hermeneutically, Weber stood in the tradition of Wilhelm Dilthey, as Talcott Parsons recognized and as, more recently,
H. P. Rickman insists. The materials from the Dilthey corpus
which Rickman has organized and edited in his *Pattern and
Meaning in History*, show that not only Weber's concept of *Verstehen*, but also his view of the life-world, derived from Dilthey.[29]
With an obvious takeoff on Kant, Dilthey called his hermeneutical enterprise, "A Critique of Historical Reason." Noting how the
individual is involved in the interactions of society because its
various systems intersect in one's life, he describes the effort of the
mind to determine the systematic meaning of the world which
links these converging factors. He declares:

> The task can only be accomplished if the individual pro-
> cesses, which work together in the creation of this system,
> can be sorted out and it can be shown what part each of
> them plays, firstly in the construction of the historical course
> of events in the mind-affected world and, secondly, in the
> discovery of its systematic nature.[30]

Already hinting at the specific terms that Max Scheler and others
were later to use in their hermeneutical projects, Dilthey describes an interpretive enterprise that was to be developed by
both Weber and Scheler: "Understanding is the rediscovery of the
I in the Thou; the mind rediscovers itself at ever higher levels of
interconnectedness; the sameness of the mind in the I and the
Thou and in every subject of a community, in every system of culture and, finally, in the totality of mind and universal history,
makes the working together of the different processes in human
studies possible."[31]

Vast as was the range of Weber's research, he set himself to a
far more modest enterprise than did Dilthey and made no claim
to universal inclusiveness. Dilthey rejected the notion that mean-

ing derived from a metaphysical or any other structure outside of life itself, and thereby defined his position over against Hegel or Marx. He was careful to stress the importance of the parts to the whole of life, of the individual's identity in relation to the community. The pattern of meaning in life is not shaped by ineluctable causal forces, either: "There is only a loose progression from the presupposition to what follows it; what is new does not formally follow from the presupposition; it is rather that understanding passes from something already grasped to something new which can be understood through it. The inner relationship lies in the possibility of reproduction and empathy."[32] In these lines are the seeds of the problems and the approaches to their solution that were to occupy Weber throughout his career: the relative significance of the individual and society in social change; how innovation occurs; how religious factors contribute to the shaping of the economic order, or why it was only in Protestantism that capitalism arose. Rickman, in showing how Dilthey distanced himself both from reification of such entities as classes, ages, or nations and from radical restriction of history to the actions of individuals, offers a useful summary of those aspects of Dilthey's hermeneutics which were to be developed and refined by Weber: "We have to take into account what human beings have in common, that is, at its most general, human nature and, more specifically, the shared characteristics of nation, classes, or other groups. From this point of view the infinite variety of human nature can be explained in terms of the different degrees to which individuals possess these common characteristics. This quantitative approach, combined with attention to environmental influences, can make an important contribution to the understanding of individuals."[33] Obviously, both Weber's ideal types and his notion of world-image shared by a community were anticipated in Dilthey's work, as was his *Nachdenken* strategy for the interpretive task.

IV

The potential of this range of Weber's insights and methodological procedure for facilitating and enriching the work of the historian of Christian origins has been heightened by the impact of his thought on philosophers and social scientists during his life-time and subsequently. In his brilliant monograph on Edmund Husserl, Maurice Natanson demonstrates how Husserl's phenom-enology at crucial points is a working-out of themes from Weber.[34] And the phenomenological sociology of Alfred Schutz, whom Husserl sought to bring to Freiburg just before his death and before Schutz's flight to America, has been recognized as manifesting deep influences from both Weber and Husserl. By drawing on insights and methods of Husserl, Schutz was able to refine and develop Weber's typology, his concepts of social dy-namics, the relationship between the individual and society, the image of the world (or life-world, as the phenomenologists called it), and above all, the hermeneutical goal of understanding meaning-in-history.[35] We shall assess this contribution as it bears on the task of historical reconstruction, organizing our material around the four themes already enunciated: methodological, conceptual, epistemological, hermeneutical.

(1) Methodological

We have already noted Weber's method of analysis of phe-nomena across cultures by means of ideal types, just as we have described briefly the efforts of the history-of-religion school to in-terpret the historical aspects of one religion by the use of so-called parallels from another cultural setting. Superficially, the two en-terprises look alike, yet at least two serious fallacies lie concealed in the history-of-religions tactic. The first is the assumption that resemblances in cross-cultural phenomena assure that there is fundamental kinship. The second is that the emergence of a phe-nomenon superficially similar to that in an earlier culture is the historical cause of its later manifestation. By way of illustration: in classical Greek texts the devotees of a savior-god share a cup of mystic ecstasy; in the New Testament, the devotees of a savior-god share bread and wine — proof *ex hypothesi* that the Christians have borrowed their sacrament from hellenistic culture. Or as I have observed before,[36] Isis and Wisdom (in the Jewish tradition) both address the faithful in the form of self-proclamation ("I am

Isis" or "I am Wisdom, who"—and then follows a recital of bene-factions, cosmic and personal). In John's Gospel, Jesus speaks in precisely the same way: "I am the light of the world: he that fol-lows me shall not walk in darkness . . ." (John 8:1). Does this im-ply that the early Christians engaged in conscious borrowing or cultural imitation? Did the Isis-Wisdom tradition cause the Jo-hannine revelatory speeches? The history-of-religions answer would be "Yes." The venerable fallacy, *post hoc, ergo propter hoc* has not weakened with age, at least among those whom Samuel Sandmel has felicitously, if a bit sarcastically, described as stricken with "parallelomania."[37]

Weber's typological ground rules should have been more carefully observed. In addition to his warnings that ideal types are not historical realities but heuristic instruments, he noted that "the goal of ideal-typical concept-construction is always to make clearly explicit, not the class or average character, but rather the unique, individual character of cultural phenomena. Even when one is dealing with developmental sequences by means of ideal types, the danger is to be avoided of confusing them with reality."[38] Or again Weber declares that constructing the ideal type "is no more than a means for explicitly and validly imputing an historical event to its real causes while eliminating those which on the basis of our present knowledge seem impossible."[39] In cur-rent and traditional practice among historians of Christian ori-gins, the identification of a roughly analogous phenomenon in a culture contemporary with, prior to, or even later than the first and early second century is seized upon as providing the historical explanation for what was occurring in the nascent Christian movement. This strategy reached its zenith or nadir, depending on one's point of view, in Morton Smith's *Jesus the Magician*, where the Greek Magical Papyri, dating mostly from the third and fourth centuries of our era, are appealed to as explanation for "what really happened" in the New Testament accounts of Jesus and the apostles.[40] Other scholars have claimed to expose the his-torical base of the gospel tradition by reasoning back from the ac-counts of itinerant tricksters in the satirical narratives of Lucian of Samosata, who flourished in the later second century A.D. The warning of Weber about mistaking ideal types for reality and his pleas for making clear "the unique individual character of cultural phenomena" have both been ignored.

Although there is no indication of direct influence by Weber, Jean Piaget's observations about structures are relevant here. He rejects the notion of a fixed form of a conceptual, or social, or any other structure: "The structure is preserved or enriched by the interplay of its transformational laws."[41] Referring to the observation of C. H. Waddington about genetics, "The relation between the organism and its environment is a cybernetic loop such that the organism selects its environment while being conditioned by it," Piaget discerns a clear analogy in the development of social and conceptual structures: "It happens frequently that a structure changes its function to meet new social needs."[42] The import of this insight for typological studies and the assessment of alleged parallels is obvious.

(2) Conceptual

No single concept employed by Weber in his sociology of religion has been more widely used by historians of Christianity than his bipolar scheme of charismatic leadership and institutionalization. As an early twentieth-century historian phrased it, "Jesus foretold the Kingdom, and it was the church that came."[43] That implicit value judgment has been continued down to the present by Bultmann and his school. In his popular Jesus book, Bultmann portrayed Jesus as an eschatological prophet whose aim was to call his hearers to radical obedience to God, an attitude and response that Jesus himself exemplified, as we noted earlier. Break with family, with gainful occupation, with national aspiration, with subservience to the political power and the religious establishment — all these characteristics of Jesus conform precisely with Weber's ideal type, the charismatic leader. Bultmann's rationalistic conditioning gets in the way, however, of his acknowledging, with Weber, that an essential feature of the prophet's role is the performance of miracles. Bultmann prefers to assign that aspect of the tradition to later hellenistic influences, not because the evidence points that way unambiguously, but because his philosophical leanings incline him to admire the existential encounter with radical decision, while he finds intellectual embarrassment in a "real" Jesus who expelled demons and healed the sick.

But the distortion of the Weberian ideal type is not at an end. Bultmann regards Paul and John (in a drastically edited version of his Gospel) as the ones who understood and transmitted faithfully the essence of Jesus' call to decision, although each of these apostles expressed that message in mythological language deriving from his own cultural background. Each was concerned for individual confrontation with the divine demand; neither had a place for the church as institution. By the second century, however — according to the Bultmannian reconstruction — the gospel of radical obedience had been abandoned in favor of an organizational drive whose interests were chain of command, ritual and doctrinal conformity, and good public relations. In short, the New Testament period ends in what Bultmann and his student, Ernst Käsemann, call Early Catholicism. Although they do not overtly employ the charismatic-institutional polarity, it seems implicit in their reconstruction.

The irony, as S. N. Eisenstadt pointed out in his introduction to Weber's *On Charisma and Institution Building*, is that not only were these themes interrelated in Weber's thought, but also his major concern was for institution building, for social transformation, for cultural creativity. These processes involve crystallization, continuity, and change of major types of institutions; they demonstrate the limits of transforming existing institutional and cultural complexes, as well as the stages in building of new ones. Of central interest to Weber was "the continuous tension between . . . the constrictive and the creative aspects of institutions and social organizations."[44] Although charisma is inherently anti-institutional and antinomian, it does not necessarily lose its power with the passage of time; it can be transmitted, as we have noted, by office, by kinship, or by heredity. On the other hand, Weber described ideal types of leadership at the institutional stage as well: those who can set up broad orientations, establish new norms, articulate new goals, and implement them both administratively and by rallying support. The utility of these ideal types of leadership and of social dynamics has yet to be investigated seriously; there is much to be exploited by historians of early Christianity.

(3) *Epistemological*

In their introduction to a set of Weber's essays, Gerth and Mills remark that his correlation of world-images and social conditions paves the way for, or perhaps launches, the intellectual enterprise that has come to be known as sociology of knowledge. This aspect of Weber's work needs to be examined from at least two different perspectives: how the formation of the world-image (or life-world) takes place in a religious movement; and how recognition of this factor may aid in understanding the history of a religion.

Weber saw this world-construction as a primary task of the prophet: "To the prophet, both the life of man and the world, both social and cosmic events, have a certain systematic and coherent meaning. To this meaning the conduct of mankind must be oriented if it is to bring salvation, for only in relation to this meaning does life obtain a unified and significant pattern."[45] Yet once such a charismatic's reorganization of the symbolic and cognitive order (together with the sociostructural counterpart) has become institutionalized, the system begins to change. In the case of ethics, for example, Weber wrote that although a religious ethic receives its stamp initially from religious sources, frequently the very next generation reinterprets those claims and promises in a fundamental fashion. Such reinterpretations adjust the revelation to the needs of the religious community. He went on to observe that, even when a change in the socially decisive strata of the community occurs and exerts a decisive impact, the basic type of religion continues to have far-reaching influence on the life-conduct of the adherents, however diverse their stratification may be.[46]

The implications of this for the historian of early Christianity are apparent. The religious phenomena cannot be analyzed without serious attention to the system of "symbolic and cognitive order" as well as the social setting in which the religion functioned. But further, it is not sufficient to reconstruct "*the* Chris-

tian world-view," or even multiple static entities, such as Bultmann's "Palestinian Christianity" and "hellenistic Christianity."
Careful analytical attention must be paid to the process of transformation of the various forms of Christian community reflected
in the New Testament, including full accommodation for how
their life-worlds changed in the changing circumstances of their
epoch.

Acknowledging his debt to both Husserl and Weber, Alfred
Schutz has provided a concise description of the "world" from the
perspective of sociology of knowledge:

> The social world into which one is born and within
> which one has to find his bearings is experienced as a tight-
> knit web of social relationships, of systems of signs and sym-
> bols with their particular structure of meaning, of institu-
> tional forms of social organizations, of systems, of status and
> prestige, etc. The meaning of all these elements of the social
> world in all its diversity and stratification, as well as the pat-
> tern of the texture itself, is, by those living with it, "taken for
> granted." They consider it to be the socially accepted way of
> life for the members and the appropriate means for coming
> to terms with things. This social world is perpetuated by an-
> cestors, teachers, and authorities, and is deemed adequate
> for action and understanding, and as a guide for problem-
> solving and other forms of action. It is assumed that the tra-
> ditions should be transmitted whether we understand their
> origins or not. Through the tradition one learns to define the
> environment, what to take for granted, what are the typical
> constructions and solutions.[47]

The chief medium for communicating this life-world is the
vocabulary and syntax of language. In naming things and events,
in typifications and generalizations, are conveyed the relevance
system within a linguistic in-group. These define the subjective
meaning the group has for its members, and the social roles and
statuses of each. Schutz then observes that this description of a
shared life-world and its social dimensions are true to both existential groups and voluntary groups, although in the latter case
the system must be learned and appropriated. Here is a factor of

profound importance for historical reconstruction of early Christianity: persons were being converted to the new faith from a variety of social worlds. Even in conversion, they did not fully abandon the taken-for-granted aspects of their past. Schutz's discussion of in-groups and out-groups is directly relevant to the break between various types of Christians and various types of Jews.[48] The fact that they were employing common language and common concepts does not mean that they were operating on identical assumptions. Careful investigation must be undertaken to decipher what each meant by the language used, what were their central myths, how their processes of rationalization and institutionalization differed from each other. Schutz does not provide the answers, but he makes the historian aware of neglected or unrecognized issues and problems.

(4) Hermeneutical

After sketching out various patterns of world-abnegation as found by him in major religious systems, Weber offers a remark which is appropriate for describing the interpretive usefulness of his sociological method as a whole offered here in my paraphrase: "The constructed scheme . . . only serves the purpose of offering an ideal-typical means of orientation. It does not teach a philosophy of its own."[49] The theoretical constructed types of conflicting "life-orders" are merely intended to show that at certain points such and such internal conflicts are possible and adequate. These "spheres of value" can appear in reality and in historically important ways, and they have. Such constructions make it possible to determine the typological locus of a historical phenomenon. They enable us to see if, in particular traits or in total character, the phenomenon approximates one of our constructions; to determine the degree of approximation of the historical phenomenon to the theoretically constructed type. To this extent, the construction is merely a technical aid which facilitates a more lucid arrangement and terminology.

When Husserl called for *epochē*, that is, for withholding assent to the natural attitude toward the world, he was demanding that historians bracket their own historical conditioning. As Natanson has expressed it, "In phenomenological reduction the bracketing of history means rendering either naïve believing or self-conscious analysis explicit to reflection; thereby one is prepared for phenomenological inquiry by which one can trace out and reconstruct the path of originary constitution by which the life-world took shape."[50] Natanson observes that Schutz saw his central task as the systematic exploration of the everyday social world. In pursuing that goal he developed a conception of social action based on Max Weber, according to which human action in the world can be understood when one asks, not what it means to the observer, but what it meant to the actor. Employing the term and the basic insight of Dilthey, Schutz conceives of *Verstehen* as the means through which human beings respond to other human beings' intentions. That can be achieved only when the interpreter enters the life-world of the other.

The historian of Christian origins cannot responsibly proceed by measuring the early Christian phenomena against post-Enlightenment norms, or by resolving historical difficulties through the canons of a positivistic "scientific" world-view. We are familiar with proposals of that dismal sort: Jesus appeared to be walking on the surface of the lake because it was shallow at that spot; the disciples found an empty tomb because they went to the wrong one. What is required, rather, is to seek to reconstruct the structure of reality as it was perceived by the ancient writer and audience.

V

What is the outcome of historical work carried out along the lines of the post-Weberian methods sketched above? It does not lead to the historicist's paradise, where everything is seen "as it really happened." Neither does it lead to the theologian's *sanctum sanctorum* where ultimate truth is disclosed. But it does bring into sharper focus the range of models which were used and which may still prove useful for expressing conceptually and for embodying socially the early Christians' common claim, in spite of all their differences, that Jesus of Nazareth was God's agent to call into being the New Covenant community. In the process, these methods can help to clear away careless claims and naïve notions about both similarities and differences between the phenomena—social and conceptual—of the early Christians, of Jews in the period of the Second Temple, and of Greco-Roman culture of the period. That may sound like historical relativism, but there is at least one historian who would prefer relative precision to absolute fuzziness.

NOTES

1. Talcott Parsons, *The Structure of Social Action* (New York: McGraw-Hill, 1937), pp. 475–86.

2. Ibid., p. 476.

3. W. G. Kümmel, *The New Testament: The History of the Investigation of Its Problems*, trans. Howard Clark Kee (Nashville: Abingdon Press, 1975), pp. 51–61, where the impact of "natural religion" on New Testament interpretation is traced.

4. A detailed analysis in Kümmel, *New Testament*, p. 121.

5. Ibid., p. 132.

6. Otto Pfleiderer, *Das Urchristentum, seine Schriften und Lehre, in geschichtlichen Zusammenhang beschrieben* (Berlin, 1887).

7. Erwin Rohde, *Psyche* (Leipzig, 1890).

8. Paul Wendland, *Die hellenistich-römische Kultur in ihren Beziehung zu Judentum und Christentum*, I.2 (Tubingen, 1907), pp. 126, 131, 178–79.

9. William Wordsworth, "The World Is Too Much With Us."

10. Adolf von Harnack, *What Is Christianity?* trans. Thomas B. Sanders, 2nd ed. (London: G. B. Putnam's Sons, 1901).

11. Rudolf Bultmann, *Primitive Christianity in Its Contemporary Setting* (New York: Scribner's Sons, 1956).

12. James Frazer, *The Golden Bough: A Study in Magic and Religion*, abridged ed. (New York: Macmillan, 1927), p. 1.

13. Clifford Geertz, *The Interpretation of Culture* (New York: Basic Books, 1973), p. 359.

14. Mircea Eliade, *The Quest: History and Meaning in Religion* (Chicago: University of Chicago Press, 1969), p. 53.

15. Mircea Eliade, *Cosmos and History*, Bollingen Series 46 (Princeton, N.J.: Princeton University Press, 1954), pp. 150–51.

16. Guilford Dudley, "Mircea Eliade as the 'Anti-Historian' of Religion," *Journal of the American Academy of Religion* 44 (June 1976): 345–59.

17. John Gager, *Kingdom and Community: The Social World of Early Christianity* (Englewood Cliffs, N.J.: Prentice-Hall, 1975). Among the most perceptive studies analyzing early Christian literature by means of insights and categories drawn from sociology of religion and sociology of knowledge — especially in relation to sects and group identity — are those of Wayne Meeks: "The Man from Heaven in Johannine Sectarianism," *Journal of Biblical Literature* 91 (1972): 44–72; "'Am I a Jew?' Johannine Christianity and Judaism," in *Christianity, Judaism, and Other Greco-Roman Cults*, ed. Jacob Neusner (Leiden: E. J. Brill, 1975), pp. 163–86; "'Since Then You Would Need To Go Out of the World': Group Boundaries in Pauline Christianity," in *Critical History and Biblical Faith: New Testament Perspectives*, ed. T. Ryan (Villanova, Pa., 1979), pp. 4–29.

18. Gerd Theissen, "Itinerant Radicals," trans. A. Wire, *Radical Religion* (1975).

19. Gerd Theissen, "Soziale Schichtung in der korintischen Gemeinde," *Zeitschrift fur Theologie und Kirche* 65 (1974): 235.

20. E. A. Judge, *The Social Pattern of the Christian Groups in the First Century* (London: Tyndale Press, 1960).

21. R. A. MacMullen, *Roman Social Relations* (New Haven, Conn.: Yale University Press, 1974); *Enemies of the Roman Order* (Cambridge, Mass.: Harvard University Press, 1966).

22. Karl Jaspers, *Three Essays: Leonardo, Descartes, Max Weber* (New York: Harcourt, Brace, 1964), pp. 236–40.

23. Max Weber, *From Max Weber: Essays in Sociology*, trans. and ed. H. H. Gerth and C. Wright Mills (1946; reprint ed. New York: Oxford University Press, 1977), Introduction, p. 59.

24. Max Weber, *The Methodology of the Social Sciences*, trans. E. A. Shils and H. A. Finch (New York: Free Press, 1949), p. 93.

25. Jaspers, *Three Essays*, p. 240.

26. Weber, *From Max Weber*, "The Sociology of Charismatic Authority," pp. 245–53.

27. Max Weber, *On Charisma and Institution Building* (Chicago: University of Chicago Press, 1968), pp. 21–28, 253–67.

28. Weber, *From Max Weber*, pp. 280–81.

29. Wilhelm Dilthey, *Pattern and Meaning in History*, ed. H. P. Rickman (New York: Harper and Row, 1962).

30. Ibid., p. 67.

31. Ibid., pp. 67–68.

32. Ibid., p. 107.

33. Ibid., p. 97.

34. Maurice Natanson, *Edmund Husserl: Philosopher of Infinite Tasks* (Evanston, Ill.: Northwestern University Press, 1973), p. 112.

35. Alfred Schutz, *On Phenomenology and Social Relations*, ed. Helmut R. Wagner (Chicago: University of Chicago Press, 1970), p. 1.

36. Howard Clark Kee, "Myth and Miracle: Isis, Wisdom, and the Logos of John," in *Myth, Symbol, and Reality*, ed. Alan M. Olson (Notre Dame, Ind.: University of Notre Dame Press, 1980), pp. 149–64.

37. Samuel Sandmel, "Parallelomania," *Journal of Biblical Literature* 81 (1962); 1–13.

38. Max Weber, *Methodology of the Social Sciences*, p. 101.

39. Ibid., p. 102.

40. Morton Smith, *Jesus the Magician* (New York: Harper and Row, 1978).

41. Jean Piaget, *Structuralism*, trans. and ed. Chaninole Maschler (New York: Harper and Row, 1971), p. 5.

42. Ibid., pp. 50, 118.

43. Alfred Loisy, *The Gospel and the Church*, trans. Christopher Howe (Philadelphia: Fortress Press, 1976), p. 166.

44. S. N. Eisenstadt, in Weber, *On Charisma*, p. xvii.

45. Weber, *On Charisma*, p. 266.

46. Ibid., pp. 253–64.

47. Schutz, *On Phenomenology*, pp. 72–76.

48. Ibid., pp. 82–95.

49. Weber, *From Max Weber*, pp. 278–81.

50. Natanson, *Husserl*.

7

Royce: The Absolute and the Beloved Community Revisited

JOHN E. SMITH

ANYONE WHO LIKE MYSELF has studied Royce's philosophy over a long period of time — my *Royce's Social Infinite* was published more than thirty years ago — must keep coming back to a problem posed not only by the development of his thought, but even more pointedly by his own interpretation of that development set forth in the course of remarks he made at a dinner given in his honor not long before his death. Ever responsive to criticism, Royce was keenly aware of the objections leveled against his doctrine of the Absolute by Howison, James, and others; and he also took note of questions being raised about the continuity of his thought. In the philosophy of what has come to be called the later Royce, expressed in writings subsequent to *The World and the Individual*, the Absolute disappears, as it were, and attention is focused on the doctrines of loyalty, community, and interpretation. In the remarks mentioned above Royce was at pains to insure the continuity of his philosophy, maintaining that the notion of the community was present in his thought from the beginning.[1] Earlier on I disagreed with this interpretation in the belief that it had an ad hoc character suited to the occasion and that Royce was misreading his earlier statements in order to prove his consistency. I have changed my mind on this at least. The community idea is indeed to be found in earlier works, notably in his book on California and in *The Spirit of Modern Philosophy*, where it figures largely in his conception of the higher or more inclusive self and in his conception of objectivity as dependent on permanence and a community of ideas. This much continuity, however, does not resolve the more difficult problem of what happened to the Absolute. I shall suggest further on in the discussion that Royce was, sometimes quite imperceptibly, responding to criticism of the Absolute focusing on the reality of time, development, novelty, and individuality and that he came ultimately to believe that the doctrine of community provided a better solution to the problem of the One and the many than the Absolute with its *totum simul* consciousness apprehending all individuals as "drops in this ocean of absolute truth."[2]

I shall approach the problem of the fate of the Absolute, if that expression is not too paradoxical, in three steps: first, an account of the conception itself in terms of what I shall call Royce's fundamental conviction; second, an interpretation of the ingenious argument offered for the reality of the Absolute Knower in the chapter from *The Religious Aspect*, "The Possibility of Error"; and third, a brief consideration of difficulties encountered by his Absolute idealism and an indication of how his last philosophy was intended to meet them. I trust that you will understand that Royce laid great store by his technical skill in philosophical discussion and that the ground to be traversed is quite intricate; I obviously cannot cover it all and I shall hope not to make it more confusing.

Royce's fundamental conviction

It has been said that a comprehensive and systematic thinker, like the hedgehog in the fable, knows one big thing or has one grand idea which he or she articulates, shapes, and reshapes, in an effort to give it the fullest possible expression. In Royce's case, that idea is the reality of a time-spanning consciousness, an Absolute Self to whom all truth, and indeed error too, is known. Royce saw this idea as consonant with the biblical hope of being able to know as we are known, and he saw it as the cornerstone of the thought of Augustine. This commanding idea—that the meaning, truth, and purpose of any fragment, whether it be a momentary thought, a physical object, an event in one's history, are to be found only by appeal to a whole which is, for a finite knower, out of sight — figured in every context of Royce's philosophy. In the sphere of knowledge, no isolated judgment taken by itself and apart from a whole of experience can be deemed true or false; in self-development and the unfolding of consciousness we are always in the situation of having to be more than we are at any moment in order to understand what we are at that moment;[3] in the ethical dimension, the full understanding of the worth of a deed depends on its relation to the whole life of which it is a part; and in religion the significance of any event for our individual destiny can be fully grasped only from the perspective of a Self capable of apprehending a person's life as a whole.

Later on, in *The Problem of Christianity*, this idea was to receive a most forceful application in Royce's interpretation of Jesus' preaching about the Kingdom of God. Since each member of that company is viewed by God who has a conspectus of the totality, each of us is to regard our neighbors and act toward them not only in accordance with our limited view of their welfare but with an imaginative grasp of the way they would appear if we could know their lives as God does. Royce reiterated this fundamental conviction ever and again, and it was the copingstone of his idealism. To know the present context of experience, a particular object, an event in one's life, necessarily requires the appeal to an other, and that, in turn, to an other; if the entire process is to have unity, coherence, and permanence, there must ultimately be an Absolute Self whose experience is of the totality. Royce was indeed captivated by this vision of an Absolute Experience wherein what is apprehended by finite individuals only fragmentarily and discursively is grasped all at once, *totum simul*, with nothing omitted. As we shall see, however, the doctrine that what is, is always all there — not a new doctrine, but one to which Royce gave a novel voluntaristic twist — was to give rise to its own difficulties, not the least of which centered on reconciling this *totum simul* Absolute with Royce's very perceptive theory of the individual self as a purpose to be realized and a task to be performed.

In noting Royce's captivation with the idea of an Absolute Experience, I do not mean to say that he regarded it as sufficient merely to wax enthusiastic about the notion. On the contrary, despite the not-inconsiderable rhetoric and even unction to be found in his writings, Royce had an overweening confidence in the power of logic, and he spoke unabashedly of the need for proof in philosophy. And in fact he was convinced that in his famous argument from "the possibility of error," to which we shall shortly turn, he had established beyond all wish, hope, and even postulate, the existence of the Absolute Knower. I do not regard it as an expression of any lack of faith in rationality to say that I do not follow Royce in his belief in proof in philosophy. Proof, if such there be anywhere, is to be found only in axiomatic systems which are *ipso facto* abstract, and, despite the dream of Descartes, no comprehensive account of what there is can be cast in such a mold. Clarity of analysis, the adducing of consistent reasons, and the meeting of objections are all we can do in philosophical thought, and, in my view, that is enough. Royce clearly wanted more, and he was spurred on by his unlimited trust in versions of the self-referential argument; on more than one occasion he claimed that he could start with the premises of those who proposed to refute him and show that even they had to appeal to his truth! With regard to the particular argument from error, as distinct from the matter of proof in general, I shall say at this point no more than that I believe Royce validly showed something there, although exactly what that something is is more difficult to say than you may imagine. If my interpretation is correct, his argument is of a transcendental sort, and that is no matter of linear proof.

The argument from the possibility of error

How seriously Royce regarded his account of error can be seen in his later reference to it in *The Spirit of Modern Philosophy*. There he described the chapter from *The Religious Aspect of Philosophy* as "containing a metaphysical discussion of the proof of the main thesis of Objective Idealism."[4]

No part of Royce's philosophy can be understood apart from the fundamental assumption which has been in one way or another the cornerstone of all modern idealisms, especially those derived from that development running from Kant to Hegel. I am referring to the thesis that the key to the understanding of being is through being known. The assumption is that a proper understanding of the relation between an idea (judgment) and its object holds the key to the nature of reality. In that relationship we have something of the nature of a privileged position or unique access to reality; we lay hold of the real when we understand what it would have to be like and what conditions it would be called upon to satisfy if it were to be known and apprehended in its truth. We would never get on to our task were I to stop to consider the problems raised by this assumption; we must allow it for the argument's sake and then point out that in Royce's version of idealism the knowing involved is deeper and richer than that envisaged by more rationalistic systems. Royce introduced a voluntaristic dimension into the position, declaring that there is no "pure intellect," all logic being that of the will. The upshot is that all intellectual endeavor is oriented by purpose and intention so that the truth of any set of representations depends on what and how you are attempting to represent.

Since I have categorized Royce's argument for the Absolute Knower as a "transcendental" one, it will be necessary to clarify that notion for a start. The introduction of this way of thinking must be credited to Kant, and it represents something quite novel in the history of Western thought. Kant proposed to begin with knowledge as a fact, that is, with the assumption that Newton's mechanics and the mathematics ingredient in it are forms of objective knowledge about an existent world. Having made this assumption, he then went on to ask how this knowledge is possible, by which he did not mean how do we arrive at it from the standpoint of method, but rather what conditions must be fulfilled if we are to understand the rationality and thus the reliability of a knowledge already regarded as actual. The quest for the conditions which make the actual possible is the task of transcendental philosophy. This reflective enterprise is novel in that it cannot be carried out on the basis of either of the two classical forms of thought: deduction, and induction or probable inference. This position in the hands of Kant, and in my view of Royce too, assumes the form of an idealism because of what Kant called his "Copernican Revolution," which for our purposes will be taken to mean the reversal of the long-standing belief that in knowledge thought must conform to things. For Kant things must be understood as conforming to thought if knowledge is to be possible, and that is why what he called the a priori conditions for knowledge are to be found in human faculties of sensibility, understanding, and reason. All intellectual endeavor, in short, is dependent on synthetic activities of the subject.

Royce followed this pattern of thinking in his argument for the Absolute Knower, but he did so with a characteristic Roycean twist. Seeing that beginning with the fact of knowledge is vulnerable because the skeptic can claim that we have no knowledge, Royce began instead with the fact of error, that we make real mistakes, a claim he thought could not be doubted. Royce, then, was asking, How is error possible? and he aimed to show that it is not possible unless there really is an Absolute Knower to whom is present the whole of experience. The upshot, in Royce's view, is that anyone rejecting his conclusion is forced to hold that error is impossible, and this contradicts the facts. As I have pointed out, the argument is long and intricate, and, moreover, it is not always clear; I shall attempt to elucidate the crucial points.

The first consideration is to determine what it is for an idea (judgment) to be a "real" error. Harking back to a point made by Kant and much emphasized by Peirce, although often overlooked by many, Royce claimed that an erroneous judgment is not in error with respect to any object you please, but only in relation to *its* object, that is, the unique object the judgment aims to characterize. One can see the force of this point from a simple illustration. If I look at a blackboard on which are drawn diagrams of the conic sections and say, "That one is elliptical in shape," and someone says, "You are wrong; it is circular," my judgment would be in error only if in fact I had intended the circular figure—which I did not. Under such circumstances, one would say, "The circular figure is not the one I meant, not the proper object of my judgment, and hence I made no mistake." If I do make an error about an object, the error must be about the intended object; and if it is a real error, that object must have a tenure beyond my individual thought and intention. If this were not so, it would be impossible for anyone to make a mistake, because the judgment that the blue object I mean is blue cannot fail to be correct since that and no other object is the intended one. On this basis no error is possible. The price of this infallibility, however, is that nothing is being said about an objective world going beyond the individual mind. Royce insists that a real error must be about a real object which is at the same time the object intended by the judgment. How are these conditions to be fulfilled?

The principle behind Royce's answer to this question we have already noted; no finite thought, content of experience, or judgment can be known, thought, understood without going beyond it. In this case what we are seeking to understand is an error, that is, a judgment about a judgment. It is Royce's contention that when we say to ourselves, "This color now before me is red, and to say that it is blue would be to make a blunder," we represent what he calls "an including consciousness" which is far more complex than that of the initial judgment. Three distinct elements are included within the unity of this expanded consciousness; "first, the perception of red; secondly, the reflected judgment whose object is this perception, and whose agreement with this object constitutes its own truth; and, thirdly, the erroneous reflection, *this is blue*, which is in the same thought compared with the perception and rejected as error."[5] The inclusive thought is necessary because in a real error the object intended must be the same object intended by the true judgment in comparison with which the error is exposed, and, on his view, this comparison can be made only within the unity of a thought to which the error, the truth, and the same intended object are present. Royce concludes that this complex must be present for one inclusive thought, so that error is possible as a moment in this higher thought or consciousness which makes the error a part of itself while knowing that it is an error.

But, one may ask, Why must there be an Absolute Knower? Why cannot each individual self-conscious being realize the complex unity just described? Royce's answer, although one must work through his many restatements of the argument to find it, has two features. The first is that no single judgment taken by itself can be an error. Error is possibly only as actually included in a higher thought which provides the judgment with a completed object; for example, the object in its whole truth, by comparison with which the error is judged to be error. The idea is that if error is a fragment or an incomplete thought, that fact can be discovered by comparing it not with other fragments but only with the completed object. No finite knower possesses that object; we can intend it and find error about it, but we do not have that object available to us for comparison with our isolated judgment. Only an Absolute Knower could do that. Secondly, Royce argues, there is an infinite mass of error possible, and since the possibilities of error are infinite, there must be an infinite thought to expose them through comparison with the truth about these objects. That task is beyond the power of finite knowers of any finite collection of them.

I must leave the exposition here with apologies for not having made it all clearer. I shall, however, make three brief comments about Royce's claim. First, much of the difficulty in following the argument stems from two features in Royce's presentation. One is his having restated the case several times but with some novel feature on each occasion. The second has to do with differences in the kinds of objects he considered and the bearing these differences have on what it means to say that the infinite thought furnishes the real object of our judgment. The physical objects, things of the world, are available to us as such, even if we don't have the whole truth about them. The situation is somewhat different when we consider the knowledge of selves. In a discussion I have omitted, Royce availed himself of a humorous remark made by Mark Twain that in every conversation between two people, there are six participants—the real John and the real Thomas, and their respective ideas of each other and of themselves. His point is that a real error on John's part about Thomas must be about the real Thomas. While John can *intend* that Thomas, the complex unity of thought, feeling, and the like, constituting the real Thomas is not directly available to John, but only to a Knower who possesses the whole and completed truth about Thomas. The point is ever the same; a real error requires that it be about a real object, but its meaning as an error consists in its being compared with the corresponding true judgment about the same object present to the same inclusive thought. What Royce is assuming here, but not admitting as clearly as he might have, is that a singular erroneous judgment can be exposed as such not by comparison with a fragment, but only from the standpoint of a Knower who possesses the whole truth about a complete object.

This brings me to my second point: for Royce, everything depends on the knowing purpose involved. It is not the object as such that we seek, but the truth about it; and this is the reason Royce needs a completed object or the whole truth about that object and no other to counter all the error that is possible. Only an Absolute Knower has that truth, and that is why such a Knower is required for explaining the possibility of error.

My third point follows directly from the preceding; it concerns the transcendental character of the entire argument. The point of such an argument, one must remember, is not to offer a touchstone for determining when we have made a mistake in a particular case, but rather to specify the conditions which make error as such possible. If error, any error, is actual, then the conditions for its possibility cannot themselves be merely possible but must be actual as well. It is for this reason that Royce claims the actuality and not just the postulation of the Absolute Knower. About this feature of the transcendental argument, Royce was right; the point goes all the way back to Aristotle's claim that the actual cannot be accounted for solely on the basis of possibility.

Whatever difficulties there are in Royce's position, I think he should be defended against one misunderstanding of which some of his critics, including James, were guilty. Royce makes no claim, as James seems to have thought, that the knowledge of the Absolute Knower is available to us to be used as a standard for judging particular judgments. James's famous exclamation, "I say, Royce, damn the Absolute!" was prompted by the common-sensical idea that it does us no good in the way of knowing to know that the Absolute Knower knows it all, because that knowledge is inaccessible to us. But here James missed the point — and this would remain true even if Royce's entire argument were fallacious. The Absolute reached in the argument is an implicate, a condition necessary for explaining error and the truth which makes error possible. The parallel with Kant's *Critique of Pure Reason* in this regard is instructive. The *Critique* tells us what knowledge of an object means and the conditions which make it possible, but the *Critique* by itself does not enable us to determine the material truth or falsehood of this or that judgment. So it is with Royce's argument; it tells us what an error is and why an Absolute Knower is required if the fact of error is to be made intelligible, but that account itself does not provide us with any formula for ascertaining in a given case whether we have made an error or not.

Absolute idealism, community, and interpretation

One thing remained constant throughout Royce's philosophical career: his commitment to idealism as the only satisfactory metaphysics. "A doctrine," he has written in *The Spirit*, "remains, in the metaphysical sense idealistic, if it maintains that the world is, in its wholeness, and in all of its real constituent parts, a world of mind or of spirit."[6]

The shape of that idealism, however, did not remain fixed. Even if we allow, as I think we must, that there is continuity between his earlier and later thought as regards what may be called the "social principle" and the reality of community, his conception of the spiritual reality was altered both in response to criticism and as a result of the influence of Peirce's theory of interpretation. The dropping of the language of the Absolute in his last writings is not the least of these alterations. I shall select three focal points at which Royce showed concern to rework his ideas in an effort to do justice to certain features of experience which, as it seemed to some, had been subordinated by his uncompromising idealism. These points are the status of the self and the reality of finite individuals; the recognition of time as a real order allowing for novelty; and the solution to the problem of the One and the many. In considering each of these points in turn, I shall have to simplify matters somewhat because of the extensiveness of the relevant discussions, but I trust that I shall not distort Royce's views in the effort.

To begin with and remaining on a commonsensical level, the most obvious uneasiness about Royce's Absolute was expressed in the fear that its all-encompassing unity meant the disappearance of individual finite selves endowed with some measure of autonomy. James gave expression to this uneasiness when he described Royce's world as a "block universe" whose grade of unity is so tight that there seems to be no room for possibility, indeterminacy, contingency, and creativity. In short, for James, such a world could have no open future. Apart from his more rhetorical pages in which he celebrated the completed unity of the one Self, Royce never envisaged the Absolute as undifferentiated, and, in fact, it is one of his major criticisms of mysticism that it so often results in an undifferentiated immediacy wherein everything finite is absorbed. Royce, it is clear, rejected such a view, but it remains to be seen how well he succeeded in doing justice to individual selves within the confines of his Absolute idealism.

In his Gifford Lectures, *The World and the Individual*, Royce set forth a novel theory of being, the fundamental thesis of which is summed up in the formula "To be is to be the fulfillment of a purpose." According to this view, what there is represents the will or purpose of the Absolute Self who intends this world and no other; every being in it must be seen as this individual and no other, since all belong to one and the same system. The idea that will or purpose defines individuality is of the utmost importance because it figures largely in Royce's conception of the individual self as an overarching purpose or plan. The self, in the end, is a task to be performed, calling into play the active powers of each individual. There can be no doubt that Royce envisaged for each individual the need to identify himself or herself in some form of contrast to other selves, the world, and God. Each will have, says Royce,

> the really deep and important persuasion that he *ought to possess* or create for himself . . . some one principle, some finally significant contrast, whereby he should be able, with an unified and permanent meaning, to identify that portion of the world's life which is to be, in the larger sense, his own, and whereby he should be able to contrast with this, his larger Self, all the rest of the world of life.[7]

Individuals, then, are such that they are identified by the projection of and the persistent effort to realize a purpose providing the unity and identity essential for selfhood. In my own language, I refer to this aspect as the expression of "what I mean to be." That we are here dealing with something undeniably individual is clear; Royce continues,

> Now this purpose, I maintain, is indeed your own. As nobody else can share it, so nobody else can create it; and from no source external to yourself have you derived it.[8]

That is a strong declaration of uniqueness and individuality.

There is, however, the other aspect of his idealism noted above; the whole of being represents the realized purpose of the Absolute Self so that we have not to do merely with what I mean to be, my purpose, but with what "I was meant to be" from the standpoint of that Self who intended me and no other. How are these two aspects to be brought together? Here Royce meets a problem by no means unknown to the Western philosophical, no less than the theological, tradition. In my view, although he did seek to bring both the "I mean" and the "I was meant" into some form of unity, he cannot solve the problem on the basis of his Absolute. The reason is that a completed and fully determinate self or object is what the Absolute now possesses, and if this is so, it is difficult to see in what sense it can be said that my individual purpose as it now stands before me has not been derived from any source external to myself. If, of course, Royce means that the Absolute Self is not external to me in the sense that two beads on a string are external to each other, well and good. But what holds me apart now from that completed self which the theory demands and cannot do without? The problem is endemic to an idealism which allows the real no tenure apart from will and mind and is therefore forced to identify that real with a totality or completion of meaning and knowing. Short of this completion, we have nothing at all. That is the perennial problem of Absolute idealism.

Having suggested why I believe Royce cannot reconcile the two aspects ultimately, let me call attention to the great strength of what we may refer to as his proximate solution. Long before Sartre, and even Marcel, Royce had the idea of the self as a plan or project, an essentially ethical task. He never wavered on the basic point that the self is not a datum given to direct perception, nor is it some combination of conceived universals. The self is a living unity extending over time, and the unity is provided by a purpose to be realized. Unlike Sartre, however, who identifies the self with freedom, Royce saw the role of destiny, of Providence in religious terms, and the need to acknowledge the existence of factors and conditions in the makeup of an individual that cannot be put down to freedom alone. If the world is not just so much brute fact but is intended as the fulfillment of a purpose, then I must find myself already endowed with capacities, talents, interests answering to what "I was meant to be." In short, whatever freedom I have to realize what "I mean to be" must be limited. Nevertheless, these capacities and endowments, Royce contends, do not organize and direct themselves — to do that is a task to be carried out by me and no other.

From my standpoint as this individual there is a life-plan to be framed and pursued, and neither task can be performed by anyone else. Again, from that standpoint I am not to regard my completed and fully determinate self as all there in advance. But, as I have pointed out, if the argument from error stands, there is no way in which Royce can avoid the necessity of the completed object if he is to have any object at all. This is the root of his problem. In fairness, however, I should say that Royce would have pointed in reply to his ingenious theory of the Actual Infinite set forth in the supplementary essay to *The World and the Individual*, where the totality is said to be found in the form or purpose generating all its members and not in a *seriatim* completion ending with a final term. I cannot discuss this here, beyond saying that it points in the direction of an open end to the world process which Royce was to stress more and more later on.

I shall telescope the remaining two points — time as a real order allowing for novelty, and the conception of community as the final solution to the problem of the One and the many — since they are intimately connected. Of crucial importance was Royce's discovery of Charles Peirce's theory of signs and interpretation. Royce gladly acknowledged his debt to Peirce in this regard, but he assumed sole responsibility for the special applications of the theory to problems in the philosophy of religion and especially to the task of reinterpreting Christianity in terms of what he called the essential Christian ideas. To anticipate those applications, I shall mention the two relevant for our purposes. One is Royce's fastening upon the connection between time and the open-ended nature of the interpretative process; and the other is the double claim that interpretation is unique and not reducible to other cognitive forms, and that it is especially suited for the achievement of understanding between selves and consequently for the realization of communities of persons.

Peirce had argued as a general thesis that all thought takes place through the medium of signs which have the distinctive triadic character of (a) pointing to an object, state of affairs, or anything we can intend; (b) embodying some meaning, qualification, or determination of that thing; and (c) addressing themselves to a potential reader or mind capable of interpreting what the sign means through the use of other signs. There is a more exact formulation of sign-functioning as a triadic relation of sign, object, and interpretant, but that might prove more confusing than enlightening for our purposes. Royce sought to bring out the peculiar features and role of interpreting signs by contrasting interpretation with the two basic faculties of the human mind bequeathed by Kant's analysis in *The Critique of Pure Reason* — perceiving and conceiving. *Perceiving* has as its object a thing, datum, complex of fact which is present to us and apprehended directly. *Conceiving* aims at defining the universal and repeatable characteristics of things and their structures and relations. Royce was well aware that, while Kant had held that only a synthesis of the two can lead to knowledge, a debate has continued from Plato to Bergson and beyond as to whether one of the two is fundamental and the other derivative. More important, however, than the resolution of this problem is the assumption that the dichotomy presented is exhaustive and that there is no other cognitive process. Royce denied this assumption in a most telling way. Not only are perceiving and conceiving self-limiting processes — the former comes to rest in the presence of the datum and the latter has done its work when the ideal type of the fact has been determined — but neither taken alone is equal to the task of interpreting signs. Consider his example of the weathervane. Perceiving the device as an object present and describing it by means of concepts are both possible for someone who does not know how to read it, that is, to interpret the meaning of the device as a sign indicating the direction of the wind. Unless one understands that the vane is a sign and knows what the position of its movable part means, one can do no more than look at the object and describe its features; one cannot interpret. Interpretation, moreover, is not self-limiting, because every reading of a sign takes place through an interpretation which is itself a sign addressed to a future interpreter. The process is essentially social, since every sign is a sign of a mind that was, and is addressed to a mind that is yet to come upon it.

Adopting Peirce's earlier claim that the self is not the proper object of either perceiving or conceiving since it is essentially a conversation of interpreted meanings, Royce declared that interpretation is the only appropriate cognitive process whereby selves come to know themselves and each other. This notion is at the root of the doctrine of community, illustrated at an elementary level in the process of translation and then extended by Royce to include religious, moral, political communities based on traditions extending over long periods of time. When translators confront a text in a given language, they encounter the signs of another mind; in translating this text into another language they produce a second set of signs addressed to a future mind; and interpreters say, in effect, to that mind: "What I say to you is what the text says to me." There is thus a linkage of meaning, via the office of the interpreter, between three minds—the writer of the text, perhaps long gone, the present interpreter, and the future mind who, in reading the interpretation, becomes related to a mind in the past.

It should now be evident that through the doctrine of interpretation, Royce is attempting to provide a solid foundation for a real time-order. Seen from the standpoint of an individual, the present self interprets the past self to the future self. I recall today that some weeks ago I promised to return a book at some determinate time in the future. The reference to both memory and anticipation led Royce to consider the ability of otherwise distinct selves to extend themselves in both directions by identifying themselves with certain events in the past as part of their own history, and by identifying themselves with certain hoped-for events forming part of a future not yet actualized. Such ideal extensions are the substance of what he called communities of memory and communities of hope. The community comes into being when many distinct selves find themselves accepting as part of themselves and their own biography a common past and a common hoped-for future. The experiences, persons, and events, for example, which form the substance of religious communities, are preserved in the sacred literature of the community, available as signs to everyone present to interpret them. When one identifies oneself with this past and regards it as belonging to one's own history, he or she is at once linked through spiritual bonds with all other selves making the same identification. In commemorating the deliverance from Egypt, for example, the members of the Jewish community give thanks to the Lord for delivering *us* from bondage. Each individual, in saying "we" and "us," is making an identification with that common heritage which all share. The same phenomenon is evident in national communities; consider that in his Gettysburg Address, Lincoln did not say "the forefathers," or "some forefathers," but "our forefathers," a clear expression of the identification by all participants of themselves with a tradition shared by all.

We cannot follow Royce's extended application of the doctrines of interpretation and community to what he called "the problem of Christianity" and his account of the social dimension of religion supremely exemplified by the Beloved Community. However, let me bring the discussion to a close by defining more exactly the nature of community as Royce saw it, and how it serves to relate the One and the many. To begin with, Royce, like Aristotle and Hegel, regarded community as a distinct type and level of being,[9] not to be understood in terms of adding or summing individuals. Royce repeatedly insisted that if one thinks of a one, and another, and another, and so on, it will not be possible to arrive at a community, but only a collection. Understanding what a community is depends on seeing, first, that genuinely distinct individuals are required, and, secondly, that these individuals become linked to each other in virtue of the fact that they are all linked to the same third reality. For the existence of a community, three conditions are required: the power of the individual to extend his or her life in time; a number of distinct selves capable of communicating with each other; and the inclusion by the ideally extended selves of some events which are for all of them identical.

The first condition depends on Royce's thesis that the self is no datum either of perception or conception, but a life which is interpreted and interprets itself over a course of time in accordance with purposes and reasons determining what that life shall include and how it will be identified. As regards the second condition, the existence of individuals in communication, Royce was emphatic, in his own words, "that a community does *not* become one, in the sense of my definition, by virtue of any reduction or melting of these various selves into a single merely present self, or into a mass of passing experience."[10] The point is crucial and often overlooked. Suffice to say here that were there no many there would be no problem of how to relate them to the One. Anyone who supposes that Royce wants to absorb individuals into a community has misunderstood him.

The third condition is in many ways the most important because it points to the unifying spiritual bond enabling us to say that though there are many members, there is but one body. Insofar as all members acknowledge as belonging to their own past a heritage of faith, of deeds, of insights, they form a community of memory such that each member knows about all the others the fact that they are identified with the same past he or she acknowledges. And so with the community of hope engaged in accomplishing some goal — what Royce usually called a cause in performing deeds aimed at helping to realize that goal. Each individual knows that the others accept as part of themselves that hoped-for future and are committed to the common task of contributing to its realization. The many are One in virtue of their relation to the common third reality, but they remain many since this very relationship contributes to their own fulfillment as individual persons. One loses one's life in the cause, only to find it again through individual but cooperative endeavor with fellow beings unified by a bond of love and loyalty.

Recognition of the discursive and temporal character of the

process of interpretation, and of the dynamic life of communities through their members in history, no longer made it necessary for Royce to adhere to the *totum simul*, or "all at once" conception of consciousness characteristic of his earlier thought. A dynamic development of life and spirit in a historical order has now taken precedence over the previous conception of a completed Absolute. And, in fact, as I have noted, that term disappears and is to be found, if at all, only in the faint echo of an Ideal Interpreter which, if my memory serves me correctly, makes but one appearance in the pages of *The Problem of Christianity*. Instead, we have a new orientation in Royce's thought leading into a possibly creative future. At the end he was expressing the hope that the historical process would move in the direction of realizing a community of all humanity in which spiritual ties of understanding, loyalty, and devotion would prove strong enough to overcome the conflicts and divisions among people which lead ever and again to those two distorted forms of human relations — collectivism and individualism. The former is a One without a real many, while the latter is a many without a real One. Royce's vision of community points to a form of life transcending these distortions because it is a unity of a One and a many which allows for both without sacrificing either.

NOTES

1. Speaking of his career and intellectual development, Royce said, "When I review this whole process, I strongly feel that my deepest motives and problems have centered about the Idea of the Community, although this ideal has only come gradually to my clear consciousness" ("Words of Professor Royce at the Walton Hotel at Philadelphia, December 29, 1915," *Philosophical Review* 25:3 [May 1916]: 510).

2. Josiah Royce, *The Religious Aspect of Philosophy* (1895; reprint ed., New York: Harper & Brothers, Harper Torchbooks, 1958), p. 441; cf. Josiah Royce, *The Philosophy of Loyalty* (New York: Macmillan, 1908), p. 395.

3. "In order to realize what I am I must . . . become more than I am or than I know myself to be. I must enlarge myself, . . . go beyond my private self, presuppose the social life . . . " (Josiah Royce, *The*

Spirit of Modern Philosophy [Cambridge, Mass.: Riverside Press, 1892], p. 215).

4. Ibid., p. vi.

5. Royce, *Religious Aspect*, p. 423.

6. Royce, *Spirit of Modern Philosophy*, p. xiv.

7. Josiah Royce, *The World and the Individual*, 2 vols. (New York: Macmillan, 1899–1901), 2:274.

8. Ibid., p. 294.

9. This does not mean, as nominalists and individualists invariably suppose, that a community is something that still continues to have some sort of being even if there were no members! This conception misses the point.

10. Josiah Royce, *The Problem of Christianity* (Chicago: University of Chicago Press, 1968), pp. 255–56.

8

Homo Homini Deus Est:
Feuerbach's Religious Materialism

MARX W. WARTOFSKY

> Religion is from the outset con-
> sciousness of the transcendental
> arising from actually existing forces.
> This more popularly.[1] — *Karl Marx*

Introduction

I DO NOT PROPOSE to give any detailed reconstruction of Feuerbach's philosophy of religion, or of his distinctive and problematic conception of species-being (*Gattungswesen*), or of his equally
problematic materialism. Rather, I would like to raise a question
not about Feuerbach, but by way of Feuerbach, namely: "Is
there a viable materialist conception of religion?"

This is a less simple question than it appears to be. Plainly,
there are materialist conceptions of religion, from Epicurus
through Marx and Engels, which explain religion as a function of
material human needs, and of the material conditions of human
life which give rise to these needs. The question is: Are such theories viable or adequate to explain the phenomenon of religious belief? A viable conception of religion is one which doesn't simply
explain religion away, but rather explains its origins, its distinctive cultural and historical forms, its persistence in various institutional contexts, its changes and development, its continuing
and present existence in the modes of belief and action of individuals. The question of whether there is a viable materialist con-

ception of religion is therefore a question of whether any of the presumptively materialist theories meet these requirements. What would it take for a materialist theory of religion to do so adequately?

The focus on Feuerbach is prompted by the fact that he gives the first and most fully elaborated materialist explanation of religion in modern times, in a way which attempts to preserve the reality of the phenomenon, and not merely to discount it. The burden of my title is the kernel of Feuerbach's thesis: "*Homo Homini Deus Est*" ("man is a God to man"). Feuerbach proposes that religious consciousness, revealed in its "true essence," is the human recognition of the human as divine, as the highest value, and as bearing within itself the grounds of infinity and perfection. That Feuerbach sees these divine qualities in the actuality of human existence, in the materiality of human need, feeling, and consciousness, and in the sociality of the human form of life is the intent of my characterization of Feuerbach's view as "religious materialism." But Feuerbach's theory fails. The failure is, nevertheless, important. For it opens up the possibility of an adequate theory in the most serious way and also anticipates the most serious difficulties that an adequate theory would have to resolve. Indeed, it is the critique of Feuerbach which seems to me to be the path to salvation—at least to theoretical or philosophical salvation. In Engels's play of words on Feuerbach's name, *Feuerbach* is the "fiery brook" which was the "purgatory" through which German post-Hegelian thought had to pass. This "fiery brook" still serves as the purgatory through which our own conceptions of religion have to pass, if they are to transcend the limits of the past.

In this paper, therefore, I propose to do several things: (1) To pose the general form of the problem that a materialist theory of religion has to solve—namely, the problem of transcendence. (2) To sketch Feuerbach's formulation of the problem, first negatively, in the form of Feuerbach's critique of theology, then positively, in terms of what he took to be a humanist resolution of the contradiction in theology. (3) To consider why Feuerbach's theory may be called a "religious materialism." Here I will question what is "materialist" about this materialism, and whether any materialism, properly so-called, can be characterized as "religious," or whether this is simply a *contradictio in adjecto*. (4) To sketch the philosophical and theological alternatives in the traditional conceptions of transcendence, and to explore whether a materialist theory of transcendence is possible. (5) To present the Feuerbachian and Marxian views of transcendence which, it seems to me, begin to formulate the concept in a materialist way. Here, I hope to show that dialectic — the Hegelian dialectic, in its transformations by Feuerbach and Marx — provides the clue to a materialist theory of transcendence, first, as a dialectic of consciousness, and then, as a dialectic of praxis.

What will have happened, by this time, to the notion of materialism is perhaps the crucial question of this paper, and also a crucial question to me, personally, for it concerns the wider question of how Marxism is to be understood, and whether it is viable. It should be clear, from this introduction, that I take the question of transcendence to be the conceptual heart of the matter, and that I take it, therefore, to be central to the characterization of religion. Whether or not there can be a viable materialist conception of religion hinges on this point. There can be, only if there is a viable materialist theory of transcendence.

Transcendence: a first approach

The reason that I approach the question of transcendence by way of Feuerbach is that he offers a striking and radical reformulation of the traditional theological problem. The traditional problem concerns the relation of God to the world, and it arises from Christian theology both as a general question of religious consciousness, and in a specific historical setting.

First, as a general question: no conception of religion can be viable if it doesn't deal with the present, with the concrete realities of present human life, in both their sordid and glorious details. At the same time, no conception of religion is viable if it doesn't deal with what transcends the present, with what is grasped as beyond the actual and the particular. The problem for traditional theology (and metaphysics) was how these apparently incompatible, if not indeed contradictory desiderata could be held together. The Christian mystery, the center of Christian faith, lay in the identification of these opposing requirements: of the present moment with eternity; of life here and now with everlasting life; of human finitude, suffering, and sin with infinite being, joy, and redemption. The Incarnation of the divine served Christianity (as it did pre-Christian religions) as the living metaphor, the concrete embodiment of this apparent contradiction. Christ was human, a living, suffering, dying individual; and was also God incarnate. The infinite and eternal God was identical with the finite and temporal human individual.

Feuerbach saw, in this paradox of faith, the very essence of Christianity. But he saw it as a rational contradiction only on the interpretation demanded by theology — namely, that God was nonhuman, superhuman, wholly other. In *The Essence of Christianity*, Feuerbach argued that this theological insistence upon the separateness of the human from the divine is in reality — nontheologically or anthropologically — nothing but the separation of the individual human being from his or her own species-nature; and that religious consciousness resides in the awareness of both the species-nature of the individual, and of the separation of the individual from this species-nature. Thus, he writes that his task is "to show that the opposition of the divine and the human is nothing but the opposition between human essence and the human individual."[2]

However, the traditional theological problem of transcendence also arose in a particular historical setting. And to that dimension, Feuerbach pays scant attention. The question is: Why did Christian theology formulate the notion of divine transcendence as it did? The burden of Christian theology in its early phases — whatever its sources in Greek or Jewish thought (or in their Philonic amalgam) — was to counter pagan identification of God (or of the gods) with nature (with natural objects or phenomena) or with any given human or ethnic character of a local sort. The task of theology was, both theoretically and practically, to counter idolatry. God, who creates the world, must stand beyond the world. God must be in some sense wholly other, precisely in not being limited to the conditions of finitude and transiency which are the sources of human need, suffering, and death. God is ultimately different, and this ultimate difference constitutes transcendence.

The difficulty which traditional Christian theology posed for itself in this formulation of transcendence is that this self-same transcendent God had also to see, to touch, to succor, to care for, to provide, to judge, to show mercy, to recognize, to hear, to understand, to heal — not in some realm beyond the world of finite, concrete, and daily human existence, but just in that very world itself. The transcendent God had also to suffer and die, to be born of woman, to bleed, to cry, to eat and drink. The infinite had to become, not symbolically, but actually, existentially finite. To worship Christ as a symbol of the Godhead would have been to substitute one idolatry for another. Symbols are not gods. So belief in God had to be belief not through Christ but in Christ.

Theology was then caught between the demands for a transcendent deity, distinct from the gods of the idolaters, and the demands for an immanent, embodied, incarnate deity, accessible to believers. Where theology posited the Incarnation as a mystery of faith, Feuerbach took theology to be the embodiment of a contradiction, precisely in that this theology sought to assert both rationally exclusive demands in a rational way. He argued that the belief of believers is not contradictory, for belief is not a matter of reason, but of feeling, of felt need. Belief is the activity of the practical imagination to supply what is needed in the imagination to realize the demands of feeling. It is, in effect, not yet rational because it is not a matter of asserting propositions. It is prelogical, the work of the heart. It becomes contradictory and rationally insupportable when it is transformed into rational terms, subject to the dictates of logic. Theology, Feuerbach argued, is the perversion of belief. The theory of transcendence, as in the rational theory of incarnation, is outright contradiction. It asserts mutually exclusive propositions. So runs, in brief, Feuerbach's critique of traditional Christian theories of transcendence.

And yet, Feuerbach himself had a theory of transcendence. How can that be? If Feuerbach were to have such a theory, by his own strictures, and on the grounds of his own critique, then in it the transcendent could not be conceived to be wholly other and yet identical with that from which it is wholly other. Yet, insofar as the divine—for Feuerbach's transcendent is the divine, and nothing less—is fully immanent, identical with the human and the worldly, in what conceivable sense could the divine be transcendent at all? The trick is to ground the transcendent in the human, but in such a way that it is human beings who, by their very nature, create the transcendent in the course of their characteristic activity. Thus Feuerbach's solution to the traditional problem is not to offer an alternative to the solutions already posed, all of which he rejects as self-contradictory, in that systematic critique of theology which comprises his major work, *The Essence of Christianity*. Rather, his solution is to radically reformulate the problem itself. He does this by taking it as a genetic question: How does the transcendent originate? How do human beings, finite flesh-and-blood creatures, individuals, arrive at such a consciousness, and what, in effect, is it a consciousness of? What is its object?

For Feuerbach, the object of religious belief exists, and not merely as a fiction of the imagination. Rather its exists in a full-blooded, ontological way, no less so than does the believer. In fact, the object of belief in the transcendent is oneself, the believer! Religious consciousness is nothing but human self-consciousness, whose object is the human itself.

Feuerbach's move, then, is to take the human as a consciousness of self which is at the same time a consciousness of an other like oneself. "Self-consciousness exists . . . by the fact that it exists for another self-consciousness; that is to say, it *is* only by being acknowledged or 'recognized'." This rough paraphrase is not Feuerbach, of course, but, recognizably, Hegel, in *The Phenomenology of Mind*.[3] Feuerbach takes Hegel's formulation as a basis, and elaborates it to mean that consciousness of oneself as a human being requires the recognition of oneself as a species-being. The condition for human individuality, as human, is the bond of consciousness in which the I knows itself to be an I only in relation to a Thou. The community of *I*'s and *Thou*'s, the human community or species-being, is therefore constituted in this essential mutuality of recognition itself. The being which the individual consciousness takes as the object of such human recognition is thus as much *I* as *Thou*, as much other as self, as much community as individual.

Now for Feuerbach, this species-being is the living, material community of human beings, and therefore an embodied or concrete universal. It is this species-being which is the object of consciousness of the transcendent. But there's the rub. For the individual is existentially finite, and a finite consciousness. Yet such a human individual's consciousness, even of this finitude, is a recognition of one's own finitude only with respect to, and by contrast to, the existence of others like oneself. One recognizes oneself to be human only in recognition of one's common humanity, one's human "essence," to use Feuerbach's term. And the representation of this human essence, this species-nature, is a recognition of that which lies beyond, transcends the limits of one's own individual finitude. The human consciousness is, in Feuerbach's view, this double awareness of one's separate and finite individuality and one's common, universal, or shared nature.

Insofar as the human being recognizes the separation of the self from others, one aspect of one's essential humanity is realized: one's own distinctiveness, existential uniqueness, the "I." Insofar as one recognizes one's universal, shared, or mutual nature with others, in the relation of I and Thou — since only individuals exist — another aspect of one's essential humanity is realized. But it is this otherness, this species-nature transcending the separate "I," which becomes the object of the consciousness of transcendence. Taken as symbolic "other," this Being becomes invested with characteristics no individual Thou can possess, but which expresses the potentiality of the community of *I*'s or *Thou*'s. It transcends the limits of any individual's existence or capacities. This abstracted "other" is then taken to be a transcendent entity; in short, a God. But in reality, this "God" is only the hypostatized community of individuals, misidentified with its symbolic representation in consciousness. Human dependence on other human beings becomes identified with human dependence on this "Other," beyond the limits of individual finite human existence. This "Other" becomes deified as that Being which stands over and against the concrete individual existence of *I*'s and *Thou*'s.

One step more. This new Being, this image of communal existence, becomes *God*. But Feuerbach says, if we recognize the genesis and nature of this God as "nothing but" the alienated form of human-self-consciousness, then we recognize what this "God" in truth is: *"Homo Homini Deus Est"* ("man is a God to man"). From this, there follow all the Feuerbachian aphorisms: "Theology is esoteric anthropology," and others.

The transcendent, as an object, has on the one hand been identified with the mystified, mistakenly hypostatized representation of the community of human beings, but has now, on the other hand, been demystified, recognized in its concrete existence as the flesh-and-blood community of human individuals itself. It is not the case, therefore, that an individual human being, as such, is or can be God; but only that God, as transcendent Being, is in living fact the community.

However, if the human is the divine, then the divine would seem to be a being of consciousness only, and not a material being, for species-being, the awareness of oneself in the relation to the other, is an intentional constitution of the community, in the act of mutually recognizing self-consciousnesses. In what sense can one say that Feuerbach goes any further than Hegel, in *The Phenomenology*? Is Feuerbach's humanism anything more than an identification of Hegel's *Idea* with human self-consciousness? If Feuerbach's view is to be understood as a materialist conception of religion, wherein lies its materialism?

Religious Materialism

If *Homo Homini Deus Est*, then Feuerbach's materialism must lie in his conception of the human being, or the person. His materialist conception of religion (if indeed he has one) must construe the object of religious belief as a material being, and the praxis of religion as a material praxis. However, there are two ways to interpret this requirement of materialism. The first is to argue that the object of religion is the material human being and that therefore religion is about this material being, but that religious consciousness concerns this being not in its concrete existence in the world, but only as an object in consciousness. Thus, the praxis of religion is belief, and belief, as an activity of consciousness, is not a material praxis but rather a mental praxis. Or (to be fully fair to Feuerbach, in this interpretation), belief is a praxis not simply of thought or of intellect or of reason, but rather of feeling. It is a matter of expression of a conscious need or want or wish, by a thinking-feeling-willing being; but the expression of this feeling or desire is in the imagination. The arena of this praxis of belief is therefore the imagination, and the activity of the imagination is not itself a material but a mental activity. Therefore, though the object of religion is material human existence, the praxis of religion is not a material praxis, but rather a reflection in the imagination *of* the material praxis or life-activity of the species.

The second interpretation of the requirement of a materialist conception of religion is that both its object and the activity of the subject as a religious consciousness are material. On this view, the praxis of belief would itself have to be construed as a material praxis. Belief would not simply be a matter of feeling or desire reflected upon in the imagination, but indeed, practical belief. The object of belief would still be an object of the imagination, but the imagination would no longer be an activity of merely inward or mental reflection, or even a matter of external representation of the object of belief. Rather, the representation itself would serve as a model for its embodiment in the world. It would reveal itself not only as purpose, or end of action, but would become actualized in that very activity. Such belief, then, is the activity of practical objectification, material praxis. It would not only interpret the world, it would also change it, in accordance with the imagination of what such a change would bring about.

Such an interpretation of the requirement for a materialist conception of religion raises two questions: (1) Why should such an object of belief as the human being, as species-being, be regarded as "material"? What is "materialist" in this reading of "material human existence," especially if we are talking not alone of individuals, but of their social species-being, their universality? What is, in short, a material universal? Is it no more than the Hegelian concrete universal? And if it is more, what do "concrete" and "material" signify here? (2) Why should such a materialism, however it is construed, be characterized as "religious"? Why not say, instead, that the "religious" has in fact been left behind, once the transcendent is no longer an imaginary or hypostatized entity of thought, but becomes instead the very activity of transcending the limits of the present in practical activity?

Feuerbach answers these questions in a variety of ways, and I cannot here offer more than a brief sketch of his thought. I can also say that his resolution of these questions remains tentative, problematic, and inadequate. But he does raise the problems, and raises them in such a way that the nineteenth century and a good part of the twentieth are taken up, both intellectually and practically, with the problems which Feuerbach proposes, and with a critique of his inadequacy.

First, what does Feuerbach mean by "material" or "materialism"? Certainly not the mechanist materialism of eighteenth-century natural science, or natural philosophy. He is concerned with material nature — the physicochemical stuff that is the condition of human existence. But materialism in terms of Feuerbach's humanism is focused on material needs. Thus, in his grossest version of such a "materialism" of organic nature, he repeats, with Moleschott, the adage with which he has unfortunately become identified: *"Der Mensch ist was er isst"* ("man is what he eats").

But the main focus of Feuerbach's materialism is his theory of *Sinnlichkeit*, ("sensateness" or "sensibility"), which is an interesting but confused empiricism in which the human sense organs themselves are the primary mode of our activity and our knowledge. *Sinnlichkeit* has also the connotation not only of sensationism, in the traditional epistemological sense, but also of the affective, intentional mode of our activity, in the awareness of needs and desires. In Feuerbach's case, this awareness is interpreted fundamentally as an awareness of two sorts of needs, which are closely related: the material need for bodily sustenance, from which there originates our feelings of dependence upon nature; and the social need for other people, interpreted not only as sexual need, but as a need for others in affirming and realizing our social or communicative nature. From this need there originates the feeling of dependence upon others not only for our bodily existence, but also for our spiritual existence, as self-conscious agents. Out of this need, of course, comes the awareness of ourselves as species-beings. *Sinnlichkeit*—both sense-awareness and also awareness of our dependency on nature and on other human beings — then functions, for Feuerbach, as the direct source of our ontological conviction that the world beyond us, both the natural and the human world, exists. Insofar as transcendence means the recognition of the not-myself, which at the same time has its being-for-us in relation to our sensibility, then this *Sinnlichkeit* is, for Feuerbach, the means of our self-transcendence.

Yet what are we to make of the sense of the term *religious* in Feuerbach? True, he writes: "My philosopy is — *no* philosophy; my religion is — *no* religion." Yet he is the philosopher of religion *par excellence*. He wants to save religion from its alienated, mystified form, reveal it to be the very arena of human self-recognition in thoroughly this-worldly terms. He wants to deny to religion that which makes it a fetter on the human mind. He wants to reveal the "secret of religion," namely, the divinity of the human as the thoroughly human understanding of its own nature. He writes that the true atheist is not the one who denies that God exists, but the one who denies the existence of the predicates of God — love, justice, mercy. These are divine predicates, but the object of which they are predicated is the human. Feuerbach, in effect, wants us all to become true believers, but not believers in the image of human essence, which is God; rather, believers in the existing reality of which this is the image, which is the human. In this sense, religion is, in Marx's phrase, "the consciousness of the transcendental arising from actually existing forces."[4] Feuerbach's materialism, insofar as he understood "actually existing forces," was certainly not Marx's, or Engels's. It was the materialism of social existence, but not yet of this social existence conceived in its determinate political, economic, historical forms, or modes of action. Thus Marx could write that Hegel, in *The Philosophy of Right*, was far in advance of Feuerbach's understanding of society or of concrete social beings.

Yet Feuerbach's materialism is a religious materialism in a sense which goes beyond the characterization of religion as simply the consciousness of species-being as the transcendent object of belief. It is religious in that it gives full recognition to the affective life, to the qualities of commitment, care, need, hope which make of human desire something infinitely different from animal need-awareness or animal gregariousness. With Hegel, Feuerbach says, "The animals have no religion." That is because the object of the animal's awareness cannot be the species. One may argue, against this, that species-recognition in animals does exist; that it is innate or instinctive; or even that it is acquired; and that it exhibits itself in maternal care, in mating, in gregariousness; and that it may be explained in terms of natural selection, by the adaptive advantages which distinctive species-recognition affords to species-survival in animals. But Feuerbach is pre-Darwinian, in this respect. Also, he is acutely aware of the difference that speech, language, representation, make in distinguishing animal from human consciousness. It is the capacity to envision the universal and the transcendent as an object of imagination which allows for intentional human agency, especially in respect to the future. It is this capacity which marks off human from animal life. Marx was to propose a historical materialism, in which this conscious intentionality became the hallmark of creative human praxis. It was praxis undertaken to satisfy conscious purposes and needs, thus a praxis in which human existence, and its material conditions, could be raised to the level of a conscious object which guided activity and gave rise to rationality. Marx's sketch, here, is largely unfulfilled as yet. But it presages a notion of historical transcendence based in the very features of human social praxis.

In Feuerbach's account of the nature of belief, there remains a rich source for the fuller realization of a theory of such praxis, emphasizing its subjective, felt, or affective dimensions, as well as the distinctively human, rational dimensions. These dimensions may not, properly speaking, be "religious," but they represent what remains the province of religion, and has not yet been adequately realized in the theories of social, political, or economic praxis. In this sense, Feuerbach's religious materialism, in all of its inadequacies, poses contemporary problems for any materialist theory, including historical materialism, which may then have to reappraise its foundations radically in order to be able to account systematically and viably for this fundamental aspect of human belief and human activity.

Transcendence: a second approach

Feuerbach's religious materialism thus provides an approach to a materialist theory of transcendence on two grounds.

First, he proposes (within the limits of his humanist materialism) a materialist interpretation of the transcendent object of religion — of God — as the embodied, living human community or species-being. Second, he proposes, or suggests, a materialist interpretation of the method by which religious consciousness achieves its recognition of the transcendent object, namely, by the activity or the praxis of belief, or faith (*Glauben*). But now it is necessary to take a second look at the concept of transcendence, this time not so much in terms of the problem that theology poses for religious consciousness, but in terms of the philosophical or metaphysical formulations of the problem.

The standard theories of transcendence in metaphysical thought, as well as in theology proper — at least in the rationalizing theologies that Feuerbach attacks as "speculative" — posit the transcendent either as a rational presupposition, or as the independently existing reality to be discovered by thought, or as a sheer convention of language or thought. Or else, they immerse the transcendent indistinguishably so that it is mystically and mysteriously identical with what it transcends. It is mind, thought, penetrating the veil of sensibility, that uncovers the universal, that transcends particularity, that overcomes the transiency and disconnectedness of things, that grasps what lies behind, beneath, beyond, and either discovers or invents the conceptual order of things.

Well, this is, of course, a method. But it is only adumbrated in the traditional views. Its elaboration as an explicit process — indeed, one may say, its discovery as a method — is due to Hegel. Since the issue is transcendence, I will focus on only one aspect, but, to my mind, the crucial one in this method. The method is dialectic. But what is it a method of? It is precisely the method of overcoming particularity, finitude, the disconnectedness of things. What Hegel takes it to be is the very nature and process of consciousness, of thought itself. Whatever Hegel's debt to Kant, to Fichte, and others, he alone develops rigorously and systematically the step-by-step account of how thought passes from the immediate here-now, to what is other, to the not-self, to the relation of subject to object. The method, simply, is difference, or negation. *I* am distinct from the *not-me; now* is different from *then; here* from *there;* the bud from its flower — homely distinctions to be sure. And if only these, if simply difference alone, then not yet dialectic; rather, what Hegel calls abstract negation. *Omni determinatio est negatio* ("every determination is a negation"). So what? To be a *this* is not to be a *that*. But mere difference is not yet the relation between *this* and *that*, how *this* bears on *that*, how *thisness* depends on *thatness*. It is the relation of the present moment to what lies beyond it, of the finite individual to what is external to that individual, that marks for Hegel the passage of thought from dumb and brute immediacy to synthesis, meaning, understanding, thinking. In this way, thought, establishing the relation of the object of thought to itself, makes its own what lies before it as its object. The sheer otherness of its object becomes appropriated. In the Hegelian jargon, this otherness is overcome, transcended, negated, *aufgehoben*, raised up, so to speak, into a content of thought, into its own content.

Nothing can be an object for thought, in Hegel's terms, without at the same time having become such an object. Thus the total or abstract — that is, disconnected — externality of what lies beyond this activity of thought becomes an object for thought only on condition of this appropriation.

The mysteries and horrors of the Hegelian dialectic are well-enough publicized to have scared off two to three whole generations of Anglo-American philosophers. But its point is relatively clear, after all, if we take it in homely fashion. We get beyond ourselves and our present moment by activity upon what lies ready to hand. The wider we cast the net of our activity, the more we connect this with that, in a widening circle of relations. The sense of the process as a whole points to the totality of all the relations we would discover and appropriate, were we to continue the process to its infinite limits. It is this *notion of totality* which we grasp heuristically as the very object of the process of thought. We do not grasp the totality in its actuality, however. (This would be the fabled Identity of Knowing and Being which marks dialectical philosophy from Plato to Hegel.)

So, with Hegel, we have got ourselves a transcendent object of sorts, here. But, in effect, we have turned the transcendent object into no more than an object of consciousness, to be appropriated by thought and in thought.

Here is where Feuerbach's critique of Hegel begins, and

with it, his critique of speculative philosophy as a whole. Earlier, Feuerbach had explored the relation of thought to belief. His argument was that speculative philosophy had either ignored or subordinated belief or faith to thought, or had, in good dualistic fashion, simply excluded it from the system of reason. In talking about Descartes as a philosopher and as a Catholic, Feuerbach says that Descartes held his reason and his faith apart. He writes, "Descartes himself excluded belief from the domain of thought; he accepted his belief in an unconditional way, without thought or criticism or inquiry, as it was handed down to him."[5] At this stage (in 1838), Feuerbach's humanist theory of religion was fully rationalistic. What the religious belief in God really comes to is the recognition, by human beings, of the divinity of their own thinking consciousness, as constituting their human essence. "So bifurcated is man," he writes, "that he affirms — or at least imagines he can affirm — in belief what he directly denies in reason! A split in man, a contradiction which will remain . . . so long as religion is not recognized as man's own true essence, as identical with his reason."[6] In Hegel, philosophical awareness comes to the fore; belief remains reason's dependent. It is, at best, consciousness's representation to itself of its own rational essence in the form encumbered by the imagination, by sensuality, by sense-imagery, by anthropomorphic personality. The philosopher's God, by contrast, is stripped of all these sensory, imaginative, and personal embodiments.

But, Feuerbach complains (against his own earlier views as well, since this had been the thesis of his Hegelian dissertation [1828]), this identity of reason and human essence, or species-being, is a mere thought-unity, not the real unity of living, flesh-and-blood human beings. That real unity grows, instead, out of the demands of feeling, of need, of the recognition of the other *not* as an object of abstracted thought or reason, but as an object of love, of need, of feeling-dependency, of sensibility — in short, as an object and as the content of *Sinnlichkeit*. Now, to be fair to Hegel (especially to the Hegel of the *Jena Realphilosophie*), he too had generated the intentionality of thought, of consciousness, from desire, from felt need (*Begierde*).[7] But, Hegel argued there, the satisfaction of desire, of need, in the practical appropriation of its objects in consumption, leaves no trace in consciousness. It is animal desire, which vanishes without a trace, or is transcended in the incorporation of the objects—for example, food—which satisfy it. Human beings create the satisfactions of their needs in embodied, external form, by labor, by the use of tools—so says Hegel in the early writings—and thus they objectify this desire in the external forms of those relatively permanent, not immediately consumed means that are created in order to carry out the activity of satisfying desire. Here the object of consciousness is tied directly to feeling, to need; and insofar as belief posits, in the imagination, the image, the projection or representation of what would satisfy it, belief itself—not simply as representation, but as intention bound to the fulfillment of a represented need—is thus concretely bound to activity, to practical realization of needs.[8]

Feuerbach's critique of Hegel (which overlooks this earlier theory of practical activity) is that Hegel sees the activity of satisfaction as mere thought activity. The Hegelian dialectic, therefore, is characterized by Feuerbach as a monologue of thought with itself; whereas what is needed is a dialogue of thought with feeling, with belief, with sensibility, with the empirically felt or sensed other of thought. Feuerbach proposes, therefore, that the method of transcendence—not of imaginary, ideal transcendence in consciousness or in thought but of real transcendence, in "real" life, that is, in feeling, needy, practical life—that this method of real transcendence lies in belief, faith, the transformation of the imagined community of thought into a real community of living, feeling beings. Thus Feuerbach sees the method of transcendence, by which finite individuals overcome their isolation and recognize themselves as species-beings in the act of fellow-feeling, in love. This truth, says Feuerbach, is represented in the faith of believers in its imaginative and mystified form: "God is love." The human self-consciousness which had its realization in thinking the other, in Hegel and in the early Feuerbach, here gives way to a self-consciousness which achieves itself in feeling.

Feuerbach writes: "Man becomes self-conscious in terms of his object: the consciousness of the object is the self-consciousness of man."[9] But the object of love is the other as human, the Thou, which responds to our feeling with feeling. The dialectic here becomes a dialectic of feeling, in the communion of shared and re-ciprocal feeling. The condition for the transcendence of individ-ual finitude is community, and this community is a community of feeling. This transcendent object, taken as the object of feeling, is by virtue of that alone a religious object, according to Feuerbach. God is, in effect, the externalized representation of this fellow-feeling. And feeling transforms its object from an object of mere dispassionate perception into an object which is related to the practical, the wished for, the satisfying—in short, the good. En-dowed by feeling with value, the object of belief, as against the object of mere speculation or thought, becomes an other which is appropriated by belief.

Feuerbach provides a method of transcendence in his theory of belief. But it remains a praxis of belief, not yet a material praxis, not yet the concrete activity of transcending the present. In this sense, Feuerbach falls behind Hegel in two fundamental respects: he fails to recognize the domain of the political and the economic as the concrete domain of practical human activity. He recognizes these aspects only abstractly, whereas Hegel, in *The Philosophy of Right* (especially in the section on "The System of Needs") and elsewhere, raises this domain to theoretical impor-tance at least. Feuerbach also fails to recognize the historicity of human self-transcendence. True, like his master, Hegel, Feuer-bach is also a master of the history of ideas and the history of reli-gion. But historical praxis as real transformation and transcen-dence of the present lies beyond Feuerbach's ken.

Yet, the praxis of belief provides a method which points to-ward a materialist theory of transcendence. It is no secret that Marx's critique and appropriation of Feuerbach focus precisely on Feuerbach's notion of "material," practical, concrete, sensu-ous existence, and that Marx faults Feuerbach's notion of the human as not yet concrete or differentiated enough. That Feuer-bach's thinking-feeling-willing creature of needs, who is at once an I and an I-Thou, is still too abstract a being, is the burden of Marx's *Theses on Feuerbach* and his longer critique and discus-sion in *The German Ideology*. The nub of his criticism is that a resolution in consciousness—even in practical, believing "reli-gious" consciousness which posits real human need as its object—is not enough.

It is just this ahistoricism which Marx criticized in classical political economy. And insofar as Feuerbach conceives of species-being as an ahistorical essence — whose development simply consists in the progress of its self-revelation in consciousness, but whose object of consciousness, species-being, remains a fixed and unchanging being — Feuerbach, too, falls under the interdiction of ahistoricism. To be fair, Feuerbach does have a strong sense of natural development, anticipating a theory of the natural evolution of the human species.[10] And indeed, he sometimes suggests just the notion of historical self-creation of the species by its own activities which is so central to Marx's thought. Thus, Feuerbach writes:

> Man cannot be derived from nature! True! But man as he directly emerged from nature was only a natural being, not a man. Man is a product of man, of culture and history. There are even plants and animals that have changed so much under human care that they (the original forms) are no longer found in nature. Would you then take recourse to a *Deus ex machina* to account for their origin?[11]

Programmatically, and in temperament, Feuerbach is open to the conception of human self-transcendence by historical practice, not only in consciousness or belief, but in modes of material and social existence. But it is not given to Feuerbach to develop this conception. Engels, in his critique, attempts to explain the limitations of Feuerbach's views in the context of the development of the natural sciences of his time, not yet imbued with the notions of process and evolution which were shortly to develop. Engels also adduces Feuerbach's divorce from active political life and intellectual exchange, in the long years of his rural existence in Brucksberg, as reason for his failure to comprehend the historical, political, and economic processes at work in Germany.[12] Still, Feuerbach's theory makes of religious belief the very ground for material transcendence, once it is realized what the role is which such belief — demystified, self-conscious as to its object, the human — plays in shaping the nature of practical activity itself.

Seeing the present historically permits one to appropriate the past as more than merely temporal beforeness. The brute pastness of the past, its inexistence, is transformed from abstract negation as time, to determinate or concrete negation as *aufhebung*, as what has become embodied, incorporated in the present. Thus history makes the past our past, and it is our past that provides the determinate conditions for present activity. What is this recognition in the present of the creative possibilities of human achievement, of the species-capacities for perfectibility, but belief? Belief, faith, is thus not the misdirected anticipation of what is superhumanly possible, but the anticipation of what is humanly possible. The mere projection in the imagination of possibilities as objects of contemplation is thus not true belief, or faith, but passive, regretful, and impotent reflection. True belief is active belief, the belief whose object is seen as the realizable future, made by human effort and action. Such belief, therefore, entails not only idly imagining future possibilities but regarding them as possible on the grounds of the present itself. But the present, here, is not an object of reflection, or of the passive, contemplative consciousness. Just as history is appropriated as value, made one's own as heritage, so too is the present comprehended as the realm of creative activity which ever transforms it, and makes of time a measure of activity, of change.

Belief, here, becomes commitment, care for the future, anticipation of what is to come in the mood of positive expectation. In short, it is hope. Hope, as active belief, animates purpose, and provides the normative element in teleological work and action. Purposes, needs, wants are posited not only as abstract goals, but as felt, value-laden ends, or, as Feuerbach would say, objects of the heart.

Such transcendence of the present, and of the limits of finite individuality, as an anticipation of a future realizable by social, communal practice — if not in one life, then in the ongoing transcendent life of the species — is as material as it can be, because it is the practical transformation of the present by human activity: technological, social, political, and ideational. It is no mere interpretation of the world, but that interpretation of it which leads to changing it. But such change, such revolutionary praxis has as its animating spirit a vision of human possibilities which sees the divine as within the grasp of our own creative activity, and as the object of our hope. Such a theory of belief, as a materialist theory, exceeds the bounds of contemporary materialism, which has as yet no consistent theory of hope, or of this sort of recognition of the transcendent. But the transcendent, thus conceived, is within the realm of human possibility. And a theory of hope as active, practical, efficacious belief in such human possibilities, is needed.

NOTES

1. Karl Marx and Friedrich Engels, *The German Ideology*, 3rd rev. ed. (Moscow: Progress Publishers, 1976), p. 102.

2. Ludwig Feuerbach, *Sämtliche Werke*, ed. W. Bolin and F. Jodl, 10 vols. (Stuttgart: Fromann Verlag Günther Holzboog, 1903–1911), 6:17.

3. G. W. F. Hegel, *The Phenomenology of Mind*, trans. J. B. Baillie (New York: Macmillan, 1931), p. 229.

4. Marx and Engels, *German Ideology*, p. 102.

5. Feuerbach, *Sämtliche Werke*, 4:287–90, n. 39.

6. Ibid., 4:175.

7. G. W. F. Hegel, *Jenenser Realphilosophie II, Die Vorlesungen von 1805–1806*, ed. G. Lasson (Leipzig: Felix Meiner, 1931), 20:194f., 213–17.

8. Ibid.

9. Feuerbach, *Sämtliche Werke*, 6:6.

10. Ibid., 10:19–20, 26–27; 8:161–65. See also my discussion of this in Marx W. Wartofsky, *Feuerbach* (London: Cambridge University Press, 1977), pp. 397–401.

11. Feuerbach, *Sämtliche Werke*, 10:237.

12. Friedrich Engels, *Ludwig Feuerbach and the Outcome of Classical German Philosophy*, in Karl Marx, *Selected Works*, 2 vols. (New York: International Publishers, 1936), 1:439–40, 450.

PART III

The Reality of God

9

Hegel as Theologian

J. N. FINDLAY

THE AIM OF THIS LECTURE is not to study Hegel's account of Christianity or of other religions, whether in the *Jugendschriften* or in
the *Phenomenology of Spirit* or in his mature writings. Its aim is
to study the Hegelian Absolute or Absolute Idea, not as a terminal
concept satisfactory to the ever-developing dialectic of philosophical reason, but as a concept — or rather an object — satisfactory to
the unconditional dedication and devotion of religion, something
that can be unconditionally worshipped if anything at all can.
Hegel, of course, regards religion as a somewhat imperfect approach to philosophy, as something that uses the *Vorstellung* — the
mythic, representative idea — as opposed to the pure concept, and
something that approaches its object in the obscure mode of feeling or *Andacht* rather than in the lucid mode of conceptual thinking. It is, however, clear that, even in his professedly scientific
writing, Hegel at key points produces passages that are steeped in
mystical feeling, and that inculcate a profoundly worshipful, religious view of the world. I shall cite only a few of such mystico-
religious utterances to prove my point. Thus at the end of the Introduction to Self-Consciousness in the *Phenomenology* Hegel
speaks of Spirit as "this absolute substance which, in the complete
freedom and opposition of distinct self-existent consciousness, is
the unity of the latter, the I that is a We, and the We that is I. Consciousness has in self-consciousness, as the concept of Spirit, its
turning-point, at which it leaves the colored show of this-world
sensibility and the empty night of the supersensible behind, and
enters into the spiritual daylight of the present." Similarly, in *En-*

177

cyclopedia #159 he says that "the thought of necessity is rather the dissolution of its hardness, inasmuch as it is the coming together of its other with itself. It is a liberation which is not the flight of abstraction, but one that has its own being and positing in the other actuality, through which, as actual, it is bound by necessity. As self-existent this liberation may be called 'I', as totally developed, free Spirit, as sensation love, as enjoyment blessedness." Similarly he tells us in the *Zusatz* to *Encyclopedia* #234 that "unsatisfied desire vanishes once we realize that the final goal of the world is always just as much accomplished as for ever accomplishing itself," and in the *Zusatz* to #239 that "the Absolute Idea may be compared to the old man who makes the same creedal responses as the child, but in whom they have the meaning of a whole lifetime." In these and countless other similar utterances Hegel looks through the appearances of finite existence to an object which, though difficult of capture by ordinary phrases, nonetheless seems capable of illuminating and transfiguring everything. If what these passages express is not religious I do not know what is, and Hegel, like Saul, must undoubtedly take his place among the prophets. And among the same prophets we shall of course have to find a place for Aristotle with his notion of an Absolute Being whose thought is a thinking on its own thinking, and the love of whom is the source of all life and movement in the cosmos. And it is of course obvious that Platonism is religious with its trinity of the One or God, the *Eide* and the absolute thought that envisages them, and the World-Soul which imposes them on the imperfect changeable world, and which also, in the writings of Proclus, draws a very Hegelian distinction between the Absolute's three moments of μονή or *Beisichsein*, πρόοδος or *Entasserung*, and ἐπιστροφή or return to self. Hegel's theology is a Germanic version of the theology of Proclus, something which is also true of a great deal of prior medieval thought.

We have, however, to inquire into the relation of an Absolute, as the sort of ultimate construct built up by Hegel and other like-minded philosophers, to the religious constructs covered by such names as Yahweh, Brahman, Dharma, Tao, and so on. Philosophers have a discipline, not always consciously cultivated, that may be called Absolute-theory, and it is valuable to consider its relation to the religious articulation of an object of cultus and devotion. What shall we say are distinctive marks of a philosophical Absolute? An Absolute, we may say first of all, has being in the fullest sense admitted by a given ontology, and must not merely have being as in some sense dependent upon, or adjectival to, or derivative from, something else, or representing only some object or goal toward which something else tends, or some modification or modality which pertains to something else. *Id quod in se est et per se concipitur* is Spinoza's definition of his Absolute; and whatever is in something else, or requires to be conceived in terms of something else, is not in this sense an Absolute. Hence absolute wisdom or purity or velocity or whatever are not Absolutes in our sense, provided, that is, that they are not conceived as self-subsistent, but as properties of something else that is such.

The prime category to which an Absolute belongs will of course differ from ontology to ontology: an Absolute may be an individual existent, on which everything else depends for its derivative being, but even here there are choices. Space has been found by some to be as good an absolute existent as the total universe has been found by others. But the prime category to which an Absolute belongs may not be that of the concrete individual at all, but rather something universal on which particular instances are regarded as being ontologically dependent. Here we have hypostatic, Platonic-type Absolutes which may be qualitative or relational or arithmetical or propositional or psychological or axiological: Unity itself, Truth itself, Mind itself, *Bewusstsein überhaupt*, Goodness itself, and so on. These Absolutes only function as such if the ordinary ontological priorities are inverted, and if particular cases are regarded as depending upon universals as their *Archai*. To many such an inversion seems absurd, though to myself the ordinary ontological view seems absurd, since I am not sure that I have ever encountered a real particular. There are further Absolutes that mysteriously combine the roles of different categories: the Absolute of Aquinas, in which essence and existence are one and the same, combines the advantages of individuality with Platonic-type universality. All these options will become relevant when we consider the very unusual Absolute of Hegelianism.

An Absolute has in the second place the logically interesting property of existing irremovably or necessarily: the notion that it should not be there is not coherently entertainable, though it may of course be incoherently entertained. For an Absolute must be something on which not only all actual being is dependent, but also all possible being, and, since its being covers all possibilities, there can be no possible situation in which it would not be actual. The only possible way in which the tables could be turned upon such an Absolute would be to hold that it is itself incoherently conceived, that there can be no such thing as an entity which exists of necessity. This is a step which Kant seems to take in some of his utterances which, however, apply only to phenomenal senses of existence, perhaps, and not to some noumenal sense that we can understand but not know about. Absolutes, in short, stand in the strange predicament of being either necessary or impossible: they cannot occupy the middle ground of being something that possibly may be and possibly may not be, though for us epistemically both alternatives are entertainable. An Absolute, of course, further has to have some sort of an essential content which is as necessary as its being. What necessarily is will have to have this essential content, and this content will be wedded to its being. Such content may, of course, specify itself further in a large number of nonnecessary ways, but the total range of such ways, and the mechanism for actualizing them, will have to be inherent in the Absolute, and covered by its necessity. There can, in short, only be a single essence of the Absolute, and there cannot therefore be alternative types or sorts of Absolute, though for us, operating tentatively and epistemically, there are of course many alternative Absolutes, material Absolutes, spiritual Absolutes, propositional Absolutes, axiological Absolutes, and so on, and also the grand option that there are no Absolutes at all.

From these general determinations we advance to a few evident corollaries. First, that an Absolute is unique and single, both in reality and possibility. There can be no other Absolutes than the unique Absolute which actually is. Second, that an Absolute cannot be internally composite, nor compounded, of parts or aspects or functions that could exist separately. It is totally itself in whatever part or function or aspect that can be distinguished in it, and hence is profoundly simple or unitary. Thirdly, that an Absolute must have some internal moment through which it determines such contingencies as are not part of its necessary essence, though included in the latter as possibilities. On some views, such as that of Spinoza, no such moment is required, since everything in every possible manner follows the nature of the divine or infinite Substance, and neither the content nor the order of its modes could be other than it is. Hegel is not, however, an absolutist of this Spinozistic type, which is, we may hold, incoherent; he admits many irremovable contingencies in the free functioning of his Absolute.

We may in the next place hold, what is implicit in all that we have said, that an Absolute must have omnitude, must be all-comprehensive. There must be nothing actual or possible that does not fall within its purview or its power, and even the nonexistent and the impossible must cling precariously to its skirts as being what its essence or its existent elaborations exclude. This omnitude, I need not say, is a very religious property, and is often identified with infinity, though there are senses of the infinite in which it need not coincide with omnitude. Hegel's True Infinity is, however, a self-identical, undivided pervasion of all that is thinkable or existent, however limited or distorted, and there are many beautiful passages that testify to this. An Absolute, further, must be intellectually appeasing: it represents what is self-caused and self-explanatory as well as being the cause and *explanans* of everything else. Many philosophers, such as Kant and Herbert Spencer, are content to affirm the unknowability of this ultimate appeaser, though it is questionable whether such a negation is not covertly positive. Hegel, however, believes that there is nothing lacking in lucidity in his Absolute; it leaves no questions unanswered that can coherently be raised. And, in the last place, an Absolute, to be fully an Absolute, must embody and integrate in their highest form those values which we esteem supremely, and which we hold up as ideal goals to be pursued by everyone, and for everyone. Values of this intersubjective sort are so much a part of the phenomenal world as it is given to us, and have so strong an appearance of the inescapable and the irrefragable, that they necessarily seek a home or a source in the concept of the Absolute

Ens, and crown it with an appropriate perfection. I am not saying that some thinkers have not believed in value-free Absolutes,
and that the values embodied in different conceptions of the Absolute have not differed widely; it is, however, part of the notion
of an Absolute to embody all the values that are held to be inescapable and true, whatever the precise sense of this last adjective
may be. Those who have opted for value-free Absolutes have generally believed that there are no values that are true. The Absolute must not only satisfy the intellectual quest for understanding, but also the emotional and practical quest for what is in all
respects totally appeasing and good.

I have enumerated a number of features of an Absolute, but
must at once admit that there are many defective and imperfectly
developed Absolutes which do not measure up to my list. There
are, for example, imperfectly developed Absolutes which, in their
quest for omnitude, include evil in their Absolute, without showing how it can be made to accord with the element of value in it.
And there are Absolutes which seem to admit other Absolutes
alongside of themselves, without anything but a vague unity, a
Diké, or whatever, that unifies them. And there are Absolutes
that simply ignore the demand for omnitude, and leave certain
sectors of being unexplained, such as the being of consciousness in
certain materialistic systems. And there is of course infinite difference of view in regard to the essential content of an Absolute,
whether this be individual or spatiotemporal or physical or psychical or what not. And there are, of course, inadequate Absolutes built on an ultimate contingency: they merely happen to be
there, and everything else happens to be a mode or a dependency
of them. I should, however, hold that all forms of thought covertly admit Absolutes even if they are such unsuitable things as
logical space or ordinary language or sense-data. And I think it a
worthwhile project to develop the logic of Absolutes independently of any contentful theory as to what the Absolute actually
is; it is better to engage in a project clearly and self-consciously
than to do so in a confused and muddled manner. Hegel, I may
say, does not develop any Absolute-theory in independence from
the theory which is his own. One has to collect what he thinks an
Absolute is from the many contexts in which he mentions it. And

though he discusses the three traditional proofs of the existence of God, this does not provide a complete account of the conditions that an Absolute must fulfill.

Nonetheless the interest in tracking down the Absolute is throughout essential to Hegel's dialectic; his logical categories are said to be no more than a set of definitions of the Absolute, and his dismissal of concepts as inadequate is always done in the light of some conception of absolute adequacy which becomes clear only in its actual working out. Those who do not think in terms of Absolutes find Hegel's transitions profoundly mystifying and unconvincing. They do not see why we can't be content with clear, finite determinations merely because they are not all-comprehensive, or why infinities must be bad because they admit of no final summing up, and why mechanical explanations are inadequate because they do not reveal an outcome as present in the sum of its conditions, or why all finite purposes must be regarded as forms of an absolute purpose which aims at nothing beyond its own purposiveness. There seems to the nonabsolutist nothing attractive about the re-entrant concepts in which Hegel delights: identity in difference, the vision of self in what is other, the self-repulsion which is at once self-attraction, the interiorization which involves externalization, and so on. If one is not in quest of something which has the curious properties of an Absolute, Hegel's dialectic will always remain for one a closed book; it is at all points an ascent to the Absolute. It is for this reason that I shall now try to indicate the peculiarities of the Hegelian Absolute, since I think it, all in all, to be the best Absolute that there is, that is, if one adds to it a few touches borrowed from Plotinus and Proclus. I may say that I do not regard my own description of an Absolute as in any way mandatory: it merely indicates the general thought-area in which Absolutes are to be looked for.

Hegel's Absolute belongs, of course, to his prime ontological category, all other categories being parasitic upon this one. What is Hegel's prime ontological category? It is that of the concept or notion or *Begriff*. The Hegelian Absolute is, in fact, the highest and most universal of all *Begriffe*, the concept of concepts or universal of universals, the Absolute Idea. What is the status or nature of a *Begriff* as such? It is not a concept in the sense of something which merely exists as an internal modality in human subjective life, in virtue of which persons understand or interpret the data of sense-encounter, and come to recognize them as being such and such, or as being thus and thus circumstanced. It has, of course, these Kantian functions, but they are not what it intrinsically and principally is. It is not, either, a mark or feature which the mind discovers in concrete individual entities, and which, by its repeated appearance, enables the mind to sort them out into classes. Nor is it, of course, any individual existent in the universe or any individual spirit that tenants it. Nor is it merely a deep structure which we think of as underlying and explaining the manifest surface of phenomenal things, and becoming actual in and through them. There is no way of evading the answer: a *Begriff* is a subsistent, Platonic entity which exists freely in its own pure medium, though having necessary relation to the acts and attitudes of the human spirit, and to concrete natural realities set out in space and time. It can exist in a liberated, abstracted form in a spiritual intelligence, but can also exist in a sunken, "petrified" form in one or other natural object or process, and has, further, in virtue of this dual possibility of being, a purely logical, intrinsic being of its own, in virtue of which it can be held apart from the thinking minds that employ it, and the natural objects that embody it, and be seen purely in respect of its own content and its relation to other ideal forms.

A *Begriff* is, further, no mishmash of disparate, independent features or marks, arbitrarily or contingently bundled together, but can only be characterized as a unity, of which its features are merely sides or "moments," a very characteristic Hegelian term. To separate such features, even ideally, is in fact an incredibly magical exercise, on which the *Begriff* avenges itself by angrily snapping its sundered aspects together again and making us aware of their necessary mutual belongingness and inseparability. Thus all the varied features of such a *Begriff* as life or number or causality belong ineluctably together, however much we might like to sunder them and number them, in the fashion of formal logicians, as (a), (b), (c), and (d). And it is the intimate belonging together of all the moments of a *Begriff* that represents to the mind their congenial intelligibility, what makes them genuine entities of reason, things that can be understood, and in whose light the welter of the particularity can likewise be understood. And Hegel believes further, like Plato, that the embodiment of *Begriffe*, whether in natural or spiritual instances, can deviate considerably from the rational unity which the *Begriff* inself embodies. The *Begriff* may appear in subjective, mental life in the confused form of a pictorial *Vorstellung* or image, or in the equally confused form of a feeling in which nothing is distinctly conceived. There may also be an intrusion of alien and irrelevant material in such confused cases of conception which may require to be dialectically purged. And in the instantiation of *Begriffe* in existent, natural realities, there may, as in Platonism, be many imperfect or deviant exemplifications: a magnet, by its extension, may not plainly manifest the inseparability of its two poles, a living body may not succeed in embodying the health which is its concept, and a particular political state may deviate far from being the unity of free, mutually recognizing persons which it is the *Begriff* of a state to be. And even on their own purely notional plane, *Begriffe* may exhibit a conceptual malaise springing from their autonomous self-sufficiency, on the one hand as incarnations of the total notional system, together with, on the other hand, their necessary interdependence on other members of the same total system, so that they seem to waver or melt into their opposites. Thus pure Being, divorced from the positive determinations which give it content, and from the alien determinations which delimit it, shows a disposition to melt into its sheer opposite Nothing, and not in fact to be what it is at all, a malaise which the force of the *Begriff* itself dialectically corrects, by achieving a living synthesis of a partless unity with its differentiating moments.

Begriffe, then, are remarkable amphibians, present and alive in subjective, mental life, in objective existence, and also in a hovering state between these two modes of existence. And on all these planes they are not merely existent facts or appearances, but are also envisaged by Hegel in a vivid mythology of action, as always doing things and effecting results which are descriptively at least distinct from themselves. *Begriffe* suffer from internal repulsions which cause them to sunder themselves into distinct forms; they also suffer from countervailing attractions which cause them to collapse into identity or immediacy, to negate their negations, to be where they are trying to get to, or be what they are only trying to be, and so on. The interpretation of this mythology is comparatively easy when one is dealing with mental life or with existence in space and time, for there, of course, it spells itself out in the form of temporal process, which is for Hegel the externalized form of his notional dialectic. A mind can work toward the complete articulation of a concept and toward its application to phenomenal facts, its freeing from irrelevances and inconsistencies and gaps in explanation. And an organism can develop toward the complete articulation of its inherent *Begriff*, and an inorganic substance toward the fulfillment of its inherent gravitational, chemical, electrical, and luminous capacities. A social system can similarly develop toward a full organization of persons and classes, with their characteristic patterns of interaction and their developed rights and duties. On the ideal plane, however, where there is no time, how can there be action? Concepts are such as both to hide themselves off from other concepts and to have their own distinct *Ansichsein*, and also to require union with the other concepts from which they have thus notionally severed themselves, and to realize that union in another richer concept. In such self-separation and in such return to unity, we have, moreover, a notional analogon of temporal process. The one-sided abstraction can be imagined as moving out of its one-sided isolation and passing over into a richer notional synthesis. The metaphor of action is, therefore, well-founded, and we understand time better when we see it as a sensible analogon of a set of timeless relations with similar logical properties, rather than seeing the latter as an analogon of time. *Alles vergängliche*, Goethe tells us, *ist nur ein Gleichnis*, and Hegel has tried to tell us what it is a likeness of.

It is, however, all-important at this point to make plain that any pluralism of *Begriffe* is itself, for Hegel, only a *Gleichnis*, and that behind all *Begriffe*, in the plural, is *der Begriff* in the singular, the concept or universal as such: this is present and active in them all, and responsible, in a transcendent sense, for all their necessary and their contingent relations. *Der Begriff* is not a specific concept, but the Principle, or *Arché*, of differentiated, intelligible unity which is present in all concepts and illustrated by them all. And it is the presence of the one absolute *Begriff* in each species and subspecies that gives to each the inner completeness that the understanding delights in: it is because the one *Begriff* is present, whole and entire, in every one of its species or specimens that each entity is capable of being looked at apart. It can be so separated, since it is not a mere part of a dismembered Absolute, but the whole Absolute functioning in a given phase or mode, and, like the monads of Leibniz, embracing everything from a particular angle or point of view. Hegel's Absolute is much more Leibnizian than Spinozistic: he puts the All into everything, rather than everything into the All. For Hegel, further, the *Begriff* essentially specifies itself into all the specific *Begriffe* that fall under it: it is not separable from the total range of its specifications, but is itself differentiated in them. And it specifies itself, not only in its proximate species, but in all more remote specifications, and even reaches down to completely specific *Begriffe* of individual things, to which Hegel allots concepts, as Plotinus was later to do. A good individual or a good work of art, for example, is one that lives up to its own individual notion (*Encyclopedia* #178). And of course all the necessary relations of specific *Begriffe* with one another are themselves part of the operation of the one *Begriff* present in them all. All this is prefigured in the Platonic conception of the *Eide* and their ordered unity, as all specifying the single *Arché* of Goodness and of all the instances of such *Eide* in the spatiotemporal world, or in the thoughts which apprehend them or apply them, as derived from the same, single, transcendent Goodness and intelligibility. The continuum of *Eide* in the *Phaedrus*, and the Communion of *Eide* in the *Sophist*, also anticipate Hegelian conceptions.

There are some in my audience who will no doubt resent all this active mythology: they will object, as Aristotle objected, to the activity or agency ascribed to ideal, timeless entities, and will see in all such talk mere poetic metaphor. My own books on Plato have had to encounter a great deal of adverse criticism because they attempt to justify the great Platonic inversion of seeing the individual as a function of the universal, rather than the other way round. I cannot, however, depart from my stance of seeing this as a legitimate and illuminating way of viewing things. It is of the essence of universals to be capable of instantiation. Their instantiation, however, does not create an independent realm of instances, but a realm of modalities essentially dependent on the patterns they instantiate, and having no substance or content apart from these. *Begriffe* are not given intelligibility by having imperfect, vanishing illustrations, but the illustrations acquire what intelligibility they possess from the *Begriffe* that inform them. Hegel is so much of this mind that he sees in a person's ego or thinking self, which Kant called the "transcendental unity of apperception," no more than a high-grade exemplification of the *Begriff* as such, the active universality involved in all our acts of thinking, in all the categories involved in such acts, and in the comprehensive unity which they all build up; our ego is in fact nothing but the *Begriff* in action (*Encyclopedia* #63, 24 *Zus.1*).

Some of the features of Hegel's conception of *Begriffe* lead, further, to well-known logical peculiarities which have occasioned great scandal, and which it is here our task briefly to elucidate. Hegelian concept-language often appears to violate the Law of Identity, in that entities are identified with entities which are also held to be other than they: the whole Hegelian philosophy is in fact a transvestite Walpurgis-night in which everything dons the garments of everything else. In this night propositions also seem to dance about with their explicit negations, thus violating the Law of Contradiction. Such goings on are not what Cambridge and Oxford, England, or Cambridge, Massachusetts, can countenance. It is plain that when one is talking about an instance, as an item in the thing-world, that the logical Laws of Identity, Contradiction, and Excluded Middle hold in the ordinary manner. An instance cannot at once instantiate and fail to instantiate a given *Begriff*, nor can it at once be identical with, and also diverse from, an instance of the same *Begriff*. When, however, we treat an instance as merely a *Begriff* in instantiation, it can while retaining its separate identity *as* an instance be identical with another instance of the same *Begriff*. Both instances are the same *Begriff* elsewhere instantiated, a situation no more remarkable than that the Morning Star is the same as the Evening Star, but at another time and place in the heavens. And the *Begriff*, *qua Begriff*, is itself in all its scattered instances, and yet in a sense participates in the diversity of its instances, and can thus also be said to be alienated from itself. And *Begriffe* of course both are, and are not, the higher *Begriffe* which they specify, and the lower *Begriffe* that specify them. And where specific *Begriffe* verge continuously into one another, as they normally do, each wholly specific *Begriff* is merely a vanishing moment in the unfolding of its generic *Begriff*, and is nothing but the latter in such a vanishing moment, and is as such also all the other vanishing moments into which it unbrokenly passes.

Plato, as I have said, was well aware of the eidetic continuum, and of the difficulty of finding precise joints at which to cut it. At no point in a world of universals do we in fact find the precise, well-assorted, unconfused things that the ordinary application of the logical laws seems to demand. But these laws are not in fact violated, provided one salts one's discourse with a liberal admixture of ἤ's or *qua*'s or *insofar as*'s. A universal *qua* specified thus or thus, or *qua* instantiated here or there, behaves differently from a universal *qua* simply itself or in some other capacity, and one must follow Athanasius in neither confounding the moments nor dividing the substance. The whole dialectic of early Christian theology is in fact impressively Hegelian: Arians, Nestorians, Monophysites, Patripassionists, Sublapsarians, and so on, all find difference in identity, or identity in difference. And Hegel's *Begriff*, like Athanasius's God, is above all a Trinity. It brings together in its impartible unity the three moments of *Allgemeinheit* or universality, *Besonderheit* or specificity, and *Einzelheit* or individuality. These moments are as different as chalk is from cheese, but since they are all only the moments of the one and only *Begriff*, they do nothing to disrupt its unity. The same universality, in virtue of being universal, specifies itself in many different ways, and instantiates itself in an infinity of cases. But it remains the one unbroken, unbreakable unity in all these self-multiplications, self-repulsions, and self-alienations, and in fact only is a unity because it is thus self-multiplying, self-repelling, and self-alienated. Identity for Hegel is never analytic but always synthetic, and it is only by not being oneself that one can truly be oneself.

In no field, however, are the antics of the self-alienating universal more remarkable than in the field of self-conscious Spirit. I, the particular person who is speaking to you, am an instance of self-conscious Spirit, and Dr. Orgel, my honored commentator, is another. Self-conscious Spirit, you see, is intrinsically *sprödig* ("brittle"), to use Hegel's homely adjective; it breaks up into spirits who are irremediably sundered from one another. Dr. Orgel is not myself, and I myself am not Dr. Orgel, and, at a certain level of discourse, the twain will never meet. Nonetheless we both instantiate self-conscious Spirit, and are in fact self-conscious Spirit in a moment of *Einzelheit*. And insofar as we thus both simply are our informing universal, we are also the same as one another, and this is what I recognize when I respect the acumen and probity of Dr. Orgel. But self-conscious Spirit, also, *qua* universal, is intrinsically specified and instantiated and cannot be universal if it is not. We can therefore say that it is only because I am not self-conscious Spirit that I am self-conscious Spirit, and that self-conscious Spirit only isn't me because it is me, and that I am Dr. Orgel only because I am not him, and that I am not Dr. Orgel only because I also am him. All these are childish antinomies; one is merely turning the *Begriff*, like some jewel, around in one's hands, and watching the ever-varied flashes that beam from its various facets. The logical Law of Contradiction is in them not so much violated as transcended; the sort of separately packaged things it wants us to talk about are no longer available.

Hegel's Absolute, the *Begriff*, is therefore as multiform as Proteus. It has the supreme form of being, *Allgemeinheit*, which includes *Besonderheit* and *Einzelheit* in itself. It is ineliminable and necessary. It actively specifies and instantiates itself in every conceivable manner, and only is itself in doing so. It is, moreover, unique and unrivaled, and can suffer neither diremption nor composition, but is always present, whole, and entire in all its modalities, thereby lending them such self-sufficiency as they appear to have. It satisfies the needs of the intellect, once one has got used to its queer ways, and since its forms are also declared to be the patterns of goodness for individuals, it satisfies our feelings for value. It is in fact a transcendentally good Absolute, and the best that anyone has ever excogitated.

I should like at this point to dwell on a further characteristic of Hegel's Absolute: its essential teleology, its necessary progression from forms that inadequately express itself to forms that express itself ever more fully and adequately, until a consummation is reached where adequacy, as far as its form is concerned, is total. It is this dialectical aspect of Hegel's thought which brings it into the closest relation to our religious aspirations toward what is best and most perfect, since all the phases of the progression have an axiological as well as an ontological aspect. The most perfect being of Anselm seems to be slowly constituting itself by stages, though at the end it becomes clear that it was always there from the beginning, whole and entire. It is like the way in which each member of the real number-series is incorporated into those that follow, and in which all are incorporated into the transfinite numbers which, though they are not to be found in the ascending series of real numbers, nonetheless are the number of the whole preceding series.

The exigencies of time forbid me to go into the details of the Hegelian dialectic, except to say that they distinguish, integrate, and arrange in progression the three basic manners in which the *Begriff* expresses itself: (1) its being as a pure universal or category on the plane of abstract thought, differentiated into a ladder of ascending forms or categories; (2) its self-alienation in time and space in a ladder of inorganic and organic forms ascending from inert mechanism to fully developed and differentiated life; (3) its development through the forms of self-conscious Spirit, first opposing itself to the externality of natural objects, then dominating the latter and creating a second, social nature congenial and amenable to itself, and then, finally, achieving full self-consciousness in the three forms of art, religion, and philosophy. The *Begriff* here achieves full consciousness of itself as responsible for everything in the world, as being the active universality which lies behind every natural or spiritual form, and which has no goal beyond itself. It is important to note that it is in the art gallery or the atelier, in the public church or the private devotional closet, and in the philosophical seminar, where Hegel preferably is the presiding genius, that the Absolute finally reveals itself for what it is, and reveals itself, moreover, as consisting wholly in this self-revelation.

In the short time that remains to me I wish to make a few remarks about the religious value of Hegelianism, and about Hegel as a theologian. Religion is the attitude of worshipful self-dedication to what incorporates all values, and this must include in its object the ontological perfection which, I think, Hegel furnishes in the richest possible manner. His Absolute is certainly not an individual person external to ourselves, after the fashion of the less reflective fundamentalisms of the Jewish, Christian, and Islamic religions, the religions of individualism and of formal logic. But these religions themselves, in their more reflective forms, have been profoundly transmuted by Platonism and neo-Platonism, and the God of Augustine, Anselm, and Aquinas has much more of the character of a Platonic *Eidos* than that of a transcendent individual. God is Truth itself, very Beauty itself, Goodness itself, even Being itself independently subsistent, rather than a specially high-grade case of these exalted requirements. It is only where one has a regressive fundamentalism, even in the comparatively high-grade intellectualism of a Barth, that one is very far from Hegelianism. The most deeply thought religious forms of Christianity, Judaism, and Islam are close to Plato and also to Hegel. And Hegelianism is of course in harmony with the nonindividualistic religions of the East, where, however much people may feel devotion to real or mythic individuals, they still set universal principles such as Dharma, Tathātā, Brahman, or Tao beyond them.

It seems to me that reflective religious persons must content themselves with a relation to something which, while essentially revealed in conscious persons, and more eminently there than anywhere else, also transcends personality as much as it transcends other forms of instantial being. And the logical gambits of Hegelianism suit the mysteries of religion better than anything else: the presence within us, and also beyond us, of a universal Spirit which both is and isn't ourselves, and which only is the one because it is also the other. There is here as much *bhakti yoga*, devotional union, with a person as a devotional individual may need, and also as much *jñāna yoga*, the union of knowledge, or of *karma yoga*, the union of work, as other sorts of individual may require. I myself follow the last form of yoga rather than the others, though my devotion to work takes the form of writing philosophical discourses. Hegel's theology is of course not orthodox, but then neither is the theology of Saint Thomas, whose God, in whom essence and existence are one, is certainly far from the very personal God of Moses and Jacob.

Perhaps, however, from the standpoint of Christianity, the Hegelian religion is remotest from the Christian in the manner in which it treats the person of Christ. For to Hegel it is the idea of an incarnation, of the Absolute Idea conscious of itself in a human individual, that is the all-important thing. The particular historical embodiment of this idea was not, *qua* individual, important, and had to pass away and be replaced by the presence of the Holy Spirit in the Christian community. Jesus, however, certainly believed in his unique messianic role, as channeling the action of the Divine Spirit to all who accepted him in that role, and he also plainly believed in a future kingdom in which the sensuous and the spiritual would be united, and which would be presided over by himself, after he had gone through a preordained ordeal of repudiation by the ecclesiastical and secular powers that be. To these beliefs Hegel accords no credence except as mythic presentations of eternal spiritual truths, and I myself cannot help seeing Christian belief in the same light as Hegel did. Such a demythologization will not, of course, recommend itself to many sincere Christians, and to these I recommend that they live by the light that they themselves feel and know, and not by philosophical conceptions that represent the best that can be had by other sorts of religious people, to which I, fortunately or unfortunately, belong.

I wish to end this essay by dealing with what I consider the most serious defect of Hegelianism: that it is wholly this-worldly, and altogether lacks an otherworldly dimension. For I believe that the full achievement of the Absolute must involve the perfection of human souls, and that, as Saint Paul and Kant have taught us, if the soul's life ends with the death of its body, then are we of all people most miserable, or rather the universe itself is most miserable, since it begets spiritual entities of infinite value and promise, and then simply lets them lapse back into nothingness. I believe that the world must contain a dimension in which we shall be liberated from the compulsions of matter, though not at first from the dear vividness of sense—though we shall ultimately be liberated from this also—and from the *Aussereinander* of space, and the *Nacheinander* of time. Our spiritual education demands in fact a long series of incarnate lives, whether on this planet or others, interspersed with periods of purgation or vacation, in which we shall live freely among images and thoughts, until at length we are ready to incorporate into the timeless thought of the Divine Reason itself. There the instance will be one, without loss of distinction, with the universal that it instantiates, and with all other specifications and instantiations of that universal. The eternal Idea, the active universal, will then actually be all in all. This is not a new message, being a familiar doctrine in the writings of Plato and in the scriptures of the great Eastern religions. It also was the creed of one considerable philosopher who is now once more being written about, and whose work I was recently rereading. I mean John McTaggart Ellis McTaggart, the bizarre Hegelian of Cambridge, who died in 1925, and who tried to prove time to be no more than a self-contradictory appearance, a series of terms which masks a timeless series of inclusions and which seems to march forward to a glorious final consummation of fulfilled love, but which, however, when we reach it, or rather seem to reach it, will prove to be a state in which we always timelessly were, or rather are.

10

Nietzsche and the Crisis of Nihilism

ERNEST L. FORTIN

WOULD NIETZSCHE BE HAPPY with the current surge of interest in his writings? Probably not, especially in view of his low opinion of professional philosophers and an almost pathological fear of being misinterpreted by his readers. But no one will accuse him of having underestimated his own originality. On the theory that the more novel one's teaching is, the less likely it is to be accepted by one's contemporaries, he once suggested that people should not be allowed to read *Beyond Good and Evil* until about the year 2000.[1] He might easily have said the same of *Zarathustra*, which is typically subtitled "A Book for Everyone and No One." The problem is further complicated by his aphoristic and often oracular style, the self-confessed evolution that he underwent over a productive period of less than twenty years,[2] and above all the unfinished character of his thought. Paradoxically, Nietzsche, who shares with Marx the dubious honor of being the most outspoken of philosophers, is at the same time the most secretive writer of his generation. It is therefore not surprising that the interpretation of his works should continue to give rise to serious disagreements on the part of competent scholars.

Was Nietzsche the radical innovator that he claimed to be,[3] the herald of a new gospel,[4] the first philosopher in whom the entire tradition of Western metaphysics finds its fulfillment and therewith its ultimate transformation?[5] To these and similar questions Walter Kaufmann responds with a resounding No![6] For all his iconoclastic bombast and his manifest opposition to the ruling consciousness of his day, Nietzsche is anything but the irrationalist and the immoralist that his Marxist adversaries have made him out to be. Neither is he simply a reactionary bourgeois who found an artificial solution to the creeping decadence of the modern world. According to Kaufmann, his blunt defense of reason in the *Gay Science* proves sufficiently that he had no desire to turn his back upon it.[7] His dislike for Christianity, as distinguished from Christ, is unmistakable, but even then he only attacked it on the ground that it denigrated reason. The same holds for his criticism of all philosophical systems, to which he objected not because they were too rational but because, by refusing to question their own assumptions, they were not rational enough.

As regards Nietzsche's call for a sweeping "revaluation of all values," Kaufmann is of the opinion that it cannot in any way be construed as an all-out assault on morality itself, since its sole purpose was to rid contemporary morality of the ingredients of hypocrisy, comfortableness, and laxity with which it had long been infested. Like Kierkegaard, Nietzsche was attracted to both Christ and Socrates; but whereas Kierkegaard preferred Christ, Nietzsche opted for Socrates, whom he sought to emulate by vivisectionally applying the knife to the counterfeit values of his time. Accordingly, his moral program is not a new legislation. It aims at restoration of the old values, which had previously suffered a drastic revaluation at the hands of Christianity. By revaluating the revaluation or negating the negation, Nietzsche has in fact performed a positive and much-needed task.[8] To reproach him with having hastened the advent of nihilism, as many have done, is to overlook the fact that he merely helped topple what was already falling and pave the way for the recovery of the genuine virtues that centuries of Christian living had successfully repressed.

While one should be grateful to Kaufmann for having denazified Nietzsche and rescued him from the crude prejudices to which his reputation had fallen victim between the two world wars, one wonders whether his stunning rehabilitation does full justice to the complexity of the subject at hand.[9] A closer look at Nietzsche's concept of nihilism, which receives short shrift in Kaufmann's treatment, will, I hope, bring to light a number of elements that coexist only in an uneasy tension with, and perhaps even flatly contradict, the Socratic ideal to which Kaufmann points as the core of the Nietzschean enterprise.

The concept of nihilism

In his last and most controversial book, Nietzsche predicted that his name would one day be associated with a crisis the likes of which had never been seen on earth.[10] The nature of that crisis is best expressed by the word *nihilism*, which occurs with increasing frequency in his works from the year 1886 onward and which designates what he gradually came to perceive as the fundamental fact of European history. Although the term itself is older than Nietzsche, having been applied by Turgenev and others to a growing number of young radicals who challenged the traditional values of Western society in the name of scientific progress,[11] it is fair to say that it acquires in his later works a depth of meaning that goes far beyond anything that attaches to it in the literature of the nineteenth century. The reality to which it refers is not a specific world-view, comparable to other contemporary or older world-views, but a pervasive phenomenon engulfing the whole of modern life and thought — the spiritual style, so to speak, of the Western world. In its most advanced pre-Nietzschean form, it is coextensive with historicism or historical relativism and manifests itself most clearly in the final repudiation of all absolute or eternally valid norms of conduct. As such, it constitutes the root cause rather than the consequence of the corruption and moral decay of modern society. Its motto is "Nothing is true; everything is permitted,"[12] which represents the only consistent and legitimate response to the emptiness of life without a compelling horizon of values.

The distinctive features of the new movement will come into sharper focus if we glance briefly at the two philosophical positions to which it seems to bear the closest resemblance, skepticism and classical conventionalism. Skepticism, in contrast to nihilism, is essentially ahistorical. It is not bound to a particular historical configuration and presents itself as accessible to human reason at all times. It merely regards all notions of right and wrong as based on the arbitrary decisions of the community and makes no effort to correlate them with the conditions that prevail in actual societies at any given moment.

Classical conventionalism, represented philosophically by Epicureanism and, on a more popular level, by the Sophists of antiquity, is likewise ahistorical. It, too, rejects the commonly accepted principles of justice and morality on the ground that they have their source in human convention rather than in nature. It shares with its foremost competitor, the natural-right theory of Plato and Aristotle, the fundamental distinction between nature and convention, as well as the notion of the superiority of the former over the latter. Like the natural-right theory, it views philosophy as an ascent from public opinion to private knowledge or as an attempt to grasp the eternal order whose existence is presupposed by, though only imperfectly reflected in, the officially sanctioned dogmas by which societies are governed. Yet it refuses to consider justice as something desirable or choiceworthy for its own sake. By nature, human beings seek their own pleasure or their own aggrandizement, if need be at the expense of others. The rules of morality on which society depends for its well-being are nothing more than an expedient invented by the weaker members of that society to defend themselves against the encroachments of their betters. They are not inherently binding and serve only to obscure the normative character of nature, to which the wise person must turn for a true understanding of the goals of human existence.[13]

Nihilism, on the other hand, does away with the dichotomy between nature and convention altogether. One might say in a provisional way that it looks upon all right, legal or otherwise, as conventional. As opposed to both skepticism and conventionalism, it does not pretend to be coeval with human reason but is said to be related to an unprecedented situation in which all notions of right and wrong, and indeed the very distinction between right and wrong, have become questionable. Its emergence is linked to the catastrophic context of the present crash of all horizons or the total dissolution of all viable syntheses of meaning and value.[14] It culminates in the view that no value or set of values, whether it be those of civilization or those of cannibalism, is demonstrably superior to any other value or set of values. Its essence is summed up in the formula "God is dead,"[15] which, as its paradoxical wording indicates, is to be taken not as a simple profession of faith in atheism and hence as a theoretical statement belonging to the same order of truth as its opposite, theism, but as an emphatically historical statement calculated to bring home to us the uniqueness of the predicament within which it comes to light. It should be added that the God whose demise it proclaims stands not only for the Christian God but for all other gods as well.[16] In the highest instance, *God* is synonymous with the transcendent realm of metaphysical ideas and ideals from which, ever since Plato or at least the hellenistic and Christian interpretations of Plato, the sensory world of human experience was thought to derive its significance. Since, as we are told elsewhere, the gods themselves now "philosophize,"[17] or, to express the same view in less metaphorical terms, since there is no truth to be found in this or any other world, human beings are left without anything by which they might take their bearings. Like the madman to whom the announcement of the death of God is entrusted in the *Gay Science*, they suddenly find themselves "straying as through an infinite nothing."[18] The crisis that they face is a *total* crisis, provoked by the structural disintegration, not of this or that particular ideal, but of the whole world of classical and biblical thought which had hitherto made possible and supported all forms of civilized life as we have known them or could imagine them. All moral precepts having been revealed to be matters of blind preference, it would be sheer foolishness or hypocrisy to allow oneself to be determined by them in one's actions. At the extreme limit, anything that anyone will dare to do becomes permissible.

Thus understood, nihilism is only the last stage in a process that has already lasted for a century and whose roots stretch back to the origins of the philosophic tradition. Its remote ancestor is none other than Socrates, the "prototype of the theoretical man,"[19] who destroyed the primal unity of Greek cultures by establishing reason as the master of the instinctual life. It is to Socrates that the West owes the "sublime metaphysical illusion that thought can penetrate the deepest abysses of being."[20] Via Christianity, what was nonetheless only a "tendency" in Socrates has since come to inform and dominate all subsequent modes of thought up to and including historicism, to the degree to which it still adheres to the notion of scientific objectivity.

The point to notice, however, is that the present crisis was not generated from without but is the end product of an internal and thoroughly moralistic development. Had Western civilization merely succumbed to a more powerful external enemy, it could have gone down with honor, proud of itself and convinced of the superiority of its own cause. As it is, it bore within itself and from the outset the seeds of its ultimate destruction. The theoretical impulse at work within it made it inevitable that sooner or later its supreme values should not only be devalued but should "devalue themselves."[21] Indeed, once the belief in a suprasensory world of eternal ideas is seen to be without foundation, any attempt to cling to it becomes a mere pretense. At this point truthfulness turns against itself and puts an end to all forms of self-deceit.[22] In the name of intellectual probity or honesty, the last of our remaining virtues,[23] one is compelled to face that most terrible of all truths, the truth that there is no truth. It may be observed that in the process truthfulness itself, whose role as a moral virtue was strictly provisional, is called upon to disappear, leaving room for the single virtue that characterizes Nietzsche's philosopher of the future, the new historical sense.[24]

The basis of nihilism

The Nietzschean view regarding the illusory character of all objective norms and standards is sometimes said to be rooted in the experience of history, which confronts us with an apparently endless array of conflicting goals and ideals and thus seems to call into question the intrinsic validity of all human goals and ideals. There is considerable doubt, however, as to whether the evidence supplied by history warrants the conclusion that nothing whatever is right by nature. History reveals that the ideals pursued at different times by different individuals or groups of individuals often contradict one another; it does not prove that they refute one another, and it says even less about their relative merits or the possible superiority of one over the other. Natural right would be free of controversy only if its principles could be shown to be immediately available to everyone. If, on the other hand, the discovery of these principles is contingent on the use of properly cultivated reason, as most natural-right theorists argued, one would normally expect people to disagree about them, but one would also be inclined to ascribe these disagreements to human error rather than to any defect in the theory itself. In short, what the experience of history taken by itself suggests is that the knowledge of what is right by nature is difficult, not that it is impossible. Furthermore, the awareness of the indefinite variety of human ideals was never absent from the philosophic tradition and was even regarded by older thinkers, not as an argument against natural right, but as the necessary condition for the emergence of natural right. For without such an awareness, it would not dawn on anyone to look for an understanding of justice that is grounded in something other and presumably higher than human agreement or consent.[25]

In light of these remarks, one is led to conclude that the view espoused and philosophically elaborated by Nietzsche is predicated not on the experience of history as such, but on a particular interpretation of that experience, prompted by and growing out of the prior conviction that theoretical knowledge of any kind is not only difficult but impossible. It goes without saying that a complete analysis of Nietzsche's position on this score would require a much lengthier discussion than space and time permit. At the risk of considerable oversimplification, I shall limit myself to a bare summary of the argument as it occurs in the first chapter of *Beyond Good and Evil*, which offers as clear and concise a statement of the issue as is to be found anywhere in his works.

As already noted, philosophy was originally conceived as an attempt to understand all things in the best possible manner by the sole use of one's reason. Its aim was to replace the opinions about the whole that most people share, but never question with a genuine knowledge of the whole. To be sure, it never contended that a perfect knowledge of the whole had been reached or was even attainable. To the extent to which the whole remains elusive, it defies any perfectly lucid and rational account that one might be tempted to give of it. Yet philosophy does not stand or fall by its ability to answer all questions or even by its ability to provide a final answer to any of them. It requires for its justification only that human reason have access to the fundamental problems, as well as to the limited number of alternative solutions to those problems. It is thus more properly defined not as wisdom but as the love of wisdom or the unending quest for wisdom. However much philosophers may have disagreed among themselves in the past, they were nevertheless united in a common search for a common truth.

This desire to know or, as Nietzsche calls it, this "will to truth"[26] is what eventually proves to be most problematic. Philosophers, who are notorious for questioning everything, have never seriously questioned their own impulse to raise questions. All of them gratuitously posited the existence of a pre-established order, which each one claimed to have discovered and articulated more perfectly than any predecessors or rivals. Like Oedipus, they took it for granted that the riddle to be solved existed outside of themselves and did not think of asking what "in them" had caused them to seek an answer to it in the first place.[27] At no time did it occur to them that the mystery could conceivably lie with the inquirer rather than with the object of inquiry. Even their disagreements were at bottom barely more than lovers' quarrels, serving only to confirm them in their love for an object whose existence was never doubted. Their systems are universally based on a dogmatically asserted premise which, upon examination, turns out to be a delusion. In Nietzsche's phrase, they are nothing more than "beautiful and strong asses,"[28] some more impressive than others perhaps, but all of them equally stupid. Contrary to popular belief, one finds nothing in them that is impersonal or detached. Philosophers are really lawyers who defend their own causes by means of arguments invented after the fact.[29] Their thought is best described as a species of unconscious autobiography, which invariably tells us more about the authors themselves than the reality they purport to investigate.[30]

It follows that there is no permanent order of being to be uncovered anywhere, just as there are no permanent problems of being to which a solution of some kind, however tentative, might be sought. All human thought rests finally on premises which, far from being self-evident, are imposed upon us by history or by fate. Thought necessarily belongs to a particular perspective, which it can enlarge but which it can never transcend and beyond which it has no meaning. One can of course analyze its conditions, but since by definition the analysis is itself historically conditioned, it remains subject to the same basic criticism. The ultimate at which one arrives in analyzing any thought is a free act of the will in the light of which everything else is understood but which is not itself in the light. The same goes for Nietzsche's own philosophy, which must likewise be seen as an interpretation.[31] The only feature that distinguishes it from other interpretations is that it is conscious of the fact that it is an interpretation. Its sole claim to superiority is that, as the first perspective to be aware of the law of perspectivity, it ranks as the highest possible perspective. What we end up with, then, is not just a new philosophy but a new *type* of philosophy which parts company with the whole tradition of philosophic thought by denying the very possibility of philosophy as it had always been understood.[32]

The self-overcoming of nihilism

We scarcely need to remind ourselves that the notion of historical perspectivism did not originate with Nietzsche, since it was already present and operative in much of earlier nineteenth-century historical thought. If Nietzsche is to be credited with anything, it is rather with having been the first to perceive the nihilistic consequences of that insight. As he saw it, the immediate danger to which it gives rise is not that, once persuaded that nothing is true, human beings will feel free to embark upon ruthless and destructive courses of action, but that they will henceforth lack the incentive to do anything at all. Human greatness hinges on one's willingness to devote oneself heart and soul to the pursuit of a noble cause. It presupposes that one is convinced of the righteousness of that cause and prepared to make whatever sacrifices may be required. Yet it is doubtful that one who has glimpsed the ephemeral character and hence the ultimate vanity of all such causes will ever be motivated to sacrifice oneself for any of them. Human life can only thrive within a limited horizon.[33] It requires for its well-being a protective atmosphere that restricts one's vision and blinds one to the injustice implied in the choice of any goal. By disclosing all specific horizons as mere horizons, perspectivism necessarily destroys those horizons and poisons the wellsprings of human activity. It teaches not only that all ideals are perishable but, inasmuch as life is inseparable from injustice, that they deserve to perish.[34] Its truth is in fact a "deadly truth,"[35] breeding inertia or apathy and leading in the end to the blessed narcosis of a life dedicated only to the pursuit of comfortable self-preservation or the satisfaction of one's bodily needs.

The long-range but inevitable result of this state of affairs is the complete degradation of the human race or the universal domination of the lowest human beings, who are not even aware of the extent to which they have degenerated, who no longer have any desire to rule or to be ruled, and whose sole ideal, if it can be called an ideal, is that of the single fold without a shepherd.[36] The depths to which the modern herd animal has already sunk is nowhere more clearly visible than in the barbarism that afflicts the bulk of present-day art. By opening themselves up to all sorts of foreign influences indiscriminately, contemporary artists have forfeited any chance of developing a style of their own. The tasteless amalgamation of heterogeneous elements with which their works present us is symptomatic of the plight of the modern world in its totality, which knows everything but is incapable of loving anything and is itself nothing.[37]

This is not to suggest that there are no legitimate uses to which the practice of history may be put to remedy the situation. Insofar as it furnishes us with examples of former greatness, it could still stimulate activity and provide a necessary antidote to the evils of the present. It is thus more proper to say that what we suffer from is not history itself but an excess of history or an overdose of the antidote.[38] Interestingly enough, the modern historical movement, which bears most of the blame for these evils, was originally in the service of life and probably would not have survived had it not been nurtured in its infancy by an ardent love of the fatherland. Its first promoters were dedicated patriots whose attachment to their national past was intensified by the crushing defeat that they had recently been dealt by the Napoleonic armies. The misfortune is that the learned habit acquired in the process soon took on a life of its own, which persisted long after the springs of piety had dried up, transforming itself into an insatiable curiosity for anything old and greedily devouring "every scrap that falls from the bibliographical table." What had begun as national history became universal history, carrying in its wake a "restless cosmopolitanism" which preserves the corpse but is utterly incapable of instilling new life into it.[39]

It is nevertheless true that the situation just described represents only the most acute form of nihilism yet reached by Western thought. For the most part, the nihilism typical of nineteenth-century society is, in Nietzsche's view, only an "imperfect" or "incomplete" nihilism,[40] which shows itself under two different guises, one optimistic and the other pessimistic. The first of these is the cheerful or serene nihilism of the free spirits who rejoice in the death of God ("God is dead, thank God!") but cling that much more firmly to the faith in Christian morality and the dignity of the human being. Its fashionable representative is the liberal theologian David Strauss, who proclaims with "admirable frankness" that he has ceased to be a Christian and hails Darwin as a great benefactor of humanity, but whose boldness is limited to words and who thinks he can continue to live as if nothing had changed. The fallacy in Strauss's argument is that it assumes that one can get rid of the architect and keep the building or do away with the lawgiver and still claim the protection of the law. A more consistent Strauss would have realized that his premises lead straight to a "new Hobbesian war of every man against every other man."[41] Christian belief and Christian morality go together, to such a degree that the latter cannot long survive the death of the former. As Nietzsche puts it in a later reference to the essay on Strauss, "When one gives up the Christian faith, one pulls the right to Christian morality right out from under one's feet."[42] More generally stated, if traditional speculative thought is jettisoned, then traditional morality, which is rooted in it, will also have to be forsaken and replaced by a totally new morality that has nothing but the name in common with the older moral doctrines. Without knowing it, Strauss is living on borrowed time. His naïve optimism, inherited from Hegel and illogically maintained after the abandonment of the Hegelian notion of the end of history, is more aptly described as philistinism, or, if one prefers, cultured philistinism.[43]

The inconsistency is not Strauss's alone. It is characteristic of the entire modern democratic movement and its unruly tail, socialism, with their cherished belief in progress, their inherent low-mindedness, their utter dedication to mediocrity, and their slavish resentment of all forms of superiority. Both of them are unconsciousness heirs of the Christian tradition,[44] which have merely replaced the authority of God with that of reason and exchanged the otherworldly goal of everlasting bliss for the earthly happiness of the greatest number. Severed from their Christian moorings, they must suffer the same fate. The same applies to anarchists, who would gladly overthrow bourgeois society for the sake of a better world but cannot imagine anything radically different from the values they set out to destroy.[45]

Side by side with this optimistic nihilism one finds the morbid nihilism of the pessimist, who, far from taking pride in the accomplishments of contemporaries, has become thoroughly disenchanted with the flatness of modern life and seeks to escape from it by every possible means. The new mood is discernible in the romantic longing for a heroic but irretrievable past, or, for those who find the past too remote, in such other forms of evasion as the cult of art for art's sake or Schopenhauer's futile attempt to annihilate the will through an act of the will.[46] All of these attitudes are reflective of the generalized paralysis with which the age is stricken, and in none of them do we encounter anything like a genuine revaluation of values.

To these more or less developed forms of nihilism Nietzsche opposes his own brand of nihilism, which he labels "active nihilism," and which is identical with the epoch-making shift from historical consciousness to hermeneutical consciousness, or, to state the matter in terms that more closely approximate Nietzsche's own, from theoretical historicism to radical historicism.[47] Assuming that the belief in objective truth is indispensable to all higher forms of life, one might at first be tempted to substitute a new myth or a "mighty lie" for the deadly truth of historicism.[48] But it does not take much to see that this solution, which is the one that Plato had adopted, will no longer work. For one thing, a fabricated myth is not a genuine myth and will always lack the effective power of a genuine myth. For another, the demands imposed upon us by our newly acquired intellectual probity are such as to preclude any recourse to lies, however beneficial or well-intentioned.

Nietzsche's solution consists not in rejecting but in accepting and radicalizing the historicist premise regarding the relativity of all truths by applying it to scientific history itself. That solution comes to sight when one begins to perceive the essential limitations of scientific history as well as of all other forms of objective knowledge. The trouble with nineteenth-century historicism is that it did not take history seriously enough. It presumed to be able to arrive at a genuine knowledge of the past and failed to take into account the fundamental disproportion between life, which presupposes a commitment to substantive principles of thought and action, and modern historical science, which renders any such commitment impossible. As a mere onlooker, the scientific historian is in no position to recover the substance of the past, for it takes a committed person to understand another person's commitment. What is resurrected is not the past itself, which can only be grasped by what is most powerful in the present, but an impoverished version of it.[49]

There is an entirely different conclusion to be drawn from the nihilistic devaluation of all values, which is that human beings can now do consciously what their predecessors could only do unconsciously and under the false assumption that they were complying with God-given or otherwise demonstrably valid norms of behavior. They are at last free to create their own values in a manner that no longer suffers from any of the limitations under which people had previously labored. The name given to this radically new project is the "will to power," as opposed to the old will to truth on the one hand and the will to mere life on the other.[50] Its most perfect embodiment is the "superman," who has yet to come into being and whose coming is by no means assured, but in whom Nietzsche's redeemed humanity finds its ultimate meaning. It needs to be stressed that the new project is itself the product of an unpredictable creative act, which as such is not deducible from the experience of nihilism, although it assumes it and remains in complete agreement with it.[51]

The dilemmas of Nietzschean nihilism

The Nietzschean attempt to overcome nihilism from within and on the basis of its own premise is open to a number of serious objections. Nietzsche was fully aware of them and was forced to devote greater attention to them as time went on. Not the least obvious of these objections is the seeming contradiction implied in the thesis that there are no timeless truths, which at first hearing has all the earmarks of a timeless or transhistorical truth. If all philosophy is interpretation, it is not easy to see how Nietzsche can exempt himself from his own verdict and claim for his philosophy a finality that he denies to every other philosophy. The truth of relativism cannot be asserted absolutely. One has to assume that, as a mere interpretation, Nietzsche's philosophy is itself provisional and subject to revision. The objection need not be decisive, however. On purely logical grounds, it may be countered by saying that the radical dependence of thought on fate is not a truth that is accessible to human beings as human beings. It is the preserve of one and only one moment, namely, that privileged moment in which human thought is given an intuition into its own nature and becomes, as it were, transparent to itself. It thus remains uniquely historical, differing from other historical insights only by reason of a peculiar self-awareness that it, and it alone, happens to possess.

The more pertinent objection concerns the hierarchy of values postulated by the antithesis between the "superman" and the "last man," which, as an expression of the will to power, can with equal reason be thought to lack any objective status. The objection is only partially resolved by the observation that, since the superman distances himself from the last man by creating his own nature, his superiority is not to be judged in terms of any eternal or pre-existing standard but is itself its own standard or measure. For even if this should prove to be the case, one could still ask whether, in the absence of any assignable limits to what it can do, the will to power is not capable of overcoming itself by decreeing the abolition of the superman, along with the entire hierarchical structure of being to which his appearance gives rise. Nietzsche apparently thought that the clue to this thorniest of all questions lay in the notoriously difficult doctrine of the eternal recurrence of the identical, on which the whole of his philosophy was finally made to turn. By guaranteeing the return of all things exactly as they have always been, and hence of the last man as well as the superman, the eternal recurrence rules out forever the possibility of an eventual total degradation of humanity. It views the past, with all its fragments, its scattered parts, and its horrible accidents, not as something to be conquered, as Hegel and Marx had taught, but as something to be affirmed and willed as the necessary condition of the redemption of the human race.[52]

To my knowledge, no one today subscribes to any of the three closely related doctrines that lie at the heart of Nietzsche's philosophy: the will to power, the superman, and the eternal return. This is not to say, however, that the problems which Nietzsche attempted to solve by means of these doctrines can be safely disregarded by anyone who remains committed to a historical understanding of human existence. I shall mention only three such problems with which subsequent thinkers have had to contend and to which, as far as I can see, no completely clear solution has yet been offered.

The first has to do with the guidance that the new kind of thinking initiated by Nietzsche is able to provide in human affairs. Nietzsche's highly unsystematic philosophy may with some justification be seen as an extreme reaction against Hegel's completely systematic philosophy, which was wholly oriented toward the past and which did away with the need for ethics altogether. From that point of view at least, Nietzsche shares one of the major concerns of pre-Hegelian philosophy, which was to direct human action. The question is whether that concern can be adequately met by the substitution of historical standards for the now discarded universal standards. There are, admittedly, no concrete norms of behavior to be derived from past history, which is essentially nonrepeatable. Moreover, unless one is convinced beforehand that the victorious cause is necessarily the best cause, one would hesitate to say that the acceptance of an emerging trend or consensus is always preferable to the rejection of that trend or consensus. Given the lack of any identified or identifiable moral norm, all that remains, it seems, is a unique kind of formal ethics which takes the form of an appeal either to Nietzschean creativity or to its more recent analogue, Heideggerian authenticity. Both appeals are fraught with difficulties, a full discussion of which mercifully lies beyond the scope of a brief essay.

The second problem is related to the manner in which, on the basis of the Nietzschean premise regarding the historicity of human thought, one is able to understand any of the older or non-historical philosophies for which the new philosophy was intended as a replacement. Unlike modern scientists, who can rest content with their theory as long as it produces the desired results, philosophers are never dispensed from the obligation to retrace their steps and reassess their starting point. The choice of their own way necessitates the consideration of alternative or competing ways, which cannot be dismissed until such time as they have been thoroughly examined and found wanting. This amounts to an admission that continued efforts at self-understanding are inseparable from an effort to understand others as well. According to Nietzsche and his followers, however, such an effort can never be expected to yield more than limited results. One cannot possibly hope to understand the authors of the past as they understood themselves; one can at best understand them differently.[53] Yet the rejection of any or all of these authors necessarily entails a criticism of their respective positions and hence the implicit claim to have understood them better than they understood themselves. Furthermore, one fails to see how the impossibility of an objective or detached understanding of an older author can be established from history itself. There is no denying that the authors of the past have been understood differently by different people over long periods of time. But one cannot infer from that observation that none of the interpretations that have been given or could still be given of them is the correct one. In order to be absolutely certain that it is not, one would have to know both the author's thought and that of the interpreter. Since a completely objective knowledge of the first and perhaps even of the second is supposedly impossible, one is left without any real basis for judgment.[54]

The final unresolved problem concerns the notion of a privileged or absolute moment with which Nietzsche's philosophy and any strictly historical philosophy is inescapably bound up, an absolute moment similar to the one presupposed by Hegelian philosophy, although obviously not identical with it since it is no longer dependent on the assumption of the completedness of the historical process. The existence of this absolute moment is vouched for

by the fact that the discovery of the fundamentally historical nature of human thought coincides with the rise of nihilism or the
collapse of all horizons, which alone makes that discovery possible. More simply put, the discovery of the historical nature of human thought is itself historical or historically conditioned. It belongs properly to our time. For that reason, it was not shared and
could not have been shared by earlier ages, all of which were
firmly convinced of the objective validity of their own norms and
values. For the same reason, one must oppose that the situation
within which it arises will sooner or later give way to a different
situation calling for a different type of hermeneutics. Yet neither
in Nietzsche nor in any of his successors do we find the suggestion
that a major change in philosophical orientation is to be expected.
If anything, the insight into the historicity of human thought is
regarded as definitive. It is here to stay and is not likely to be affected by future developments. One wonders in that case
whether the new hermeneutics does not again claim for itself a
universality or an infinity that is implicitly ruled out by its own
admission of the finite character of all human experience.[55]

The movement of Nietzsche's thought may be described as a
movement from history to nature which bypasses the primacy of
reason and sees nature itself as a creation of the universal will to
power.[56] That movement has been correctly diagnosed by Heidegger as a relapse into traditional metaphysics. Whether Heidegger succeeds in purging Nietzschean philosophy of the metaphysical remnants with which it remains infected is a question
that may conveniently be left to others to decide. The relapse
does, however, reveal a greater closeness of Nietzsche to Socrates
than the thrust of the preceding argument may have led us to
think. Nietzsche's fascination with Socrates is undeniable. There
also appears to be little doubt that he looked upon Socrates as his
most formidable adversary. It is significant that he is himself the
first philosopher to have taken issue with Socrates, who, as the
originator of philosophy, had previously been immune to all attack even on the part of those who rejected the whole of classical
philosophy. That his first book, the *Birth of Tragedy*, should have
dealt in the main with Socrates, and that an important segment
of one of his last books, the *Twilight of Idols*, should be entitled

"The Problem of Socrates," is ample evidence that Socrates was from the beginning and remained to the end the crucial problem. It likewise suggests that the victory which he claimed to have won over him may not be as final as he himself would sometimes have us believe. Nietzsche's entanglement in the thicket of the idea of values was due in large part to the influence of Socrates. According to Heidegger, that entanglement is the reason for his failure to attain "the true center of philosophy." But, as Heidegger is also quick to point out, "Even if a future philosopher should reach this center — we of the present day can only work toward it — he will not escape entanglement, but it will be a different entanglement. No one can jump over his shadow."[57]

Nietzsche's valiant endeavor to resurrect a mummified Socrates, if only for the purpose of refuting him, raises two questions, which may never be fully answered but which can no longer be avoided. The first is whether Nietzsche's new perspective is indeed broader than, and therefore superior to, that of his antagonist. The second is whether, beyond the indefinite variety of particular perspectives with which history acquaints us, there is not *the* perspective or *the* horizon which lends meaning to all of them and renders the disagreements among philosophers intelligible, even though it may never suffice to resolve them.

NOTES

1. Friedrich Nietzsche, *Selected Letters of Friedrich Nietzsche*, ed. and trans. Christopher Middleton (Chicago and London: University of Chicago Press, 1969), p. 256, letter of September 14, 1886, to Malwida von Meysenbug.

2. Ibid., pp. 285–86, letter of February 19, 1888, to Georg Brandes. See also Friedrich Nietzsche, *Gay Science*, trans. Walter Kaufmann (New York: Vintage Books, 1974), no. 370.

3. Cf. Nietzsche, *Gay Science*, no. 124.

4. Nietzsche, *Selected Letters*, p. 311, letter of September 14, 1888, to Paul Deussen.

5. Martin Heidegger, "The Word of Nietzsche: 'God Is Dead'," in *The Question of Technology and Other Essays*, trans. William Lovitt (New York: Harper and Row, 1977), p. 112.

6. Walter Kaufmann, *Nietzsche: Philosopher, Psychologist, Antichrist* (Princeton, N.J.: Princeton University Press, 1974), p. 110.

7. Ibid., p. 230, with references to *Gay Science*, nos. 2 and 359.

8. Ibid., pp. 111–12.

9. For a critique of Kaufmann's book on this score, see W. Dannhauser, *Nietzsche's View of Socrates* (Ithaca, N.Y.: Cornell University Press, 1974), pp. 26–41.

10. Friedrich Nietzsche, *Ecce Homo and On the Genealogy of Morals*, trans. Walter Kaufmann (New York: Vintage Books, 1967), "Why I Am a Destiny," no. 1 in *Ecce Homo*.

11. See in particular Turgenev's famous portrait of the "nihilist" Bazarov in *Fathers and Sons* (1862). The word *nihilism* appears to have been coined by Jacobi in his letter to Fichte, March 21, 1799, where idealism is described as a form of nihilism; cf. F. H. Jacobi, *Werke*, vol. 3 (Leipzig, 1816), p. 44.

12. Friedrich Nietzsche, *Thus Spoke Zarathustra*, trans. Walter Kaufmann (New York: Viking Press, 1954), pt. 4, "The Shadow." Also *Genealogy of Morals*, III, 24.

13. On the difference between skepticism and conventionalism on the one hand and nihilism on the other, cf. L. Strauss, *Natural Right and History* (Chicago: University of Chicago Press, 1953), pp. 10–12, 20. The distinction between skepticism and nihilism remains somewhat blurred in S. Rosen's otherwise penetrating study, *Nihilism: A Philosophical Essay* (New Haven, Conn. and London: Yale University Press, 1969).

14. Friedrich Nietzsche, *Will to Power*, trans. Walter Kaufmann and R. J. Hollingdale (New York: Vintage Books, 1968), no. 11. On Nietzsche's concept of nihilism in general, see Heidegger, "Word of Nietzsche," pp. 60–70, and Martin Heidegger, *Nietzsche*, vol. 1, *The Will to Power as Art*, trans. David Farrell Krell (New York: Harper and Row, 1979), pp. 151–61.

15. Nietzsche, *Gay Science*, nos. 125, 343; also Nietzsche, *Zarathustra*, Prologue, 2.

16. Cf. Nietzsche, *Zarathustra*, pt. 1: "On the Gift-Giving Virtue," no. 3.

17. Friedrich Nietzsche, *Beyond Good and Evil*, trans. Walter Kaufmann (New York: Vintage Books, 1966), nos. 294–95.

18. Nietzsche, *Gay Science*, no. 125.

19. Friedrich Nietzsche, *Birth of Tragedy*, trans. Walter Kaufmann (New York: Vintage Books, 1967), secs. 13 and 15. On Socrates as the "first decadent," see *Ecce Homo*, "The Birth of Tragedy," 1.

20. Nietzsche, *Birth of Tragedy*, sec. 15.

21. Nietzsche, *Will to Power*, no. 2.

22. Ibid., nos. 3–5; *Genealogy of Morals*, III, 27.

23. Nietzsche, *Beyond Good and Evil*, no. 227.

24. Ibid., no. 224.

25. See, on this point, Strauss, *Natural Right and History*, pp. 9–10, and for a concise analysis of the so-called experience of history, as it was finally understood after Nietzsche, pp. 20–22.

26. Nietzsche, *Beyond Good and Evil*, nos. 1–2.

27. Ibid., no. 1.

28. Ibid., no. 8.

29. Ibid., no. 5.

30. Ibid., no. 6.

31. Ibid., no. 22.

32. Ibid., no. 2.

33. Friedrich Nietzsche, *Use and Abuse of History*, trans. Adrian Collins (Indianapolis: Bobbs-Merrill Educational Publishing, 1957), secs. 1 and 7.

34. Ibid., sec. 3.

35. Ibid., sec. 9.

36. Cf. Nietzsche, *Zarathustra*, Prologue, 5.

37. Nietzsche, *Use and Abuse of History*, sec. 4.

38. Ibid., sec. 10.

39. Ibid., sec. 3.

40. Cf. Nietzsche, *Will to Power*, nos. 18, 22, 28, et passim.

41. Friedrich Nietzsche, *David Strauss, the Confessor and Writer*, trans. Anthony M. Ludovici, in *Thoughts out of Season*, pt. 1 (New York: Macmillan, 1911), sec. 7.

42. Friedrich Nietzsche, *Twilight of Idols and the Antichrist*, trans. R. J. Hollingdale (Harmonsworth, Eng.: Penguin Books, 1979), "Expeditions of an Untimely Man," 5; cf. Nietzsche, *Will to Power*, nos. 19–20.

43. Nietzsche, *David Strauss*, sec. 8.

44. Cf. Nietzsche, *Beyond Good and Evil*, no. 202.

45. See, for example, Nietzsche, *Will to Power*, nos. 753, 784.

46. Nietzsche, *Genealogy of Morals*, III, 5–6; *Twilight of Idols*, "Expeditions of an Untimely Man," 24; *Will to Power*, nos. 82–85, 843–49, 1021.

47. Cf. Nietzsche, *Will to Power*, no. 3 ("radical nihilism") and no. 22 ("active nihilism").

48. Nietzsche, *Use and Abuse of History*, sec. 10.

49. Ibid., sec. 6.

50. Cf. Nietzsche, *Beyond Good and Evil*, nos. 1, 13.

51. Nietzsche, *Will to Power*, Preface, 4.

52. Cf. *Zarathustra*, pt. 2: "On Redemption," and, for a further elaboration of the doctrine, pt. 3: "On the Vision and the Riddle" and "The Convalescent."

53. Cf. Heidegger, "Word of Nietzsche," p. 58. On the antecedent history of that particular formulation of the problem, see O. Bollnow, *Das Verstehen: Drei Aufsätze zur Theorie der Geisteswissenschaften* (Mainz: Kirchheim, 1949).

54. See, for a similar assessment, D. C. Hoy, "History, Historicity, and Historiography," in *Heidegger and Modern Philosophy*, ed. M. Murray (New Haven, Conn., and London: Yale University Press, 1978), pp. 329–53.

55. On this subject see the remarks by L. Strauss, "Correspondence Concerning *Wahrheit und Methode*," *The Independent Journal of Philosophy* 2 (1978): 5–7. The connection between the approaching "world night" and the new hermeneutics is likewise emphasized by Martin Heidegger, *An Introduction to Metaphysics*, trans. Ralph Mannheim (Garden City, N.Y.: Doubleday, 1961), pp. 37–38, 41.

56. Cf. L. Strauss, "Relativism," in *Relativism and the Study of Man*, ed. H. Schoeck and J. Wiggins (Princeton, N.J.: Princeton University Press, 1959), pp. 153–54. For Nietzsche's use of the word *nature*, see *inter alia Beyond Good and Evil*, no. 188, and *The Antichrist*, no. 57.

57. Heidegger, *Introduction to Metaphysics*, p. 167.

11

"Christianity is the Future of Paganism": Schelling's Philosophy of Religion, 1826–1854

THOMAS F. O'MEARA

RELIGION WAS A THEME that was never far from Schelling's philosophy. His discontent with theological studies at the Tübingen *Stift* (where a shaft of Kantian light occasionally penetrated the gloom of Lutheran orthodoxy) led him to a brief period of mocking separation from all religion. By 1802, however, the 27-year-old professor at Jena lectured on Christianity as a realization of the new idealism. In 1804 at Würzburg, he faced the religious issue of creation and finite existence, and by 1809 in Munich he was probing evil, change, and freedom in God.[1]

The philosophy which concerns us, however, is that of Schelling's lectures at Munich after 1827, and at Berlin from 1841 to his retirement in 1846. These courses on mythology and revelation presented his positive philosophy, the new, empirical idealism, and they gave his excited and numerous hearers a dynamic and total system. Schelling had arrived in 1827 to help open the University of Munich. It quickly became clear that his philosophizing had taken an extraordinary turn: he was intent upon a philosophy of Christianity and revelation, upon an idealism which climaxed in an analysis of world-religion. He said in one of his first lectures: "The precise name for my philosophy is Christian philosophy."[2]

The following pages present a sketch of this philosophy of religion, Schelling's philosophy of mythology and revelation. Our concern is not so much the method of this philosophy as its content, less the transcendental structure as that thought-form's realization in historical process.

Emil Fackenheim wrote, "Few have bothered to read the *Philosophy of Revelation*. Until today hardly anyone has suspected that it is one of the profoundest works in modern religious thought, equal in impact to the works of Kierkegaard, Schleiermacher, and Hegel."[3]

Neither *Die Philosophie der Mythologie* nor *Die Philosophie der Offenbarung* was published in Schelling's lifetime. His chronic revisionism and procrastination, which previously drew the *Weltalter* back from the ink of the waiting presses, was at work here as he labored over his later manuscripts. Detailed summaries by students were circulated, exciting both friends and enemies of Schelling; these *Kolleghefte*, because of the destruction of the *Münchener Nachlass* during World War II, are now an important source of Schelling studies.[4]

After 1826, Schelling lectured only on his positive system. It had three parts: the first treated God as primal being and as the origin of the universe of beings; the second part was the philosophy of mythology; while the third culminated in a philosophy of revelation.[5] Since none of this material was edited during the philosopher's lifetime there is overlapping and repetition, and a generally confusing arrangement of the texts is the result.

The first part of the later philosophy is concerned with the nature of positive philosophy, its place in the history of philosophy, and the life of primal being. Several works treat these themes, some of which Schelling entitles introductions to the philosophy of myth or revelation.[6]

Die Philosophie der Mythologie proper has two books; the first is often titled as a unit—*Der Monotheismus*.[7] *Die Philosophie der Offenbarung* contains an introductory treatise and two books.[8] Book 2 is complicated, for while its new sections cover the triune life of God and revelation, almost half of its lectures are a summary of the philosophy of mythology.[9]

Let us locate Schelling's philosophy of religious history in its cultural context by outlining the sources upon which his interpretation of myth and revelation drew. By the end of the eighteenth century natural philosophy had become vitalist, organic, hylozoic, and developmental (if not evolutionary). This was all seen as a courageous rejection of the mechanism of the Enlightenment. From Brownianism, the dominant philosophy of medicine around 1800, Schelling drew encouragement to explore categories such as organism and polarity. The writings of H. Kielmeyer impressed him with their clear affirmation of process. In the mystical writings of Böhme and Saint-Martin, Tauler and Eckhart, Schelling found these ideas from speculative physics projected backward into the life of God. Franz von Baader's theorizing followed lines similar to Schelling's as it struggled to integrate the theology of Böhme with the new experimental science of magnetism, electricity, and chemistry. His theology of mythology would not have existed without the writings of F. Creuzer and J. Görres, pioneers in introducing oriental mythology to the West. Schelling understood that he was continuing the philosophical discussion of myth begun before 1800 by J. G. Herder, Gottfried Hermann, and K. P. Moritz; C. G. Heyne and J. G. Eichhorn were his first sources. Tilliette fills a page with a list of books on the criticism and exposition of mythology which Schelling knew. "Nothing of any importance in the literature, in German, French, or English, escaped him."[10] In terms of theology we should recall that Schelling's father was a professor of biblical languages and a published exegete. The son's education was in theology; his knowledge of the Scriptures was extensive; he was in contact with a number of romantic theologians — Protestant and Catholic — as associates, disciples, or critics.

What does Schelling mean by *religion*? What is the object which his positive system will interpret, this system worked out no longer as an idealist epistemology but as a phenomenology of religion? A tentative answer at this point can give some direction to our voyage along the linear development of what he summed up as historical movement. Spirit's history is theogony, and that process of theogony is threefold. Schelling is always and simultaneously describing three things: (1) the life of God, as God through his active potencies exoterically becomes fully himself; (2) the vital historical line of finite being (other than God but not utterly discrete from him), which has its own realization but which nevertheless bears inwardly the realization of God; (3) the history of human consciousness, both collective and individual, which is bringing to unity nature and spirit in art, in religion, and in their finest expression, philosophy.

"My task is the philosophical explanation of systems of religion and myth" (*PM*, 12:231). It belongs to philosophy to find the essential content and ultimate purpose of religion. The process which we call religion, myth and philosophy, seems to bridge the gulf between the Absolute and the finite.

Schelling usually wrote of philosophies of "myth and revelation," using less often the phrase "philosophy of religion." The object of his science is the life of the Absolute being realized in the human spirit and world history. If the Absolute becomes fully itself through "tension" and "process," the empirical record of that process is a history which prior to Christ we call myth and after him we name revelation. Revelation expresses with insight and mythology with picture a single process which brings together the ideal and real; the single process is history, religion, theogony.

Religion is the product of divine powers active in consciousness. The place of the process, the tension of the potencies, is consciousness. This consciousness is both the Godhead and the human spirit (*PM*, 11:207). The human person as the climax of the universe is placed in the midst of the three powers, open to their influence but ultimately free of each of them (*PO*, 13:348). Because of this union of freedom and spirit, the finite consciousness must live amid the influences of the powers, between a discoverable freedom and a false domineering security. Spirit is the subject of the realization of human beings as well as of God.

> The process which begins with the posited tension amid the potencies is a theogonic process — for the potencies effect it and are in themselves theogonic. But at the same time it is an extradivine process, not only a process of nature but one which we (initially) call mythology. [*PO*, 13:268]

This process will include unruliness, error, materialistic religion.

Schelling's neologism, "tautegory,"[11] explains how philosophy will interpret religion and ultimately become revelation. "Mythology is not allegorical but tautegorical — its gods really exist" (*PM*, 11:195 ff.). Allegory discloses one thing through something which is different; tautegory discloses the new through something which is the same. For Schelling human religion is not the symbolic or cultic representation of something obscure, whether that be the powers of nature or the heroes of nations. Rather, religion is the life of knowing and willing expressive of its own progress toward depth and fullness. This process is the development of ideal to real, and back again to the fully active ideal-real of Spirit.

Schelling's system is organic and developmental; it can be imagined as linear but also as parabolic. Expansion flows out from the beginning and returns with the spoils of realization: the self-realization of God as an outward motion and a return. This parabolic model was not foreign to the earlier philosophy of identity where the Absolute differentiated itself into the real and the ideal in order to become in a higher synthesis their identity. This pattern (scholars have recently begun researching its affinity with Plotinus)[12] was to serve also as the foundation for the later philosophy of creation and religion.

The dynamism of the human spirit is such that it unfolds the life of God. In Schelling's later philosophy of religion the Plotinian motif of fall and re-ascent was retained; what was new was the relocation of this pattern in the line of forward movement.

This essay looks first at the process which is both a divine becoming and a religious history, and, second, at the role which Christian revelation plays in fulfilling myth, imaging God, and completing religion through idealism.

The linear process

There is "something before being" (*PO*, 13:204–26), a ground of all being and of the universal system. Schelling's ground is a peaceful, active willing, the source of all that will be. Needful of nothing, in its ground it wills being. Since willing is forward oriented, the process will be unfolding and eschatological; since it is a process of realization, it will include both poles of the ideal-real dialectic. It is not a logic but a phenomenology of will-into-existence. The transcendental structure of Schelling's philosophy remains, but the a priori categories of the mind have become physical potencies of existence, both ideal and real.

This willing even in its infinite openness contains three movements: can, must, and ought. These three aspects of the active essence (*Wesen*)[13] of primal ground can also be expressed in terms of the subject-object schema: *Sein-können* ("potential to being") is the subject; the object is *reines Sein* ("pure being"); the subject returned through objectivity is *reines Sein nun* ("pure being now"). The final stage — begotten into factual existence — represents the union of the ideal and the real (*PO*, 13:273ff.). In the twelfth lecture of the *Philosophy of Revelation* these powers are called "*Potenzen.*"[14] In Schelling's speculative physics, his writings on natural philosophy, the potencies had already been present not as divine powers but as levels of natural organization. Remaining powers of being, they are now mediators between the Absolute and the universe, the divine will and history.[15] They are transcendental horizons of all being. We might call them vital fields. Schelling employed *Potenz* not as Aristotelian potentiality but as a striving ready to leap to fulfillment. Do the *Potenzen* solve the problem which haunted Schelling's first systems, the distinction between God and the world? They are not concepts, Schelling repeated, but determinations of the life of the absolute spirit-as-will, three personalities of the same essence (*PO*, 13: 250ff.). They are the deeper meaning of the Christian Trinity. Through the powers, the God of monotheism becomes worldwide, historical, and so trinitarian.

God is not found in the primal will, or in any one of the potencies, or in their product. The tension of the powers is the life of God. The powers are placed outside of the Godhead yet remain facets of the Godhead's primal being, will; they are both God and non-God. The world is *part* of the personal objectification of God. The polarity of freedom and necessity, of subject and object, is the bridge to the production of the world which is both free and necessary (*PO*, 13:257). The first potency delights in real possibility, in the attraction to beings other than itself. Yet, in this passage through differentiation, the totality of the divine being is neither increased nor diminished, for the All has simply moved from one "form of existence" to another.

The world is not the inner essence of God but an "exoteric appearance of the deeper theogony."[16] The plurality of the world rather than being a challenge to the unity of God is the confirmation of divine vitality. Creation takes place neither in eternity nor in time, but in a temporal zone which lies between the chronology of history and the pulsation of the burning yet unconsumed primal will (*PO*, 13:208, 280, 281). Creation resolves the ideal and the real: the first principle by its nature has only the desire to maintain itself, and the second can only go unconditionally beyond the first; a third power is drawing both to fulfillment, a power which they recognize as higher and independent (*PO*, 13:279).

Once God has led forth innumerable potentialities as realities, the structure is there for finite spirit to be more than an object, to be a living subject. The divine process continues in the life of the spirit. The external theogony ends not in the objects of the cosmos but in history made possible by spirit. The primal will manifests itself in the tension as process. Schelling's understanding of creation is different from the view that the world is a logical consequence of the divine nature (Spinoza) and different from the positing of God only as the term of his becoming (Hegel). The world arises through a divine process but one over which God as *Urgrund* stands, amid but above the potencies placed in tension.

Does God need the world? "God is God only as Lord, and he is not Lord without something over which to be Lord. But God is already, before the world, Lord of the world, Lord of whether to place the world or not" (*PO*, 13:291). Although the divine life is more than detached activity *ad extra*, Schelling no longer would compromise traditional thought by uncategorically placing a need for creation or incompleteness in God. There is an effort in the later philosophy to protect the divinity of God. There is an eternal theogony and a temporal one. In the first, time does not reach to the heart of God. The linguistic aid to accepting this is the distinction: esoteric-exoteric, while the systematic key is process. "In the three potencies, which are immanent determinations of absolute spirit in God, and in their ground the category of historical process lies rooted."[17]

Before we pursue the thread of religion further, we must briefly discuss the role for Schelling of the Fall. Searching for an alternative to Plotinian emanation and Aristotelian or Wolffian causality, in 1804 Schelling decided that the world came into an existence apart from God through a leap or a Fall.[18] He admits that such an employment of *Abfall* recalls that "very ancient idea" of original sin (*PM*, 11:205). From his first use in 1804 Schelling views the Fall primarily from the perspective of idealist ontology. There is no assertion of moral fault or free choice. In fact, though created by God's freedom in an immediate relationship to God, human persons were not yet free. They had not lived, had not struggled for mastery over self within the potencies. The Fall, then, is not a fall from an original and perfect freedom through a sin, but a creation into concrete existence so that greater freedom can be attained. For the universe the Fall means separateness and limitation. The separation of the second power from the first is *Urzufall*, and from this dissonance the being-process began.

> Man was created at the center of the Godhead and essentially he belongs at that center as his true place. As long as he is there he sees things as they are in God, not with a superficial view empty of spirit and unity . . . but in harmony with man as their head, and through man accepted up into God. [*PM*, 11:206]

But the Fall brings a change in the relationship between God and humanity.

> Once man moves away from the center, the divine unity is distorted and the periphery becomes confused, for he is no longer divine above things but he has sunk to their level. Since he wants to assert his central position and the insight connected with it (although he now stands in another relationship) he strives to hold onto the original and divine unity in a world destroyed and ripped apart. [*PM*, 11:206]

The meaning of the Fall, and of the wrath of the father-gods, is the shock of subjectivity, even of an absolute subject, now placed before objective independence. The positing of the world alienates it from God. In the Fall of the world, the Son, the world's potency, also falls. The Father is no longer completely father; the Son will regain serenity in a future, deeper subjectivity. Mirroring the Godhead, creation cannot resolve this tension unless creation becomes spirit, unless the real becomes the ideal.

Schelling's philosophy of religion is an attempt to grasp the full reality of history. For an idealist the important thing about history is consciousness-in-history, the ideal becoming the real and vice versa. History is not primarily the record of political events but the spiritual development of the human race. Thus we partake in the history of myths, in mythmaking. Mythogenesis is the process by which the essential, reflective archetypes in the human consciousness corresponding to theogony come to light. Mythogenesis is the theogonic process as played out during the first epochs in the history of revelation.

The philosophy of mythology is the first part of the philosophy of revelation. Schelling's analysis of the mythical systems of Egypt, India, China, and Greece was not only an interpretation of the totality of myth but the search for the reproduction of the triadic process in each particular system. Throughout a thousand pages of mythical systems, the word *Bewusstsein* repeated itself: the divine and human consciousness, the idealist realm where history expressed itself in myths.

The history of mythology has four epochs in which the three potencies play out their roles in the transformations and realignments of gods and myths (*PM*, 11:250). Every mythological system includes a story of concrete gods. This narrative is a telling of the race's social experience, and so it is myth which forms peoples. Nations emerge not from political pressures but from spiritual movements. "Mythology does not determine but *is* that people's fate (just as a man's character is his fate), its destiny allotted to it from the beginning" (*PM*, 11:65). Myths, like language and social structure, are a disclosure of the becoming God meeting humanity. The primacy of the ideal over the real is maintained even in the historical phenomenology of religion. Mutual development is grounded on both God and human beings as *Geist*.

Not only does myth mirror theogenesis; the history of myth records psychogenesis. The human spirit finding its way ahead to full freedom is a lesser reflection of God's own development for freedom. The world of gods arises in the human mind spontaneously, born of a necessity imposed by the original relationship (*PM*, 11:197). God's way to himself and the path of human history are one: one archetype and one image. "Mythology comes into being through a process which is necessary; its origin is lost in a realm before history. Consciousness may resist the process in certain particulars, but it cannot impede, much less reverse the whole" (*PM*, 11:193). Theogony is reproduced in the abyss of consciousness and of being. Myth has taken over the role which art and nature played in Schelling's earlier writings. The philosophy of myth is insight into and through the structures of mythogenesis (*PM*, 11:217). We recall here the previously mentioned key to Schelling's philosophy of religion: religious forms are not allegory but tautegory. The lives of the gods and goddesses are creations which pictorialize forces active in our minds and wills, and in God's. "Seen objectively mythology is in fact what it claims to be: true theogony, a history of the gods. The ultimate history of the gods is the creation, the real genesis in consciousness, of God" (*PM*, 11:198).

Although a divine process of revelation lies beneath the history of myth, religion is frequently and inevitably a corruption of spirit. God does not force ideas upon humanity but leads the race through various stages, none of which are fully false, to higher truth. True monotheism can be fashioned only out of the struggles of polytheism. The epochs are transitions to greater insight, greater freedom, gateways to that synthesis which romantic idealism had sought everywhere: in self, nature, art, state, and now finally in religion.

The truth: the Son incarnate

While every religion qualifies as revelation, Christianity marks a higher stage of that process which mythogenesis began. Nevertheless, since mythology is theogony, revelation could hardly be more; and so one asks: What is revelation? It is insight into the real process of God and of history and self; it is a free and true history (more than the myths of Greece or the reason of Kant) which is one with idealism. Neither Schelling's knowledge of theology nor his theological acumen equaled his competent survey of mythology. This was yet another field for him to study, and in the late 1820s when the need for such research made itself felt Schelling was fifty. In his treatment of Christianity he limits his exposition severely. Nevertheless, we know that he was acquainted with some of the theological literature of the time — with D. F. Strauss, with Schleiermacher, whom he considered to be the most intelligent of dogmatic theologians, and with certain of the publications of his Catholic disciples in southern Germany, who since 1802 had viewed him as a counterpart to Hegel.

Schelling treats at length only two specifically Christian doctrines: the Trinity and the Son as Christ. But first let us look at Christianity as a whole. Christianity does not fashion but discloses history; Christian revelation begins at that transitional moment when mythic history begins to return to a God it will find free and complete.

If the epochs of the worldwide history of religion prior to Christ are individually touched by error, still "the process as a whole is truth" (*PM*, 11:212). Each stage has prepared for the next, and yet the entire process is found in each moment.

> The content of all true religion is eternal and hence cannot be absolutely excluded from any epoch. A religion which is not as old as the world cannot be the true one. Christianity must, therefore, have been in paganism. . . . It is inconceivable that mankind should have remained for thousands of years without links to the principle in which alone there is salvation. [*PO*, 14:77]

The theophanies of the Old Testament do not seem to be much superior to paganism. Here we might recall that for Schelling the explicit content of any religion is the phenomenal manifestation of the deeper level, the process of theogony and human psychogenesis. Every rite and all doctrinal teachings point to something more profound: so it is not possible to locate revelation or freedom within only one religion.

If we take paganism, Judaism, and Christianity as the three great forms of all religion, the revelation of the Old Testament is merely the revelation that runs through mythology; Christianity is the revelation which has broken through this husk [paganism], and thereby transcended both paganism and Judaism. [*PO*, 14:124]

Paganism and Judaism are both prototypes of Christianity. "Christianity was the future of paganism" (*PO*, 14:142).[19]

If Schelling demeaned Judaism, ranking it amid the religions before Christ, he elevated the oriental religions before and after Christ. His knowledge of the history of Buddhism confirmed for him an organic theory of the universal process of theogonic revelation. A persecution of Buddhism occurred in India at the same time as Christianity appeared further west: this coincidence illustrated the complex but universal presence of the second potency, the Son, in the world (*PM*, 13:564). Religious consciousness is, then, collective as well as worldwide.[20]

Creation and history are the places of activity where through individualization lordship is won by the second power. When the Son becomes a power in history, human religion is elevated from the "natural activity" of the potency to its clearer revelation. What in nature is necessary and obscure becomes historical and intuitively clear. In the depth of Christian theology one can intuit that theogony which positive philosophy describes. Nevertheless, the acceptance of this revelation is not submission to dogmas explained away by reason (as the Enlightenment claims to have done) but insight into the work of God. The shift is also one from the essential to the existential order. Theogony is not only consciousness but, more, relationship to God. Revelation, Schelling says, is the movement from the rational order of nature and myth to the real existence of God active in us (*PM*, 11:250).

The history of our planet is the realm of the second potency. Fundamental philosophy sees it as *Sein-müssen* — the objective, existing counterpart to absolute subjectivity; the philosophy of revelation employs the name *Son*. Like the other two *Potenzen* the Son was actively present in every religious and mythical system, but Christianity is the final, explicit stage of his life (*PO*, 14: 77). Tilliette writes:

> It [*The Philosophy of Revelation*] is a speculative theology, an interpretation of dogmatic statements, but above all it is a philosophy of Christian *religion*. Within this vast philosophy of religion it appears as the second panel of a diptych: mythology-Christianity. The relationship of Christianity to paganism is the joint which allows the exposition to expand.[21]

Schelling's lectures on trinitarian theogony led quickly to the generation of the Son and its relation to world and history. While the Father is described at length in terms which are a union of idealism and Böhmeanism, the topic of the Spirit is not well developed either here or at the end of the system. Our conceptualization of the Trinity arises from the encounter of human consciousness with objectivity. Previously theologians had searched for a *vestigium trinitatis* in nature and religion; Augustine had found a trinitarian analogy in the operations of mind and will. This is not what Schelling means. Religion eventually discovers and affirms Trinity in God because the human individual and collective consciousness are a *Gegenbild* of God's becoming.

> Our principles lead us immediately and naturally to a teaching which is the foundational doctrine of Christianity. In *Die Philosophie der Mythologie* I showed that the doctrine of the Trinity in its roots and ground is not specifically Christian . . . but because this is the most primal reality of all there is, Christianity exists. [*PO*, 13:312f.][22]

Our entrance into the life of God is through the Son, for he is potency and Lord of our world. To beget the Son is to begin creation and history. The Son is the realization of God's freedom for being, the breaking of the necessity of not willing. "Before all willing, through the mere necessity of his being God, God, to the extent that he is being-for-itself, places himself in a second form . . . " (*PO*, 13:327). The Son is the object of the divine knowledge and will. The time of the Son is a period of exit and return, of risk and realization. Emerging out of freedom this *Potenz* finds that glory is solitude and obedience.

> The *actus* of this self-realization lasts until the time of the complete birth [of the Son]; only at the end is the Son real Son. Since this end is the end of creation, the Son is begotten at the beginning of creation, but is only realized as such at its term. [*PO*, 13:318]

Schelling's Christianity is Christology. Christ is not the founder of a doctrinal sect. He is the content of Christianity, just as for Christianity history is the content of the universe (*PO*, 14: 35). As theogony unfolds in the history of human religion, the potency of the Son is present in all religions. But a clearer moment is yet to come. Revelation from the potency active in a "natural" way yields to disclosure. This unveiling is, however, in terms of the Godhead, the apogee, the moment of furthest removal and incipient return.

Creation and history are tragic. Over against the lordship of the subject the solid assertion of objectivity appears not only as distinction but as alienation. So, the second potency's process is lonely and ends not only in Incarnation but upon the Cross. Two christological themes interest Schelling: the birth of the Son in eternity and time and the terms of that begetting, the *kenosis* of the Incarnation. Schelling's Christology is largely a historical and ontological elaboration of Phil. 2:6–8. What interests Schelling most in this biblical text is the Greek word *morphe*. Does not this show that the Son's pre-existent divinity was a form of God becoming? (*Form* for Schelling pertains to manifestation, mode of being, while *essence* is foundation, ground, and necessity.) Caught up in the epochal movement of the Godhead through the universe, the second potency cannot rest with its first form. *Kenosis* is principally, however, an idealist interpretation of existential Incarnation and secondarily the Crucifixion (more prominent in Paul, Luther, and Hegel). The philosopher singled out from the Crucifixion the Son's obedience. This is the psychological condition of the furthest alienation from the Father. Freedom before, through, and after the Cross: only the one who has the form of God *independent* of God can renounce it and through death arrive at glory *with* God (*PO*, 14:227).

It is not surprising that this Pauline passage — the divine person lowering himself into the abyss of historical existence in order to be exalted above all — was appealing. *Kenosis* is historical theogony, a Plotinian *exitus-reditus* extended downward to wounded mortality. The metaphysical tension and the alienation of the powers are set forth in historical terms while the format of ontological polarity is retained. The process of separation to attain a realized freedom continues the differentiation of the ideal realm of the subject. At the same time, the severity of death shows the event of Christ to be the ultimate objectivity. The Cross is historical and so eminently objective. Its blood marks the attainment of a far point in that lonely sphere of the real.

The resolution

The three *Potenzen* are the three Lords of time (*PO*, 14: 17ff.). The third potency is spirit. For the idealist, *Geist* is the creative force and the ultimate identity. Spirit, of course, underlies every stage of the developing universe and is the ground of mind and will. Though active from the beginning it must wait for the epoch of the second power, for only after the climactic moment of the Son can the coming of the Spirit, a time of synthesis, occur. Schelling continued to follow the pattern of his early idealist system where subject and object find resolution in a synthesis of both — the ideal-real. Only if God separates beginning from end does he find freedom and possess the infinity of created forms (*PO*, 13:273).

How does God resolve human history and personality? History has undergone two important transformations: one from divine indeterminateness to mythogenesis; a second from myth to revelation. We glimpse a third and final one. If Christianity was the future of mythology, is not idealism the future of Christianity? The pattern of the idealist system, of the Fall and its return, remains operative here; the ideal and the real in the human person are to be resolved in Spirit. Schelling's eschatology is protology; it looks backward for ideas. Existence finds climax in consciousness, history in the absolute Spirit (*PO*, 14:328). In bringing the Spirit, Christ has brought the possibility of the final era of full freedom. Freedom is the keynote of the time of resolution. The threat of chaos and evil is being subjected to science, to knowing and to fashioning freedom. All other religions must fade except the one of that revelation which is also *Wissenschaft*. Interpreted idealistically the *gnosis* and *charismata* of the Spirit (of which Paul wrote) are a knowledge which now knows no limits, no superstition. No protected corners of darkness escape its light (*PO*, 14:239, 296). In the meantime the process continues and slowly penetrates everything prior to the end. "The development after Christ will be subject to the same disturbances, restrictions and counterforces as would affect any natural evolution" (*PO*, 14:296).

The final stage of the theogonic process, the activity of the third potency in cosmic resolution, is not described at length. The reader must search carefully through the final lectures on revelation for fragments of a completion of the philosophy of religion. What is missing is an idealist ontology of resolution which would correspond to the first part of the positive philosophy, the lectures on the one primal Being leading into the philosophy of religion. Schelling's philosophical imagination seems to have been spent. Distracted by two material segments which excited his curiosity — Satanology and an ecumenical ecclesiology — Schelling deprived his linear process of a worthy conclusion. No doubt recollections about origins are easier than extrapolations of the future. "The past is known: the future believed" (*PO*, 14:222).

Conclusion

For Schelling's philosophy of religion there is a twofold conclusion. The historical denouement was curious and sad. In 1841, in the lecture hall of the University of Berlin where Schelling had been brought by the Prussian monarchy to combat Hegelianism, sat Engels, Kierkegaard, Bakunin, and Burckhardt. Each had his own expectations, his own relationship to philosophy from Kant to Hegel.[23] All were quickly disappointed; some wrote mockingly of the lectures. Schelling was too idealist for one, too Christian for another. H. E. G. Paulus, Schelling's old nemesis from Würzburg, acquired a transcript of Schelling's lectures and published the "finally revealed positive philosophy of revelation" to ridicule its author. Amid legal suit and lack of interest Schelling retired from the classroom. The philosophy of religion had attracted so many and yet in the long run had pleased so few.

The intellectual resolution to this philosophy of religion remains unresolved in the variety of opinions on Schelling. The philosophers W. Schulz and H. Fuhrmans argue over its continuity with idealism and its relation to medieval mysticism, although the previous generation of Heidegger and Tillich saw there sources for existentialism. A Lutheran reader may see in it discontinuity, a break between Christianity and other religions, a major role for the *theologia crucis* and for the framework of law/gospel. But one can also see continuity and evolution, an interplay between primal religion and revelation, between nature and grace. Perceiving the mutual reflection of theogony and psychogenesis, one might ponder an affinity with Teilhard de Chardin or with Whitehead.

Schelling's overstated identity of revelation and idealism broke down the wall between culture and Christianity which post-Reformation traditions had built. To this extent Schelling stands in the tradition of Origen, Augustine, Abelard.

Even with the reworking of this system, however, Schelling's final philosophy — the work some have called the last great attempt of idealism — remained incomplete, full of unresolved tensions. Precisely the affirmation of the positive history of revelation in Christ challenged the earlier foundation in the structures of consciousness. And, while Christ was the resolution of the life of the Trinity and the fulfillment of the world religions, an examination of Schelling's Christology of the Cross raises two questions. Is theogony a true process of a God becoming? It seems more likely that this trinitarian drama enacts only the outward life of God, who in the Godhead esoterically (as in the thought of Meister Eckhart) remains full, complete, at peace. Second, the realm of the third *Potenz* remains undescribed. This raises the questions of the continuing impact of the victory of the Christ, the future of our history, and the nature of eschatological resolution and fulfillment.

What Schelling at first glimpsed as a presentation of his ideas in certain forms of Christianity, became, precisely in its emphasis upon existential meaning for human consciousness and upon a nonmythical incarnation of the Son beyond paganism, a system whose breadth was too great and whose inner tensions were too strong. For the final system reached from the world of Kant to that of Teilhard de Chardin.

NOTES

1. Schelling's first work, his master's dissertation from 1792, was on the topic of myth in Genesis: *Antiquissimi de prima malorum humanorum origine*. It took into account Kantian philosophy and the biblical criticism of the Enlightenment; it drew upon J. G. Eichhorn (1752–1827) and C. G. Heyne (1729–1812). Literature on Schelling in English is sparse. For a survey, see my "F. W. J. Schelling: A Bibliographical Essay," *The Review of Metaphysics* 31 (1977): 283ff. On Schelling's philosophy of religion there are articles by Benz and Fackenheim; from Europe we have books by W. Kasper, H. Czuma, and A. Bausola as well as Tilliette's work, and the English translations of Tillich's dissertations. A. Allwohn distinguishes three stages in Schelling's treatment of myth: the early writings offer a rational-historical critique; the systems and the lectures on art present an interpretation within aesthetics; the final stage turns to the frameworks of history, religion, and revelation ("Der Mythos bei Schelling," *Kant-Studien, Ergänzungsheft* 61 [1927]: 78ff.).

2. H. Fuhrmans, "Documente zur Schellingforschung, II. Zu Schellings Spätphilosophie," *Kant-Studien* 47 (1955–1956): 280. Schelling takes pains to point out that his philosophy is not the teachings of Christianity, nor is Christianity the primary source of its material content. His philosophy presents universally and essentially what Christianity propounds in its own fragmented, diverse way (*Die Philosophie der Offenbarung*, 13:133ff.). References to *Die Philosophie der Offenbarung* and *Die Philosophie der Mythologie* are given in the text with the abbreviations *PO* and *PM* respectively. Schelling's *Werke* are cited according to the Cotta edition, 1856–1861.

3. Emil Fackenheim, "Schelling's Philosophy of Religion," *University of Toronto Quarterly* 22 (1952): 2.

4. H. Fuhrmans, "Einleitung," in Schelling, *Grundlegung der positiven Philosophie* (Turin: Bottega d'Erasmo, 1972), pp. 61ff. "My courses on the philosophy of revelation have been followed by a large

number of hearers, and, as far as I know, further diffused to regions out-side of Germany through copies of my dictated lectures" (*PO*, 14:232).

5. Ibid., pp. 15, 21.

6. *Darstellung des Philosophischen Empirismus*, 10:227–86; *Einleitung in die Philosophie der Mythologie*, 11:255–572; *Einleitung in die Philosophie der Offenbarung*, 13:3–174; *Grundlegung der positiven Philosophie*, ed. H. Fuhrmans (Turin: Bottega d'Erasmo, 1972).

7. The *Einleitung in die Philosophie der Mythologie* has two books: (1) *Historische-Kritische Einleitung*, 11:1–252; (2) *Philosophische Einleitung*, 11:256–90.

The *Philosophie der Mythologie* has two sections: (1) *Der Monotheismus* includes the first six lectures: 12:1–131; (2) lectures 7–29: 12:135–685. The *PM* has been translated by V. Jankélévitch into French (Paris: Aubier, 1945). X. Tilliette discusses the arrangement of these works on the philosophy of religion in *Schelling. Une philosophie en devenir* (Paris: Vrin, 1970), 2:393ff., 423, 435ff.

8. The parts of the *PO* are: (1) *Einleitung*, 13:1–74; (2) 13:175–530; (3) 14:1–334. This work has recently been translated into Italian by A. Bausola (Bologna: Zanichelli, 1972).

9. Lectures 18–23, 13:382–530.

10. Tilliette, *Schelling*, 2:408–9; cf. *PM*, 12:139.

11. The *Oxford English Dictionary* (Oxford: Clarendon, 1961), 11:115 explains "tautegorical" as a nonce-word and traces its origin to Coleridge. In a footnote Schelling mentions the English poet as his source (*PM*, 11:198).

12. Cf. W. Beierwaltes, *Platonismus und Idealismus* (Frankfurt: Klostermann, 1972).

13. *PO*, 13:232.

14. Cf. J. Schwarz, "Die Lehre von den Potenzen in Schellings Altersphilosophie," *Kant-Studien* 40 (1935): 118–48.

15. Cf. *PO*, 13:267.

16. "Here for the first time the perfect spirit exists no more as non-necessity of passing over into being but also as the freedom of accepting another being different from its eternal (self), i.e., its being-as-concept. . . . Here it can now say, 'I will be who I will be' . . . and posit the perfect spirit as God" (*PO*, 13:270).

17. W. Kasper, *Das Absolut in der Geschichte* (Mainz: Matthias-Grünewald, 1967), p. 228. Schelling would like to maintain that the theogony's expression in creation and religion is the exoteric essence of God, while the esoteric being remains lordly and serene (*PM*, 13:670). Cf. E. Schertel, "Schelling und der Entwicklungsgedanke," *Zoolo-*

gische Annalen 4 (1912): 312–21; F. Schmidt, "Schellings Begriff des Prozesses," *Zum Begriff der Negativität bei Schelling und Hegel* (Stuttgart: Metzler, 1971).

18. *Philosophie und Religion*, 6:28. "The ground of finitude lies, in our opinion, only in the not-being-in-God of things as particular which, since they according to their essence or in themselves are only in God, can be best expressed as a Fall — a *defectio* — from God or from the universe. . . . That which is placed in things to be grasped as reality, placed immediately through the idea of the universe itself as nothingness: this is sin. The life of our senses is nothing other than the continuing expression of our not-being-in-God arising out of our particularity. Philosophy, however, is our rebirth in the universe" (*System der gesamten Philosophie* [1804], 6:552).

19. "Christ is the end of paganism as well as of revelation" (*PM*, 12:521 ff.).

20. Cf. *PO*, 14:21. "The merely literal and formal content of ecclesiastical orthodoxy must be and remain something alien [to other religions]. One should not take it amiss if the astute and perspicacious Indians will not pretend to lend credence to formulas in which they find no connection with their own faith, with their own view of the world, with their own philosophy and wisdom" (*PO*, 14:22).

21. Tilliette, *Schelling*, 2:467.

22. Schelling is critical of liberal Protestant theologians who try to derive the Trinity from neo-Platonism (*PO*, 13:313); he repudiates Arius (p. 328), while he finds Pseudo-Denys to be an orthodox, ecclesiastical support for his own views (p. 323). The Trinity is not a triad of concepts — an idea, Schelling says, which has become "fashionable" (p. 314).

23. H. Pölcher, "Schelling Auftreten in Berlin (1841) nach Hörerberichten," *Zeitschrift für Religions-und Geistesgeschichte* 6 (1954): 193–215.

Author Index

Anselm, 22ff., 25
Aristotle, 22ff., 25, 35, 41ff.
Augustine, 43
Austin, J. L., 34

Barth, Karl, 53
Baur, F. C., 114
Bergson, Henri, 20, 25
Boehme, Jacob, 218
Bultmann, Rudolf, 116, 126–27
Burrell, David B., 3–4, 34ff.

Cobb, Jr., John B., 6–7, 91ff.

Darwin, Charles, 91ff.
Dewey, John, 95ff.
Dilthey, Wilhelm, 122–23, 131

Eliade, Mircea, 117

Fackenheim, Emil, 63, 217
Feuerbach, Ludwig, 9–10, 53,
    154ff.
Findlay, John N., 10–11, 24,
    177ff.
Flew, Anthony, 47
Fortin, Ernest L., 11–12, 195ff.

Gadamer, Hans-Georg, 88n.

Harnack, Adolf von, 115–16
Hartshorne, Charles, 2–3, 17ff.,
    105ff.

Hegel, G. F. W., 4–6, 10–11,
    52ff., 70ff., 93, 112–13, 166–
    70, 177ff.
Heidegger, Martin, 212
Hume, David, 17, 28, 31–32,
    139–40
Husserl, Edmund, 8, 67, 124,
    130–31

James, William, 34

Kant, Immanuel, 23, 26, 112–13,
    139–40
Kaufmann, Walter, 195–96
Kee, Howard Clark, 7–8, 112ff.
Kierkegaard, Sören, 66
Kümmel, W. G., 113–14

Leibniz, Gottfried Wilhelm, 25,
    30
Lonergan, Bernard, 35

McTaggart, John McTaggart
    Ellis, 194
Marx, Karl, 9, 154ff.
Mathews, Shailer, 94ff.

Nielsen, Kai, 44ff.
Nietzsche, Friedrich, 11–12,
    195ff.

O'Meara, Thomas F., 12–13,
    216ff.

237

Subject Index

Absolute, 9–10, 135ff., 178ff.
Atheism, 18ff.
Aufhebung, 80ff., 172

Begriff, 11, 70, 183ff., 196ff.

Charismatic leader, 8, 119ff.
Chicago school, 6–7, 93ff.
Christian origins, 113ff., 131
Christianity, 73ff., 226ff.
Christology, 78–79, 229ff.
Community, 9, 135ff.
Conceptual language, 70ff.

Divine, 19
Docetism, 60
Dual transcendence, 17, 20, 28

Ebionitism, 60
Ecclesiology, 79
Error, 138ff.
Essence of Christianity, 64
Existentialism, 27–28

Fall, 223
Feeling, 52ff.
Figurative language, 70ff.

God, 17ff.

Hermeneutics, 70ff.

Ideal types, 8, 119ff.
Idealism, 144ff.
Incarnation, 77–78
Institutionalization, 8, 126ff.
Interpretation, 148

Life-world, 67

Manichaeanism, 60
Materialism, 10
Mythology, 224

Nihilism, 11–12, 196ff.

Ontological argument, 21–22

Pelagianism, 60
Positive religion, 71ff.
Praxis, 10, 161–62
Presence, 77
Process theology, 6–7, 106–7, 109

Religious discourse, 70ff.
Religious materialism, 10, 161ff.
Remembrance, 75–76

Self-overcoming, 203
Sinnlichkeit, 163–64
Social gospel, 97ff.
Sociology of knowledge, 8
Species-being, 154